Transformations through Drama

A Teacher's Guide to Educational Drama, Grades K-8

Jerneral W. Cranston

UNIVERSITY
PRESS OF
AMERICA

Lanham • New York • London

Copyright © 1991 by
University Press of America®, Inc.
4720 Boston Way
Lanham, Maryland 20706

3 Henrietta Street
London WC2E 8LU England

Library of Congress Cataloging-in-Publication Data

Cranston, Jerneral W., 1932-
Transformations through drama : a teacher's guide to
educational drama, grades K-8 / Jerneral W. Cranston ;
photographs by Peter Palmquist.
p.   cm.
Includes bibliographical references.
1. Drama in education—United States.   I. Title.
PN3171.C675   1990   372.13'32—dc20   90-45530 CIP

ISBN 0–8191–7993–0 (cloth : alk. paper)
ISBN 0–8191–7994–9 (pbk. : alk. paper)

 The paper used in this publication meets the minimum requirements of
American National Standard for Information Sciences—Permanence
of Paper for Printed Library Materials, ANSI Z39.48–1984.

Dedication

To the students and children who have been involved in the process of making this work come to life. And to my husband who helped with the final product.

v

Acknowledgements

I wish to thank Dorothy Heathcote, University of Newcastle-upon-Tyne for being the inspiration for many of the ideas in this book and for her dedication to the use of drama in the classroom. Thanks should also go to: the teachers and children at Alice Birney and Jefferson Schools in Eureka, California and Equinox, and St. Mary's Schools in Arcata, California; my many students who helped me test all of the dramas and exercises; John Smith of Alice Birney School for his continued support; Sally Botzler of the Eureka Teachers' Center; Dr. James Waters and Dr. John Morgan of Humboldt State University for their help with Chapter 1; Patsy and Peggy Givens of PRO-PEN for invaluable suggestions on the text; Vicki Modarresi for assistance with the final proof-read. My special thanks go to Peter Palmquist for the excellent photographs.

I also am grateful Basic Books, New York, and William Heinemann, London, for permission to quote from FRAMES OF MIND: THE THEORY OF MULTIPLE INTELLIGENCES, by Howard Gardner. Copyright © 1983 by Howard Gardner.

Table of Contents

Preface

Measurement. Numbers. Ratios. The major goal of modern science has been to reduce knowledge to relationships which can be described mathematically by making measurements which result in numbers which can be reduced to ratios. Modern brain theorists call this a "left-hemisphere" activity. In contrast, the arts and humanities engage in "right-hemisphere" activities. It is my belief, and the thrust of this book, that left-hemisphere learning is not only enhanced by right-hemisphere activity, but even more that right-hemisphere activity is essential for left-hemisphere learning. As Wittrock says in his book *The Human Brain:*

> If there is any truth in the assertion that our culture stresses left-hemispheric skill, this is especially true of the school systems. Selection for higher education is based predominantly on the ability to comprehend and manipulate language—a fact which may help explain why it took so long for science to come to grips with right-hemisphere abilities. If the right hemisphere does indeed process data in a manner different from the left, we may be shortchanging ourselves when we educate only left-sided talents in basic schooling. Perhaps, when people speculate about an inverse relationship between scholastic achievement and creativity, they are really talking about the effect of overtraining for verbal skills at the expense of nonverbal capacities. Many problems can be solved either by analysis or synthesis; but if people are taught to habitually examine only one approach, their ability to choose the most effective and efficient answer is diminished. Increased understanding of how the minor hemisphere works will hopefully lead to better training in how to choose between and to use the skills of both hemispheres of the human brain.[1]

Sri Aurobindo, a yogic philosopher, wrote in 1910:

> The intellect is an organ composed of several groups of functions, divisible into two important classes, the functions and faculties of the right hand, the functions and faculties of the left. The faculties of the right hand are comprehensive, creative and synthetic; the faculties of the left hand critical and analytic...The left limits itself to ascertained truth, the right grasps that which is still elusive or unascertained. Both are essential for the completeness of the human reason. These important functions of the machine have all to be raised to their highest and finest working-power, if the education of the child is not to be imperfect and one sided.[2]

The world has grown smaller in many ways due to scientific improvements. There is no world wide famine which would reduce us all to the same subsistence level. The problems now no longer percolate below the surface, however, and we are reminded daily that survival is the generic concern of humankind. Diseases, narco-terrorism, the nuclear threat, the shrinking ozone layer, the homeless, the constant need for environmental supervision are bringing us to a recognition of finiteness.

Is this the reason why education has become entrenched in the so-called fundamentals? If we cannot go forward must we go backwards? Is the future so terrifying or so projected upon by our ignorance that we cannot conceive of anything with the kind of hope that enables a people or race to endure? If this becomes the trap we are caught in, then we're finding absolutes to fill in the cracks and no new knowledge is necessary. Children who have not yet lost that delicate balance between intuition, thinking, and feeling are affected by our emphasis on skewed priorities.

While many children already in school don't think they'll live out their years into adulthood because of these problems, the system continues to barely scratch the surface in order to avoid confrontation with already confused parents. Teachers are caught up in this myopic view, as well. Together with this fact and the absence of rights and power that should be delegated to our educational community, our teachers are crippled. And so are we, in turn, crippled by the fear to think, express concerns, wonder, hope, discuss and produce new thinkers. Either we contribute to the common ground of thought and development of the human potential on a daily basis, supporting that thought process of wonder and hope, the yearning for wholeness, the dream for a better world, or else we continue to give ourselves superficial answers which ignore the human potential.

At times it seems we are encased in a myopic perspective that breeds paranoia. It is this woodenness of opinion-oriented thought (without knowledge) that's stifling for those who want to pursue the questions: Who are we? What are we? Where are we going? — questions that are asked by philosophers, artists, scientists.

Apart from this death knoll on education we are copying the very thing we fear—not allowing controversial issues to be raised in schools, "cleaning up" the text books so that no one is offended has caused minds to remain sterile. Teaching fundamentals by rote, subduing any kind of creative energy to explore the exigencies of the human condition, teaching by fact rather than by question, the daily leak of undisputed truth— all of these dull the mind into apathy.

By not allowing the ground swell of reality an existence, by tying neat little pink and blue bows on a microscopic bit of truth, we're not only crippling our young, we're maintaining a level of stagnancy, a level below mediocrity.

Teaching and learning have always been similar to battle. In order for old ideas to be replaced, new ideas are wrestled with and finally understood. And sometime out there in the blue mist, 'the new idea' can become the seed for a new interpretation of the human task. A new interpretation breeds a new synthesis, a transcendence that will help us be even more valuable to our stay here on this green and blue planet.

A few years ago I worked in a school with fifth grade children and their teacher. Together with my college class we all performed an Indian ritual in order to come closer to some understanding of our enduring past, its life in us, and our growth to meet it and consolidate it toward our becoming in the future. The teacher wished to have his children participate in this process of becoming, particularly since many of their lives were without any form of intellectual enrichment or spiritual sustenance. He wanted his children to think about the topic of choosing leaders. (A sad day when it's necessary to bring in legendary material from a less dominant culture because the present one is so bereft of heroes.)

Afterward, four different parents called the principal to inquire about the kind of cult their children were being exposed to. I was, of course, very nervous when the teacher told me this. But he responded, "It's great. That means I'm doing something." I wish there were more teachers like this!

Recently, at a meeting on teaching objectives a group of teachers were talking about problems in society today. As glaring and horrible as the topics became, one person kept rephrasing the concern with the topic of "no focus." Suddenly the words fragmentation, isolation, alienation, separateness, cut off, and atrophy occurred to me; then the topics on the board seemed to have a ground for their existence. It was as though this person was proving her point, she was trying to express her "ground" but couldn't because of the absence of the very thing she was saying, no "focus."

The connectedness to the earth, the well-spring from which we grow needs to be renewed. The young need it continually, the middle aged need to remember it, the aged need to renew it after having distanced themselves from it. As we become caught up in life it becomes more and more difficult to remember that we were once nurtured by our collective mother. Throughout history, religions and the arts have provided such nourishment. For reasons beyond the scope of this book neither have prospered with their original vitality in this materialistic culture where newness shines over antiquity.

Transformation is the key for an educator. How can we bring this about for our students? Those who resist will find themselves without a ground or a frame, will become lost.

There are many reasons why some of our youth do not want to grow up: some have nothing to grow from; many abhor the ignorance at work among the so-called intellectual community and become cynical; some see and know a truth they don't want to lose; but for most, it is this very lack of the feeling of connectedness to the earth, to the human condition which leads towards hope and total fulfillment, a spiritual fulfillment not boxed in with words.

This text is dedicated to those people dealing with the survival of the human condition, a condition of the spirit.

1   Wittrock, M.C., *The Human Brain*, Prentice Hall, Inc., Englewood Cliffs, New Jersey, 1977, p. 105

2   Sri Aurobindo as quoted in Springer and Deutsch, *Left Brain, Right Brain* , W. H. Freeman, New York, 1985, p. 237

Guide to the Teacher

The premise of this text is that the present over-emphasis on the cognitive aspects of learning needs to be balanced by a renewal of the old-fashioned idea of "learning by doing." New research leads one to view the child in a multi-dimensional way: his sensory, kinesthetic, spacial, verbal, logical, inter- and intra-personal realms.

Schools today seem to over-emphasize factual recall at the expense of emotional and personality development. It is my thesis that factual (cognitive) information can be combined in a positive way with affective and psychomotor learning through the use of dramatic techniques; that the emotional and personality needs of the student can best be met with these same techniques; that the problems of the future cannot be solved by persons who are mindless, fact-accumulating machines, but only by those who have been transformed to be able to use their knowledge in a positive and constructive way. The goal of this book is to provide the classroom teacher with some tools using the techniques of drama to accomplish this transformation. It is assumed that the teacher has had little if any background in drama.

In Chapter One, Learning and the Brain, we begin with the most recent research in the area of the brain and learning and proceed to specific principles within the areas of Dramatic Art.

Chapter Two, The Teacher and Children, Live, deals with the psychological factors of teacher presentation and specifics on handling children within the scope of activities that are presented.

Chapter Three, Creating Your Own Dramas, shows how the teacher can put together her own material based upon her learning objectives.

Chapter Four, The Teacher in Role, shows the teacher's use of role and a continuum dealing with personal expression.

Chapter Five, Questioning, explores the use of questions accompanying the use of role and considers the on-going interaction between student and teacher and how to directly involve children in the learning process.

Chapter Six, Drama Elements, looks at specific aspects dealing with aesthetics and provides ways for the teacher to employ these in order to make drama more available to the child.

In Chapter Seven, Co-operative Learning is considered as a strategy in which the children find themselves in groups working toward a learning goal. They are introduced to the teacher's alter-ego or mannequin which may be presented in a variety of ways. The teacher has many options: to take on a role herself; to have a child take on a role; to call upon a mannequin for whom she speaks as a puppet; and/or to use this "puppet" as another role with whom she speaks. To expand her options still further, she may introduce other types of "puppets" which represent animals or forces within nature.

Chapter Eight, Writing and Drama, shows in detail how to use drama techniques to enhance writing skills. It contains the first ten Exercises.

Chapter Nine, Additional Exercises, shows the teacher how to use the exercises —Senses, Space, Imagination, Plots, Character, and Speech —to accomplish learning goals. These can also be coupled with longer dramas, expanded into dramas and used as motivation for, and depth in, learning.

Those exercises labeled "generic," have been selected because they always work; children adapt to them naturally as an outgrowth of their own play; so, it is wise to begin with these. These are also used in the follow-up sections suggested at the end of most dramas.

The Dramas in Chapter Ten are broken down into the following sections: Being Lost; Toys; Animals; The Old House; Island; Nature and the Environment; Human Nature; History and Oppression, with an introduction to each section. These sections focus on the broader prospectives by looking at the topic's relevance to present day views.

The main focus of this text is the emphasis upon the affective and psychomotor forms of learning rather than the two most often used: verbal-linguistic and mathematical-logical.

In both the exercises and the dramas suggestions for curriculum application are included. Because the exercises are more open-ended, their application is more versatile and grade levels are not included. In the dramas, grade levels are included. Once children are about eight or nine, their physical needs and particularly verbal abilities begin to coincide more with those of the adult. For this reason the type of drama requiring more kinesthetic oscillation that is suited to K-3 shifts into structures that are suggested in Cooperative Learning, small group improvisations such as *The Forest*, and structures presented in the last two sections, Human Nature and History and Oppression.

Considering the idea that drama is an imitation of life, these introductory comments are meant to help the teacher accumulate basic knowledge that guides her thinking. With the information on Creating Your Own Drama in Chapter Three and the Exercises in Chapter Nine the teacher should be able to bring forth original dramas which suit her mode of teaching.

In order to avoid the monstrous *s/he, him or her, etc.*, I decided to use *she* or *her,* when referring to the teacher or leader and *he* or *him*, when referring to the student. I have not yet become accustomed to the use of the sexless *their, them or they* as singular pronouns. The words *teacher* and *leader* are used synonymously.

Terms introduced for the first time will be in **bold** and included in the glossary.

Chapter 1

Learning and the Brain

Cultural Influences on Development

In the desolate Arctic, an Eskimo uses visual memory to remember his route through territory that an outsider would find untraversable. Students from Ghana are able to recall details from stories they are told because they have been raised in an oral tradition, while American children depend more on reading to gather knowledge. These examples show the importance of early education, role models and patterns in development. To grow, the child needs to view and perceive a model he can repeat and upon which he can pattern himself.[1]

In traditional societies each youth's relationship to the elders who instruct him assumes great importance for the success of the educational encounter. There is a great difference between the child taught in a culture composed of a single ethnic society and the child from a pluralistic society. In traditional societies, elders pass on the knowledge necessary for the survival of the culture. Pluralistic societies, on the other hand, value the germination of new ideas, even when the new ideas are rediscoveries of past wisdom.

The Two Hemispheres

We know a great deal about environmental and cultural influences on children's development. Modern research into brain function is adding important biological information which indicates that the two hemispheres of the brain are fundamentally different in their function and effect on growth.

Early research showed that the left hemisphere is dominant in respect to language, reasoning, and symbolic thinking. Because the right hemisphere seemed to lack distinct features, its functions were more difficult to determine and it became known as the "minor hemisphere." It was apparent early on that the right hemisphere controls the left side of the body and the left hemisphere controls the right. But understanding the two hemispheres of the brain is not that simple.

During the 50's and 60's, research revealed that if the left frontal lobe which is part of the left area of the cerebral cortex had been damaged, some patients could be trained to re-learn the words and names they had forgotten; the task was taken up by the right side of the brain. Patients who had received damage to the left hemisphere couldn't name an object, but they could recognize it by touch and sight.

After experimentation with many patients, the effects of lateralization, the division of the cerebrum into two hemispheres, became more clearly known. In one case the left hemisphere damaged patient could write, copy words or take dictation, but he could not read what he had written. Information could not be transmitted by the damaged area of the left hemisphere where visual images are decoded into language symbols. Disorders of the right hemisphere are less obvious since the effects are not seen to interrupt daily communication.

Some of the problems associated with right hemisphere damage are an inability to pay attention to the left side of the body, a damaged understanding of identity, loss of the sense of direction, inability to feel or understand emotions, and sometimes an increase of emotional expression. It is the right hemisphere that enables us to maintain a constant sense of who we are, and when the right hemisphere is damaged, we lose the sense of ourselves in the world, our sense of direction and even have delusions that parts of our body don't belong to us.[2]

The two hemispheres are specialized for different cognitive styles; the left utilizes words in an analytical, logical mode, while the right uses a more holistic, Gestalt mode. An example of this difference can be demonstrated briefly. A mother says to her daughter, "I'm doing this because I love you, dear," but her face, body movement and emotional tone say, "I hate you and will destroy you." The left hemisphere of the daughter's brain derives a sense of security and pleasantness from the words; the right hemisphere detects the body movement and vocal tone.[3]

Most theorists believe that the brain has evolved over thousands of years. When our primitive pre-mammalian ancestors had not evolved beyond instinct their brains did nothing more than direct instinctive responses. That was the reptilian brain, what we call the brain stem. But evolution demanded more complex thought processes and so the brain evolved to meet those challenges. Now we have access to a part of the brain which controls instinctual functions and a newer part which monitors emotions and supplies a basis upon which our will becomes active. The hypothesis that the right hemisphere is in contact with the older-instinctual-brain as well as the emotionally-centered mid-brain and serves as a bridge between these and the left-brain is revealing. [4]

The right hemisphere is still a partial mystery, since its function doesn't seem brain-like in ways we generally understand that idea. Its perception is related to movement in space, perceiving ground before figure in an effort to conceive holistically, and tapping into the unconscious processes,[5] as well as gaining a sense of identity.[6]

On thinking about the relation between the right and left hemispheres, several physical models come to mind. It would seem that the right hemisphere contains the left in a supportive, almost nurturing way, while at other times their relationship seems to be one of opposites which, nonetheless, are balanced. This balance can be seen as a harmonious interaction from which richness and quality result. For example, a pictorial description or image explaining connections between the hemispheres represents a right hemisphere approach, whereas the left hemisphere uses words to process these thoughts.

All models are useful symbols, and in this case the model is designed to represent two divergent styles of perception. The descriptions at the top are based on experimental evidence while those following are more theoretical.[7]

Left Hemisphere	Right Hemisphere
verbal	non-verbal, visual-spatial
sequential, temporal, digital	simultaneous, spatial
logical, analytical	gestalt, synthetic, analogical
rational	intuitive
Western thought	Eastern thought

In just a single moment we begin to see the unfolding of creation itself. It is as if the ancients knew of the split that science is only now finding a way to describe. We need to go back and rediscover our ancient beginnings that once tied us and disciplined us. The right hemisphere helps to synthesize and place into a gestalt a relationship of parts that includes inner development.

Hemispheric Lateralization

The concept of hemispheric lateralization is important to teachers since it does much to explain the learning styles and behaviors of the children we teach. If we understand that Johnny doodles on the margins of his math papers not because he is "bad" but because the development of his right hemisphere demands that he do so, our reaction to his behavior changes and we are better able to teach Johnny.

Differences in right and left hemisphere development show up graphically in the area of sexual differences. The commonly accepted idea is that culture plays the most important part in determining these differences by its distinctly separate treatment of each sex. Boys are expected to be more aggressive, while girls are more submissive. New research points out that many of the differences in behavior may be based on cerebral differences which are innate.[8]

Cerebral changes take place in the fetus during pregnancy. Eggs carried by the mother contain only the X chromosome. If the Y chromosome is introduced during fertilization, changes take place to create a male. Although it is not fully understood, it seems that the Y chromosome and the male hormone testosterone effectively slow the rate of development of both hemispheres in boys, particularly the left. This new hypothesis helps to explain why boys often have trouble adjusting to the type of school situation which requires sitting and neatness. While boys are still orienting themselves in space, learning balance and gross muscle coordination, girls are able to sit and write more legibly, seem more self-contained, and can begin to handle areas of learning in which the left hemisphere takes dominance.[9]

Developmental Differences

1. Auditory/Visual Development. From birth females are more sensitive to sounds, in particular their mother's voice. Female babies are sensitive to changes in tones and are startled by loud noises. In fact, the female hearing system remains much more intact throughout life than the male's, whereas a boy's visual ability is increased. Unlike his feminine counterpart, he is more inclined to take an object apart to satisfy his curiosity about the environment.[10]

2. Muscle Development. The male baby spends longer developing his large muscles, whereas females possess greater coordination of small muscles. In a test using a metronome, girls were able to respond with rapid sequential movements more efficiently than were boys. Girls could consistently tap out the beat even when it was speeded up and slowed down. The ability to keep this rhythm also reveals the connections with the left hemisphere's ability in sequential analysis, contributing to greater control in repetitive motor action seen in the specialization of speaking and reading. This speaks to the fact that the boy's spacial abilities are more intact as witnessed by having him mentally work through a maze, a right hemisphere activity.[11]

"Measure me sky. I have been little so long." -Leonora Speyer

    3. Linguistic Development. Along with the ability to respond in a sequential rhythmic pattern, the same coordination and left hemisphere connection is demonstrated by girls speaking sooner than boys, and by the fact that little girls rarely possess speech defects. Girls read sooner, handle language arts activities with greater ease, learn foreign languages faster — all skills which are monitored by the left hemisphere.[12]   More recent research reveals that in women some language processing is carried out by the right hemisphere.[13]

    These differences also speak to the girl's development of social skills. She will ask others while a boy tends to go to the source to find his facts, often bringing home the forest or the beach when he explores. A male baby will ignore his mother's voice and become fixated by a moving object showing what seems like greater curiosity about the environment.[14]

    Though it is, of course, wise to remember that there are males who become prodigious readers and females who want to participate in large muscle development during their primary years, it would be foolish to ignore the results of research studies which show young females to be primarily left hemisphere-oriented, while males tested out as right hemisphere in their beginning orientation. It is useful to teachers, especially those in elementary schools, to be aware of this broad and general pattern in order to assist them in fortifying their patience, particularly when desks need to be cleaned out. It also needs to be pointed out that each individual's learning patterns and right/left interactions are as different as fingerprints.[15]

The 'Right-Hemisphere' Child
    Just as children develop differently, so are they different in the mode or style of learning that works best for them. A visual learning mode indicates right brain dominance, while an auditory mode indicates left brain dominance. The **haptic** (Bold face type will indicate the first use of a technical word which is also found in the glossary.) mode of learning indicates the need to physically experience the learning rather than receive it verbally or visually. The haptic learner alternates between right and left hemispheres, but usually inclines toward the right or visual.
    Barbara Meister Vitale, in her book *Unicorns are Real*, offers the following list of general characteristics displayed by many right hemisphere children.[16]

    1. Appears to daydream
    2. Talks in phrases or leaves out words when speaking
    3. Uses fingers to count
    4. Draws pictures on the corners of papers
    5. Has difficulty following directions
    6. Uses forms of non-verbal communication including making faces
    7. Displays problems when using small motor movements, but the problems rarely appear when the child is doing something of his choice
    8. Recalls places and events but has difficulty in recalling symbolic representations such as names, letters, or numbers
    9. Has difficulty with phonics and needs to see the whole word
    10. Tends to be more physically active
    11. Works sitting part way out of his seat
    12. Uses exaggeration when recounting an event
    13. Often has a messy desk
    14. Has little consciousness of time when completing work
    15. Likes to take things apart and put them back together
    16. Exhibits impulsive behavior
    17. Tries to change the world to meet his own needs
    18. Enjoys physical contact like punching and poking when relating to other children
    19. Goes often to the pencil sharpener
    20. Gets lost between classrooms
    21. Often forgets why he is sent on an errand

22. Usually enjoys athletics and activity oriented subjects, but is poor in subjects like English
23. Will know and give a correct answer to a question but won't be able to tell you its source
24. Will often give responses unrelated to the topic discussed
25. May be a class leader
26. Displays nervous mannerisms like tongue chewing while working

Such a list allows a teacher more ways of viewing children and can become an index acknowledging differences in learning style based upon the developing brain, instead of the customary discounting phrase, "He is immature." So often "hyperactive" and "learning disabled" become synonymous. Since 95% of hyperactives are males we should be able to see the need for changing attitudes.[17]

Creativity

Many of the characteristics listed above describe the creative child as well, since right-hemisphere characteristics are related to qualities which are coupled with creativity. Most educators insist that everyone is potentially creative, and considering our Western cultural conviction that each child is unique, this view makes sense.

Our schools are filled with children who seem to walk to the beat of a different drummer, who have trouble adjusting to the rigidity of the typical classroom situation. Not only are those children outside the treadmill of daily activities because of their powers of imagination and intuition, but they are out of step with their peers as well. Lost in the moment, forgetting about time, a child like that is skewed in the way in which he views reality, drawing comparisons and making inferences that seem unrelated to the activities around him or making analogies which are original but seem illogical to others. To him, however, his **dramatic play** yields a different logic which he checks and measures in his attempt to find new formulas and combinations. And remember, he may be a future scientist, inventor, or artist.

Storytelling is a gift any parents can impart to their offspring in order to engage and develop their creative potential. Richard Feynman, the late physicist, told his son stories before bedtime.[18] A single loop of pile in the shag rug became like a tree, the rug like a forest, and the boy became the insect crawling through mountainous brambles until sleep overtook him. Richard Feynman, like Einstein and Mozart, is a guiding light in our understanding of intellectual and creative development.

Whenever we are tempted to think we have discovered the ONE RIGHT WAY to teach all children, the narrow path upon which each child should tread, it would be well to remember the story told by Pearce in his book *Magical Child*, about a little boy whose parents insisted that he only be taught THE TRUTH, THE FACTS. His parents were scrupulously honest and never lapsed into any of the convenient and lazy social lies with which careless parents fend off their children's queries. They did not respond to questions of birth with stork tales; they explained carefully the full mechanism of reproduction and birth, complete with pictures and diagrams. He was read no cheap bedtime fantasy tales, only literature that was sensible and informative. All was fine until the child was sent to school at five. There he was beset with problems such as nightmares, disorientation, fearfulness and an inability to take part in ordinary activities. Nothing worked to alleviate the problems, until the child was diagnosed at nine as schizophrenic. The recommended therapy was to "Read to this child, hours and hours a day. Read him nothing but fantasies, fairy tales, wild imaginative stories. Saturate him with the unreal and improbable. Animate every nook and cranny of his life with imaginary beings." We learn from the extremes.[19]

Stages of Development

Children need to be children. This we know. We also know that there are specific stages which all children must go through on their way to adulthood; indeed the whole course of human existence is a passage from stage to stage.

Though each child's own process of development is unique, many respected researchers have offered models which delineate general stages of development through which we all must pass. Probably the most notable of these model makers is Piaget, a psychologist who studied his own children and many others. Piaget's stages include:

The *sensory-motor* stage, birth to two years. The period of greatest brain development, laying the foundation for language development later on. Development proceeds from reflex activity to sensorimotor solutions to problems. Begins internal representation (experimentation in thought) and mental activity rather than only experimentation through actions.

The *pre-operational stage*, two to seven. Problems solved through representation. Language development. Thought and language both egocentric. True social behavior begins. Moral reasoning is in place, but intentionality is absent.

The *concrete operational stage*, seven to eleven. Logical operations developed and applied to concrete problems. Cannot solve complex verbal problems and hypothetical problems. Development of the will and beginnings of autonomy appear.

The *formal operational stage*, eleven to fifteen years. Logically solves all types of problems—thinks scientifically. Solves complex verbal and hypothetical problems. Emergence of idealistic feelings and personality formation. Adaptation to adult world begins.[20]

It is the later stage, from four to seven, of pre-operational development which is central to this text. This is a time when the intuition, fantasy and imagination provide the basis for later development in concept formation. It is the time of **dramatic play** or **role-play** in which both fantasy play and imitative play take place. In both, the child bends the world to conform to his model. In fantasy play, objects become anything the child has experienced. A matchbox becomes a boat then changes to an animal if needed. In imitative play there is some pressure to conform to the model observed in the adult world like playing house, doctor, truck driver. This is the beginning of learning social rules.[21]

The period of concrete operations which includes these play experiences is based upon the development of imagination which will be used as a basis for play activity up to and through the pre-teen years, from four to eleven.

It is here that we need to take heed not to repeat the example of the child who was pressured too soon to learn about reality. During this stage children prepare for the language of analogy. When the child asks those "why?" questions, we gain nothing by a long complex explanation which he has no way of absorbing. So, we tell him a story which overlaps with other threads of logic.[22] Very soon his own empirical reality will lead him to form a classification in keeping with the social context. The activity of play and use of metaphorical and symbolic explanations become the cornerstones on which true abstraction and creative thought later rests. The child is constantly going from a concrete reality, building onto his own ego reality, imitating and fantasizing from a model.[23]

Internal imagery is based upon external imagery. If no stimuli are given, no imaginative structure will form and the child will have no imagination. Without the capacity for internal imagery, the child will remain locked into sensory-motor modes by default. As in the case of watching too much television, development comes to a halt because the imagination is not stimulated. Whereas in the storytelling mode the imagination must function to receive the images, nourishing intelligence.[24]

From about age eight on, the child apes the world of adults by "trying on" the world through his interactions and in this way facilitates the emergence of more consistent abstract thought.[25]

Educational Philosophies

Prior to the current period of brain research there were many educational reform movements developed around the concept of holistic education. Rousseau published *Emile* in 1782. In this book he speaks of the child learning from nature and not being subjected to reading and writing about other people's experiences before he can fully realize his own. As far as is known he was the first to write about the child as a maturing person rather than as a little adult who needs to quickly grow up and act correctly. His legacy has been spread by Froebel, who started the kindergartens, and by Maria Montessori (1870-1952), among others. Montessori's ideas regarding stages of development appear to follow Piaget's (1896-1980) although their approaches were quite diverse.

John Dewey, the American philosopher, initiated a pragmatic and empirical course of education in the U.S. Like Rousseau, he thought that children should not be pressured into expressing the thoughts and opinions of others before they had explored their own meaning. As citizens of a democratic country which was in a constant state of becoming, transition and growth, one needed to be flexible, ready to adapt, criticize and develop new ways of dealing with ongoing concerns. This approach contrasted widely with the European model of the time, which was set upon drill and regurgitation, as is the Japanese model today.

The school was a microcosm for the larger macrocosmic environment, Dewey said. At the turn of the century he was setting up an experimental school to test his theories. One day he went to look for the proper furniture. After he explained his ideas and needs to the salesperson, she said: "You want something at which the children may <u>work</u>; these are all for <u>listening</u>."[26] Another scholar who has made significant contributions to education is Jerome Bruner, a psychologist. Central to his approach is the philosophy that any subject can be taught at almost any time if it is contained in an appropriate context.[27] Even very young children can be doing high level physics if they are deciding how the individual rainbow colors will be sent up into the sky.

Bloom's Taxonomy

During the same period that Bruner was organizing his group, Benjamin Bloom was meeting with scholars to organize a taxonomy to give knowledge a structure. Educational objectives were beginning to be sought after, and teachers needed a common vocabulary when speaking about them. Bloom named two broad areas of human learning or domains, the cognitive and the affective.

Categories of cognition include: knowledge, comprehension, application, analysis, synthesis, and evaluation. The activities which directly correlate to these categories are: remembering, recalling information, thinking, problem solving, and creating structures. The categories are briefly defined below in order to give the reader an understanding of how they progress toward a culmination of learning, and finally how the learner makes a personal contribution in the synthesis phase, thus adding to the greater body of knowledge.

Knowledge stands for recalling information. This information extends from isolated facts (The Pilgrims arrived in the New World in 1620) to knowledge of larger structures such as theories and universals.

Comprehension requires that the learner knows the material well enough to be able to use it without seeing its relationship to a larger framework and can extend it or extrapolate in order to predict a continuation or a trend. (The Pilgrims left England because of religious persecution.)

Application takes place when a learned idea which is still an abstraction is brought into a concrete situation. (Not only did the Pilgrims leave because of religious persecution but so did many other groups.)

Analysis requires looking at the separate parts, their relationships, how they form a hierarchy, are organized, and/or relate or lead to a hypothesis. (Many groups traveled to the New World for other freedoms, such as the right to work and to obtain economic security.)

Synthesis is the blending of elements together to form an original hypothesis or creation. <u>Synthesis assumes a new insight which springs from the learner.</u> (Of all the groups who came to the New World, those who fared the best were the prisoners who could literally begin again.)

Evaluation takes place when qualitative and quantitative judgments focus upon the new contribution in line with stated criteria, as to accuracy, value and purpose. (As an experiment in democracy, one must understand the difference between the needs of those immigrants who were among the earlier ones, in comparison to those at the turn of the century, and those who have come recently.)

Bloom realized that learning does not take place in an emotional vacuum; there is always some feeling state being generated, so the objectives of the affective domain emphasize a feeling tone, an emotion, or a degree of acceptance or rejection.

Affective categories include: receiving, responding, valuing, organization, characterization. Because the child's covert feelings are as significant as his overt behaviors it is difficult to make a neat list of activities or objectives to correlate with the categories as was done to describe the cognitive domain.

In discussing these steps a symbol from nature is used instead of a specific academic subject.

Receiving takes place when we become aware of a tree.

Responding occurs when we allow the tree to stimulate some action like taking a photograph.

Valuing the tree we are motivated to do more.

Organization means we have reached a level of commitment to include activities related to not only trees, but forests. We may join the Sierra Club, volunteer to help plant forests, get up early every morning to go bird watching, live in such a way that our choices are affected by this new commitment.

Characterization requires that everything we do is characterized by this new knowledge. We not only reorganize our priorities, but our new interest grows to include all areas of our life.

When we view the complete diagram (on the next page) we begin to see a model of the human intellect.[28]

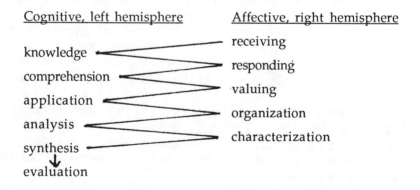

Cognitive, left hemisphere	Affective, right hemisphere
knowledge	receiving
comprehension	responding
application	valuing
analysis	organization
synthesis	characterization
evaluation	

Just as the integration of the right and left hemisphere is a necessary condition to learning, so too the harmonious blending of the affective and cognitive domains is necessary for life-learning to occur.

Learning and Teaching

When do we reach the kind of thought process which allows for the development of original thinking, for seeing connections between areas that would otherwise remain unrelated, for using the maximum of our potential brain and thinking power, and for developing techniques through which the two thinking modes of left and right can interact? This is the theme which reverberates throughout human development. The baby takes his first steps toward a toy. What motivates him, the toy or his own curiosity? There is the interaction of both subject and object, the two opposite poles which must become engaged to form a relationship. It is the process of life itself.

We do an admirable job of measuring cognition, but even with dozens of measuring tools it is abundantly clear that the score on an intelligence test, though it does predict one's ability to handle school subjects, foretells little of success in later life.*[29] Our preference for approaching affective achievement through the attainment of cognitive objectives tends to focus attention on these cognitive goals as ends in themselves without our determining whether they are actually serving as means to an affective end.

In the mid-seventies and early eighties the concept called "superlearning" crystallized this interaction between the two poles, mental and emotional.

According to Georgi Lazanov, a Bulgarian physicist, mental reserve capacities exist in our latent unconscious and can be reached through a relaxed environment, appropriate voice intonation, and use of playful techniques which authentically motivate the learner through experiential modes. A sense of authority in the teacher gives her the ability to evoke a receptive atmosphere through music, art, games, role-play which are orchestrated to open the learner.[30]

Physical knowledge of the brain and scientific studies have led to new developments dealing with gaining a better balance in learning. But the question remains: Why do some situations remain

*all of the material attributed to Gardner is from FRAMES OF MIND: THE THEORY OF MULTIPLE INTELLIGENCES, by Howard Gardner. Copyright © 1983 by Howard Gardner. Reprinted by permission of Basic Books, Inc., Publishers, New York.

in the memory over a long period of time and not others? School systems have been trying to upgrade standards, usually through the repetition of facts, drill, the basics. But these methods have all been used for at least 100 years by compulsory education and standards have not been upgraded. Though drill is important and necessary, it doesn't educate or prepare the intellect for leading an intelligent life directed by common sense.

To borrow from the old **metaphor** of the child as an empty vessel needing to be filled, imagine the right-hemisphere as a container; see it as a bowl holding individual pieces of fruit. The pieces of fruit represent the left brain. If what we want is a piece of fruit, we don't care about the bowl, but as we eliminate the fruit the bowl is slowly revealed. The only way we can appreciate the bowl is by eating the fruit. In present day educational systems, particularly in the public schools, the pressure is on to eat the fruit and after it is gone, to find some more fruit, leaving the bowl without any other function than containment. But the bowl represents the brain-mind of the child who cannot leave to discover other orchards, and who is still hungry after eating the fruit over and over again, year after year. The bowl needs to be recognized as functional. Since it represents the right-hemisphere its function is to unify and contain. It needs to be "worked" as a container by being nurtured: given stimulation by exercising images and intuition by means of storytelling and dramatic play. Somehow schools must find a way for children to become autonomous in their strength of will and character to be able to pick up their own bowl, to develop themselves so they are responsible to their own values and emotions. It is this combination of the two areas which must become integrated through awareness and practice in the classroom environment. If the child only sees the "object" but never responds to it or values it, then we as educators know his development has been neglected; his bowl is dormant. Throwing more fruit at him will not increase his knowledge.

In the last decade many systems have been introduced as ways to enhance the learning process. New attitudes toward written expression, cooperative learning, and research on learning and the brain continue. Most of these new ideas utilize modern brain research in their approach; they allow for movement, reduce stress, encourage questioning and problem solving, involve imaginative play and role play. In short, they put the child at the center of the learning environment. These systems stress process over product, they allow for individual differences in learning styles and applaud creativity. Through careful research, educational scholars are proving what the great thinkers have always taught, that for children to grow into caring human beings who use their intelligence wisely, the whole child must be taught; to focus the energies and attention of the educational process on only the limited territory directed by the left-hemisphere is to deny the child access to the full range of his potential.

In too many of our schools there is relatively little interest in the open-ended creativity that is crucial for the highest levels of human intellectual achievement. Too many teachers and administrators take refuge in slogans like "back to basics" in their unwillingness to accept the challenge of change and innovation. They too often define the problems of the school with the same limits that they impose on the curriculum, insisting on a single solution or a small set of solutions, and paying scant attention to problems with an indefinite range of solutions.

In his book, *Frames of Mind*, Howard Gardner presents seven possible approaches to intelligence which we as a species have available and use consistently in our lives. In on-going research he continues to find more intelligences, going beyond the simplistic metaphor of right-left lateralization. Like the interplay between the left and right hemispheres, all of us use most of these seven forms of learning on a simple level and probably some mix of a few on more advanced levels. They are: logical-mathematical, linguistic-verbal, musical, spacial, kinesthetic, interpersonal, and intrapersonal. Together they represent a blend of right/left characteristics. "Human beings have evolved to exhibit several intelligences and not to draw variously on one flexible intelligence."[31]

The logical-mathematical and verbal-linguistic intelligences share the area of symbolic representation and align with those cultures whose use of symbols have carried them irrevocably into the technological future. Using symbols in speaking, writing, and computing is a task monitored by the left hemisphere. Gardner points out that Piaget's work deals almost exclusively with this area, but at the same time the former states, there are other intelligences which Piaget did not recognize.[32] Through research in the last 10 years, linguistic/verbal abilities are understood to be contained primarily in the left-hemisphere; however, in some cases, particularly in women, these abilities may be localized more in the right hemisphere.[13] "It has been established convincingly that written language 'piggybacks' upon oral language..."[33]

"Traditional schools replaced the 'direct methods' of spacial and bodily intelligence, with a stress on linguistic facility---; while retaining much of the interpersonal element modern schools place increasing emphasis on logical-mathematical ability and on certain aspects of linguistic intelligence, along with a newly found premium on intrapersonal intelligence. The remaining intellectual capacities are, for the most part, consigned to after school or recreational activities, if they are taken notice of at all."[34]   This raises the question which Gardner continually asks: What about students who don't achieve in the school system because the "beat" of their drummer is not heard?

Musical intelligence: Most children's beginning speech comes in the form of babbling which merges with singing and can by two months match "pitch, loudness, and melodic contour of their mother's songs."[35] In reference to the balance between the two poles in musical thinking and teaching, a figural or intuitive approach is used in which the musical form is "felt." In contrast to this, the formal mode understands music as a system by reading the language of notation.[36]

"The facts are as follows: Whereas linguistic abilities are lateralized almost exclusively to the left hemisphere in normal right-handed individuals, the majority of musical capacities, including the central capacity of sensitivity to pitch, is localized in most normal individuals in the right hemisphere."[37]

Echoing the readiness of the child between ages four and seven to receive, respond, and value music: "...young children certainly relate music and body movement naturally, finding it virtually impossible to sing without engaging in some accompanying physical activity; many of the most effective methods of teaching music attempt to integrate voice, hand, and body."[38]

Spacial intelligence "In the view of many, spatial intelligence is the 'other intelligence'—the one that should be arrayed against, and be considered equal in importance to, linguistic intelligence."[39] "...spacial intelligence entails a number of loosely related capacities: the ability to recognize instances of the same elements; the ability to transform or to recognize a transformation of one element into another; the capacity to conjure up mental imagery and then to transform that imagery; the capacity to produce a graphic likeness of spacial information; and the like."[40] Spacial abilities cut across many fields in the arts, in engineering, and sciences— "spacial intelligences emerges as an amalgam of abilities."[41] "There is a sense of the whole, a 'gestalt' sensitivity, which is central in spacial intelligence, and which seems to be a reward for aging—a continuing or perhaps even an enhanced capacity to appreciate the whole, to discern patterns even when certain details or fine points may be lost. Perhaps wisdom draws on this sensitivity to patterns, forms, and the whole. My own view is that each form of intelligence has a natural life course: while logical-mathematical thought proves fragile later in life, across all individuals, and bodily-kinesthetic intelligence is also 'at risk,' at least certain aspects of visual and spacial proves robust, especially in individuals who have practiced them regularly throughout their lives."[42] "Dualists speak of two systems of representation—a verbal code and an imagistic code: localizers place the linguistic code in the left hemisphere, the spacial code in the right hemisphere."[43]

Kinesthetic intelligence: Kinesthesis is claimed to be the most commonly shared of all intelligences, existing as a sixth sense. "According to John Martin, a student of performance, we are all equipped with a sixth sense of kinesthesis—the capacity to act gracefully and to apprehend directly the actions of the dynamic abilities of other people or objects. Martin claims that this process comes to occur automatically. Past experiences of lifting are symbolized in a kinesthetic language, which is drawn on directly by the body, without the need for any other symbolic intervention. By the same token, when we see someone sucking a lemon, we are likely to feel a distinct activity in the mouth and throat as if we were tasting the acid; or when someone cries, we frequently feel a lump rising in our throats. Martin believes that it is our capacity involuntarily to mime, to go through the experiences and feelings of others, which allows us to understand and also to participate in art forms. He declares: 'It is the dancer's whole function to lead us into imitating his actions with our faculty for inner mimicry in order that we may experience his feelings. Facts he could tell us, but feelings he cannot convey in any other way than by arousing them in us through sympathetic action.'"[44]

"The fact that some individuals prove skilled at this kind of learning, but that it is accorded a low priority, may help explain why many promising young performers and dancers in our culture become alienated from school at an early age. If anything, the ability to mimic, to imitate faithfully, is often considered a kind of arrogance or a failure to understand, rather than the exercise of another form of cognition which can be highly adaptive."[45]

"And what of the developmental links between a child's early preoccupations and eventual inventiveness in a highly valued contemporary occupation like engineering?... 'Like practically everyone else on the team, he started becoming an engineer at about the age of four, picking on ordinary household items such as lamps and clocks and radios. He took them apart whenever his parents weren't looking.' This future engineer did not do well in high school or college until he took a course in basic electronics....Another member of the computer team was very depressed in school until he discovered that he could take a telephone apart: 'This was a fantastic high, something I could get absorbed in and forget that I had other social problems.' Such biographical accounts indicate that an interest in manipulation, in putting together (or taking apart), and in the eventual reassembly of objects may play an important formative role in the development of an engineer; such activity may also provide a needed island of reinforcement for an individual who shows scant interest (or skill) in other domains of experience."[46]

Personal intelligences are divided into the interpersonal and intrapersonal.

Perhaps these represent some of the genes which we don't receive from our parents. Recently it has been discovered that there are several "foreigners" in the original gene pool of each person which appear without any previously known relationship. That is each of us receives genes which are unique and not part of those we inherit.[47]

Personal intelligences are associated with the sense of self, self-knowledge, and "a willingness to confront the inevitable pains and paradoxes of human existence."[48]

The interpersonal mode falls on the individual's relation with the outside world. The core capacity here is the ability to notice and make distinctions among other individuals. The intrapersonal mode is the awareness of one's own feeling life. In its highest form it may be represented by the wise elder who reflects upon his own wealth of inner experiences and self-knowledge in order to advise members of his community.[49]

The patterns in both of these approaches are far more varied than are those in the other intelligences.[50] A sense of self is being formed and the inevitable balance which one comes to feel between the promptings of "inner feelings" and the pressures of "other persons."[51]

It is during the first few months of life when the infant is emotionally contained by the mother that the origins of this knowledge can be found.[52] The first stages of empathy can be seen, and the links of caring and altruism are beginning to form.[53] Also, during these early years from two to five the child is discovering things about himself by knowing about others. "There is, in fact, no knowledge and no sense of person that can be separated from one's ability to know others—what they are like, and how they view you."[54]

The hypothesis of integrating the right and left hemispheres for learning reads: as it is necessary to combine subject and object to insure development, the same combination is sought when blending the right with the left. It is what occurs when both the cognitive and affective domains are combined in teaching. Like right and left hemispheres which work together, the two learning domains can work together if the teacher is aware that she is applying them.

Synthesis

Synthesis is the holistic experience when all minor elements fold together and can be seen in a larger framework. It is the highest level in cognitive thinking and takes place after the previous steps have deepened understanding sufficiently to entice ones thought process to jump into an original concept or construction. It is the apex of one's creative thought process. Together, they form a whole, a balance, a way for impressions to last in the memory because all our faculties have been brought to the fore by the teacher's method whereby she stimulates exchanges between herself and the class through an active learning process.[55]

This type of thinking leads to conclusions which are unique, innovative, leading to wisdom.[56] It is my belief that synthesis will not take place until we integrate the two styles of mental processing together in our teaching by asking affective questions (see Chapter 5, Questioning).

The future

In a society in which the economic and intellectual freedom of the individual is extolled over the social and political realities for obtaining that freedom, many have dropped out.

The world gets steadily more complex placing more and more responsibility on educators to deal with the unsteadiness of national priorities. We face a dual problem: how to equip children to deal with a difficult future and how to bond them to a past so they care about the future.

When I ask teachers for drama topics in which they wish to involve their children, they requested topics such as: responsibility, friendship, prejudice, self-confidence, self-reliance, and cooperation — basically "right-hemisphere" topics. When these are combined into a chart, the depiction reveals how necessary the child's self-concept becomes.

SELF

non-acceptance of:	acceptance of:
prejudice	uniqueness
non-cooperation	responsibility
alienation	friendship

With the increasing complexities of life, mental and psychological survival becomes more and more crucial; we need to help children build their inner selves. What was once taken for granted now needs to be cautiously salvaged. It is not too late to rebond children, in particular those who come from difficult backgrounds.

The drama process invents a world in which the values of conservation, awareness of beauty, decision making, critical judgments, taking responsibility, cooperation, etc. are built. In a drama the child is introduced to a simulated world in which he may gain those experiences that would otherwise be lost to him. In this way he is surrounded by the richness of a particular experience. If a child has never been exposed to the richness available in the culture which he is removed from, he won't miss it. For example, in a drama, if the children are conducted into space, tension comes when they leave the earth because they've had the experience of being earthlings and so have something to remember and miss.

Recently, after I had conducted a drama about homeless people, the children and teacher talked about their own personal experiences. The children's experiences were almost anti-climatic: "My dad's in prison now, and my mother and me had nowhere to go..."; "These people who live down the street from us, sometimes I walk past and there's lots of yelling. The two older kids ran away, just left."

From a local teacher: "This week I've had six referrals to the CPS (Children's Protective Services)—four are drug related, one abuse—the kid had welts all over his back—and one neglect—all caused by parents."

In the world of the drama children begin to see and experience a reality separate from their daily lives, though one that mirrors society. The drama gives them the vantage point from which to see and make preparation. Otherwise, it is difficult to influence the ills of the culture while one is immersed in it.

A drama about the Civil War brought out the horrors of war. After the drama a blond, angelic-faced eleven-year-old said slowly during the questioning period, "I never want to be in a war." The question becomes: Do we want someone like this child making foreign policy or someone who has been buffered from the realities of war and thinks of it as fun and games—which many children do. Children already know of the problems during their pre-teen years, but if adults don't talk with them, as teens they become cynical. At this point it may be too late, because they have become a part of a peer group which has different concerns.

It becomes difficult for educators to handle questions about the constitution which guarantees, "…domestic tranquility —provides for the general welfare—for ourselves and our posterity…" Out of about five hundred children who made up the audience for a play about homelessness a few did ask: But how come it doesn't work this way?

"Hey, mister, your life's going to be in worse shape if you can't read---," a ten year old student said to the adult actor playing the role of an illiterate after the climax of a drama dealing with missing children. Children know and drama brings out what they know. Their right hemisphere learning is given structure. What they thought they knew, now, they <u>know</u> they know. The terms commitment, responsibility, cooperation, etc. are all qualities that can be bred into children through the techniques used in drama. "His (the child's) will to follow the model (form in the drama) is the same will that drives him to explore the world. He is, we might say, genetically disciplined. Just as the word 'discipline' comes from the word 'disciple', so the disciple or student follows the teacher when real learning takes place. Will is the child's mental muscularity, his power for following, which must be nurtured as any other capacity."[57] (Parentheses mine.)

The whole drama format as it's introduced in this text establishes discipline within the form. In order for the drama to work, the leader must go through a negotiation process that is like a contract requiring acknowledgment by the participants. (see p. 33, Negotiation) For example, during the beginning questioning period the children are ushered into the drama by giving their answers in connection with the life experience in question. They are in a state of paying and giving <u>attention</u>. While this is taking place, concentration is encouraged on the basis of the leader's questioning.

Gradually a relationship is constructed between the children and the subject area because the leader is requiring that the children submit to the drama during this process of negotiation, and they slowly begin their process of <u>identification</u>.

From here, <u>commitment</u> becomes apparent because their own background information is being acknowledged through questions about the topic. Slowly a world is built through simply questioning, thinking, then answering, or by using the rhetorical thought process.

Next, <u>structured activity</u> requires consistent supervision on the part of the leader providing the moments in which the theme of the drama begins to crystallize, whether it's a journey, a meeting, or a physical action. The leader must keep the single pointed concentration by narrating the images that are required, supplying related background material, and <u>intervening when necessary.</u> The teacher keeps the children on task, but it has become their 'task' deepening in significance because it has become their drama.

The leader's questions now relate to their own decisions within the drama which brings them together as artists who can look askance at the world they've given breath to, deepening their awareness, drive and commitment.

They are equating knowledge they know with what they've learned. Through questions the leader has reminded them of what they already know, providing a connection with their new learnings.

Their bonding to the larger society is taking place through the drama. They have been using the multiple intelligences, particularly kinesthetic and spacial, often left out during the school years.

Good teaching instinctively challenges student's fixed ideas by encouraging discussion of issues. This approach gets the student involved in his own learning, supplying motivation without which learning becomes futile; it leads to the open-ended creativity or synthesis without which new problems cannot be solved.

It is the purpose of this text to encourage the teacher to use her understanding of the right hemisphere taxonomy as she teaches, to ask affective questions and to make the curriculum personal so that the child may become responsible for his own learning; to insure that the step called synthesis occurs. Only through the merging, diagrammed on p. 12, can the higher levels of thinking be reached in the elementary school. It is this synthesis, the blending of many divergent threads to form a single theme, that triggers the creative process to see anew. In the chapters which follow an attempt has been made to include the techniques and methods considered in this chapter. Dramatic art contains all the human inventions at work in life; it is an imitation of life and includes the realms of art, humanities, social sciences, sciences and physical education.

NOTES for CHAPTER 1. For complete citation see Bibliography.
Listed below are authors and page numbers.

1   Pearce, 24
2   Restak , 192-195
3   Springer and Deutsch, 261
4   Pearce, 66-6, 82-84
5   Springer and Deutsch, 14-15, 260-261
6   Restak, 195
7   Springer and Deutsch, 236
8   Restak, 221-222
9   Restak, 228, 230-231
10 Restak, 223
11 Restak, 223, 227
12 Restak, 224
13 Dr. John Morgan, psychobiologist,
    Humboldt State University,
    personal communication
14 Restak, 224
15 Restak, 228-231
16 Vitale, 17-19
17 Restak, 230
18 Leighton, Ralph, private
    communication
19 Pearce,136-137
20 Wadsworth, 174-175
21 Pearce, 162-166
22 Pearce, 67
23 Pearce, 70
24 Pearce, 67, 73
25 Pearce, 69
26 Caswell, 6
27 Bruner, Ch. 3
28 Bloom I, xii, xiii; Bloom II, xii-xiv
29 Gardner, 16
30 Lazanov, Georgi, as quoted in Dhority

31   Gardner, xi
32   Gardner, 134
33   Gardner, 87
34   Gardner, 353
35   Gardner, 109
36   Gardner, 110-111
37   Gardner, 118
38   Gardner, 123
39   Gardner, 177
40   Gardner, 176
41   Gardner, 173
42   Gardner, 204
43   Gardner, 177
44   Gardner, 228
45   Gardner, 229
46   Gardner, 233
47   Gardner, 34-35
48   Gardner, 238
49   Gardner, 239
50   Gardner, 241
51   Gardner, 242
52   Gardner, 243
53   Gardner, 245
54   Gardner, 247
55   Bloom I, 162-168
546 Gardner, 293
57   Pearce. 52

"I know why drama is important.
It helps you to understand life better."
-a six-year old boy

Chapter 2

The Teacher and Children, Live

Educational Drama, like all other human activities, is easy for some and difficult for others. For some it is natural; others work hard to master its demands. But no matter our gifts or the obstacles we must overcome, Educational Drama (see Chapter 6, p.89) is worth doing, worth learning, worth experiencing.

To use this material effectively some preliminary performance skills are needed. The following suggestions should be used with individual discretion or as dictated by the needs of students.

Presence

The concept of **presence** isn't usually taught to teacher candidates, yet many teachers discover for themselves a demeanor which suggests authority to children—"this person who's our teacher is in charge."

In addition to speaking the words of the playwright, great actors like Lawrence Olivier have a presence. But even people like Olivier complain of stage fright. So, if we are to understand the process of gaining presence, we need to understand that it is a complex and very personal attribute, built over a period of time and relying on a delicate balance between abilities, motivation, self-respect and confidence.

When one stands before a group of children seeming calm, comfortable and in control, the stance itself sets up a response suggesting that children look and pay attention. There is nothing forced about it, no unstated, "I'd better show these kids who's in charge." For some people the task of presenting themselves with authority is simply not an issue. For others, however, achieving this presence takes courage and practice. To develop presence, standard acting exercises can help build a sense of inner strength that will lead to confidence.

Breathe in and out slowly. Feel the expansion in the whole torso upon inhaling, and the contraction and emptiness when exhaling. Locate a specific place in the center of your torso and get a sense that this center is growing in vitality. Concentrate on that center and feel its importance. Give it weight and substance. Feel yourself being led by that center, as if you've no choice but to follow. See and feel your breath bringing vitality, the center growing, and yourself being led by

"Give me the splendid silent sun with all his beams full-dazzling."
                                        - Whitman

the energy this concentration is providing. Walk, feeling that all parts of the body are relaxed. Close your eyes to get a better sense of your own inner strength. Basic to concepts in yoga and Eastern meditation, these practices strengthen one's inner resources. In time it will all come very naturally.

Voice

The voice has tremendous power to paint an aesthetic picture in space. If your body is the paint brush, your voice is the paint. Begin by humming. Find a comfortable pitch level and work toward low tones. Continue to feel your breath energy combine with this relaxed low vocal tone. In a slow, relaxed manner with plenty of breath, say the following phrase, "When in the course of history, one person's burden becomes another's salvation, we know the system works." Each time you cannot keep all the factors of breath, centering, relaxation, focused energy, and intoning on a hum, working together, begin humming again, and then return to the phrase. Try keeping this low tone, yet vary your pitch so that both your humming tone and speaking tone begin oscillating. Really visualize and kinesthetically feel this changing pattern. After humming it, say these lines from Walt Whitman, "Miracles, why who makes much of a miracle?/ As for me, I know nothing else but miracles."

The projection of a low vocal tone, useful for the teacher personally, can also calm and focus a class that may otherwise tend toward hyperactivity. When the teacher projects a calm presence, children are more likely to internalize a similar attitude.

Just as presence is a problem for some, keeping the voice and body moving together is difficult for others, yet it is an essential skill, particularly when working with younger children. Young children are easily involved in dramatic play, but they are also easily distracted into hyperactivity.

Narration

Using the skills discussed above, narrate a few lines of a common fable or folk tale. Let your body move both up and down, around, forward and back, to the cues your voice gives.

"When Goldilocks sat in the chair, she fell through it. (Let yourself fall.) It was too soft! She sat down in the next chair and went bump. (Show yourself hitting a hard surface.) It was too hard!"

Kinesthetic display allows the children to use the teacher as a pattern, especially when involved in dramatic play. Young children move constantly in their play. The drama experience is natural for them. An **oscillating rhythmic pattern** gauges and contains the children's natural physical energy. By constantly utilizing this rhythmic pattern in her narration, the teacher will be on top of their need to express this pattern.

The group dynamic is unified; the children will be constantly focused. For example, "Let's climb up the mountain (arrow going up); so stop a second to be sure if we should continue on (arrow going down); it's all right (arrow going up); careful, this dirt is loose here, stop (arrow going down); and place each foot down very carefully, etc.

When children are in the beginning grades, K-1, they rely on directions from the teacher; and it is customary for them to be guided in one large group activity.

Both of the above quoted passages are like a **transitional narrative** which is used in between segments of longer dramas, keeping children's feelings connected to the **subtext**, or the meaning between the lines (see Chapter 10).

Journeys

A journey is symbolic of one's life journey. It is reminiscent of the beginning step of the little child who goes toward 'life' in an object across the room. In a sense each journey is an echo of the need to explore and extend one's inner and outer world.

Usually the beginning journey has the children moving while the leader narrates and the children's eyes are open. Sometimes she will ask them to close their eyes for a moment to enable them to "feel yourself in the space." The leader's narration can help insure their belief or undermine it. For instance, guiding them through physical obstacles by saying, "bend down in order to avoid being seen," or "we need to walk carefully from rock to rock in order to avoid the reptiles," is more effective than "there are alligators around us," or "look, there's a mountain." If the physical body is motivated by a subterfuge, belief is more likely to follow. <u>Whenever children are told to look at an imaginary object without any preparation, their belief is stretched to the point of incredulity and the experience breaks down.</u> A journey must have (imaginary) physical obstacles for the journey to be successful. These insure conflict to the otherwise 'passive' television viewer. For a similar reason, the teacher will need to warn the children not to talk or else her narration cannot provide guidance. It is best to offer a reason connected to the objectives of the drama, "We need to listen for the sound of _____;" or "We can't let the _____ hear our approach or they'll hide."

The journey will be successful as long as the leader keeps her narration going in coordination with obstacles, the asking of rhetorical questions, and the oscillating rhythmic pattern. Asking them to stop and close their eyes and validate their inner senses is helpful in keeping them inside the journey. By the time children are about seven, physical journeys will not work as well since they are moving out of the pre-operational stage. It is wise for the teacher to combine visualization with narration as suggested above. By the age of eight visualizations or "in-place" journeys are recommended. (see below.)

The exercises in Chapter 9 and dramas in Chapter 10 are keyed to the journeys by means of the symbols (Jin), (Js), and (Jp). Journeys are a narrative technique and can be described as occurring either "in place" (Jin) or "horizontally through space" (Js), covering ground in movement. Some of the exercises that you will encounter are intended to prepare children for journeys and are indicated as journey preparation (Jp).

Visualization

Closely linked with the external process of narration is the inner process of visualization. Visualization is a mental journey which is appropriately carried out whenever children need to be transported into an unfamiliar environment. Narration, journeys and visualization are all connected in practice. In a visualization the prompting of mental images is usually done with the eyes closed. The average healthy person has a store of images, collected during daily activities that only need to be prompted into being. In the most successful journeys the visualization is first narrated through to its end. Then questions are asked and, lastly, it is explored physically.

During the physical exploration of a visualization the leader continues guiding, alternating images with action. "We've come to the cliff. The path winds that way and back again. Follow me...." Some quiet moments allow for each person's independent decisions to be carried out mentally, until more narration is needed. More narration is necessary to guide children's mental activity than most beginners realize, but gradually more quiet moments can be provided as the children are better able to carry through with their own inner motivation. If a child interjects a directive like, "There's a whale," the leader needs to acknowledge this, keeping her narration going while including the child's offering. "I see it...maybe it is having the same problem we are..." or "maybe we'll meet up with some whales and find out...". By keeping the narration going she is keeping the children inside of the journey, as well as adding to the richness of their visual memory.

"To hold eternity in the palm of your hand, Infinity in an hour." -Blake

Encouraging the creation of visual memory when children are young will help them to use dramatic processes later on. Children in lower primary grades move easily to spoken images, becoming kinesthetically involved while mentally absorbing the feeling quality of the image, and so develop their psychomotor skills.

The process of absorbing word qualities through visualization begins to live inside the mind and the memory, making future, more complex dramas and experiences of the right hemisphere a natural continuation of thought processes. For example, in a drama about saving a dinosaur from extinction, children who are practiced at visualizing will automatically see the dinosaur restrained by a 'joke' leash instead of just seeing an empty leash. Or, they may begin to use imaginative thinking to survive and help their fellow classmates, as in *The Island* drama (Chapter 10).

Gradually that imaginative dimension of brain power not generally used in schools will be nurtured. The drama will be enjoyed because the children will be within the process instead of outside it.

As mentioned above, <u>I have found that many children over seven years old do not receive imaginary images when a horizontal journey is used. After this age, in-place journeys or visualizations are more appropriate</u>. Adequate space is also a factor when deciding between conducting a horizontal journey or an in-place journey. By the age of eight, **conglomerate movements**, such as those used in the **machine** exercise, are also appropriate, especially if the child's inner mental powers have become tapped, used and encouraged. Focus will be more on the object in formation than on one's own self-consciousness. These mental processes are augmented through the writing process as part of the drama follow-up. If the leader continues to work with developing the child's inner thought processes through narration and visualization, it will affect the child's entrance into role and his general ability to stand before the class without feeling overwhelmed by the stares of his classmates.

Through the use of frozen **tableaus**, together with the child's enriched abilities to concentrate and focus within the drama, and develop his feeling of power, he gradually gains that degree of presence which suggests inner control and maturity.

Atmosphere (See Chapter 3 and Chapter 6 for using techniques.)

Narration is important in establishing a harmonious atmosphere. It not only bridges between action and thought for children but reinforces their developing needs to move and speak. A low, resonant and interesting vocal pattern announcing the entrance to the beauties of nature, for example, can furnish children with an aesthetically pleasant environment rather than one filled with fear or the sense of despair they may bring to school.

In the dramas dealing with ecology, time is spent enjoying the natural world, as well as looking at the problems of devastation and pollution. Most of the activities in this text consider the possibility of transforming both inner and outer environments; the outer environment is a reflection of the inner picture. Using voiced images to create a transformed environment and sustaining a dulcet and positive tone begins with the leader's own inner picture through visualization and storytelling.

What we are dealing with hinges on the child's own vulnerability and openness to receive. Many children spend needless energy trying to erect barriers because of fear. It is true that the ability to become perceptive and accept one's perceptions are based upon trust. Music and art are also introduced into many dramas and can generate this quality of trust and openness if the leader shows acceptance of the child's efforts. Timing and how the elements are introduced also become part of this overall affect. Some teachers leave the overhead lights off at appropriate times during discussions or presentations.

Reactions of Children

Children need to practice these techniques. They spend most of their hours in school trying to be quiet. When they're told they can get up and express themselves in an altogether different way, the common reactions are two extremes: debilitating embarrassment and/or the irrepressible joy of freedom, neither of which is appropriate. Children can become confused and lost when using these concepts, unless told exactly what is expected of them. The **Simon Says** approach together with **I Am Thy Master** gets them started with a clear direction.

The underpinnings for any self-expression have more to do with one's daily life than with adopting self-conscious techniques. In the use of drama, life is one's script and so is not easily shared. The very fact that anger is the most difficult emotion for children to express spontaneously, is evidence that motivation must come before expressing serious emotions. Both fear and anger are difficult because they demand a stimulus. Even an adult actor needs to find out what he's afraid of or angry at before expressing this emotion. When an adult offers a child a stimulus by using an angry person in role and invites the children's anger, Dorothy Heathcote calls this "protection into role." If the leader provides a stimulus to become angry, it is more natural for the child to react in anger. The teacher offers the child a way into the experience by initiating the emotion just as the parent offers the child a way into life. The child is immediately absorbed by the experience. This text employs the use of role by the leader to engage the child on an emotional level by causing an emotional reaction. (see Role, Chapter 4.)

Negotiation

Once an actual dramatic theme is chosen the step of negotiation is called for. As in the exercises, it is important to encourage the children to concentrate and believe, for only then will they be affected. The process of negotiation is the most important step of the drama lesson. The leader explains the demands that will be made of the children by saying: "It won't work if you don't believe." This leaves the burden of responsibility to prove that it will work on the child, and children need to feel responsible for their acts. If the leader senses any negativity, she can probe to find out its motivation, whether embarrassment or defensiveness. The negotiation process allows us to permit ourselves entry into the drama within stated limits—whatever those happen to be—which are negotiated and understood at the beginning.

The Negotiation Process

In working with a new group, I usually ask: "Have you ever seen or been in a play before? If not, then you've seen television. How do the actors know what to say? (They have a script) We're not going to have a script. What we're going to do now is become our own playmakers by making up our own words as we go along."

When working with any group, I ask questions to find out how much they know about the drama topic, which has been chosen either by the teacher or the children and teacher together. Specific types of questions are dealt with in Chapter 5, Questioning.

Last, but most important for the drama's success, is the verbal agreement we make together.

"What we're going to do is to go from the everyday world that people call reality into one we make up. But the only way we can make one up is if we're all doing it together. It's like any game. If you don't play by the rules, the game won't work. When doing a drama, if you don't believe in the reality you're making up, then it won't happen. What happens if there's a little hole in your balloon? It's the same with a drama. If anyone thinks it's stupid, then it becomes stupid. Being in a drama together is very delicate, so we have to believe. I won't be asking you to do anything you can't do. If you're having a hard time, just step out and step back in when you feel better about it." Another way is to invite them in. "Today we're going to see what it's like to---and in order to do this you need to believe. Do you think you can? If you can't nothing's going to happen for you. You're the only one who has the power to help yourself believe."

After this negotiation, there is the period of beginning questioning about the subject area to be covered, followed by a transition into the drama. The drama must be demanding of them. They must know what is expected and be given instructions. If they get up and are not in role, enthusiasm will dissipate and their involvement will be haphazard.

Generic exercises

There are about twenty exercises which always work and are discussed in the exercise section. These are open ended and can be related to almost any subject matter. The reason they work is because they remain within the child's ability range and do not make demands that cause him to hurtle prematurely into self-consciousness or less developed skill areas. Many of these exercises tend to blend the outer world of objects with the inner world of feelings, images, and attitudes.

The foundation for children's drama is children's play, and a child accompanies play with movement and sound. An extension of this same dynamic within the generic exercises is to speak with the hands as though the hands are characters. This is one step separated from the children's use of synchronized movement and sound in their own play. Another generic exercise is follow-the-leader, which is one step beyond "Simon Says." By using these exercises, the leader is offering the opportunity for children to bridge their play energy with specific ideas she wishes to introduce. Due to the lack of self-consciousness among young children, this is a ripe period for developing their expressive abilities, and it is important that fun for the sake of learning not be squelched.

When children are older, the same kind of emotional expression is more difficult; the defense mechanisms intrude and anything that is not customary is "dumb." When children react either to narration or to the leader in role they do not have to initiate the situation.

If children have not had any drama experience by around the age of eight, any role playing may seem to be "dumb," like fooling around, and they may not respect it as a skill. Their self-consciousness has grown, and together with their inability to appreciate oral expression as an art, their acting lacks depth and seems often too painful to be of merit. Generic exercises in the exercise section, Character, will assist ages eight on up to achieve spontaneity.

Most people feel silly when they are called upon to express strong emotion without cause; in drama they must feel a legitimate emotion inside themselves or it is not believable.   Children can't turn emotions on and off as well as adults. Thus the leader becomes the child's protector by helping the child react. There is little we can do for children directly in their real lives, but because we're in the world of the drama, we have a license to engage them in this very personal way. It is direct, and it will change them. Heathcote suggests that the child is trapped into a different experience and wants to pursue it in the drama. So we have to work to get them to this level, but once we have broken through they are changed forever; they have matured. Preparation for the drama helps children break through.

If the children have written a letter to give to the giant when they see him in *The Old House* drama (p. 166), 90% of the leader's work is done because the child's own investment of time has already worked to make this fanciful experience real. Drama is larger than life. By going beyond the commonness of daily living, by going beyond the classroom, we see a greater hierarchy of truisms and gain a perspective that would have otherwise remained limited.

Concentration

Several of the generic exercises emphasize concentration, keeping and holding one thing in the mind. Some of the wisest thinkers have suggested that we work best when we can keep a single item in our thoughts. This is difficult since the mind readily moves from idea to idea responding to a multitude of stimuli.

Teachers have said to me, "That's the only time he stopped jiggling all week." As adults, we know concentration is the only way we can get things done. We know it means focusing upon a task and pursuing it to completion. The experience of sending a plumb line down into our own mind and allowing it to reverberate for the length of time it takes to come up with a new thought is a process of growth that can be painful as well as revealing. This concentration is necessary when the child is involved dramatically and interacting within a group.

A generic exercise which also highlights the kind of concentration referred to is Exercise 38, *Inanimate Objects*; for children, speaking for an object is an echo of their own previous experiences in play. The object one speaks for in *Inanimate Objects* is also the object one becomes, and so is less threatening, especially to older, more self conscious children. How can anybody make a mistake when speaking for a thing, especially a thing that may look dirty, scrungy, or gross? Endowing a dirty dishcloth with feelings of rejection is just what a child does naturally. Knowing they are part of a group working in concert helps them develop an attitude of seriousness. When they begin any of these generic exercises with their group, there is nothing to do but to concentrate on the items they've been given. The leader can continue to narrate for them in order to keep them focused, either inside or outside their character.

If the leader has informed the children about the need for this type of concentration in the negotiation process, has supported the child's floundering attempts with narration, intervened using role, and worked with some preparatory exercises, then the dramas will be the logical next step toward which the children move with confidence. Through each new drama experience, the leader reminds the children of the need for concentration and belief, and each time they begin again, one more specific may be acknowledged and added.

Improvisation

Improvisation is spontaneous activity, usually using both voice and movement and often guided by a specific goal. For improvisation to work the players must have a point of departure. The five w's are referred to, the who, what, where, why, when, and often, how. These are the **given circumstances** which must be known before the acting process can take place. Each one presents a different category of human involvement to guide the child further into right hemisphere learning. They provide the subject matter of drama and fill in the answers. Who am I? Where have I come from? What am I doing? Where am I going?

By around the age of eight or nine, most children have the verbal fluency needed to improvise. The teacher can use any four line dialogue between two children as a starting point: Look/ Oh, yeah/ I think it's open/ It is...This simple dialogue is ambiguous enough to allow a myriad of possible situations —a cave, an abandoned house, a store, a school building, two ants looking into a lion's mouth. Give the children free rein to place their dialogue into any situation, with themselves playing any character. Each time they begin a new improvisation, she will add one more item to the given circumstances until they become more and more confident in their oral expression.

Just as the questions of who, what, where are answered by knowing your character, task, and location, other categories can be added by the leader. "I want you to have a conversation with your partner on the same topic, but this time think of yourself as being a particular age and see how this would affect your situation." If the teacher is striving to complete a particular assignment in language arts, she may wish to set up a **frame** within which all students would work, i.e. they are detectives looking for clues; they are trying to find an ending to their stories; astronauts exploring space. Techniques to determine shades of character, listed in order of difficulty, are: emotion, color, costume piece, age, prop, attitude, image (*Improvisation for the Theatre* by Viola Spolin).

This approach is simple, yet effective when used with children who are beginning to pass from the role-playing stage into developing a character. It is an immediate way to involve the techniques used in theatre arts and can be applied to any area of the curriculum. The simple exercises which establish a child's feeling of confidence come easily when he takes up the less threatening exercises first or reacts to the leader's narration or role. Encountering the five w's, the child begins to absorb the human qualities these characteristics represent. Each time the child improvises, he takes on one more circumstance dealing with the human condition. Just as the child must hear his own voice while singing, so he must also experience the medium of drama, perhaps in small doses using the exercises at first, followed by beginning group work in which each child has a definite task. In conjunction with these improvisations, the leader is free to come and go in role. And finally, the leader may wish to adapt any of the drama scripts which are appropriate for her group and objectives.

Audience

The audience is alluded to throughout the text. It is a given in any activity at some point and a step into the evaluative stage of the cognitive domain when the creator becomes critical of his design. Arthur Koestler and others speak of this step in mystical terms. You are watching yourself going through the process from a different vantage point, as though outside or above your own body. At some point in all the activities included in this text when the group is involved, we can begin to imagine ourselves in the eyes of others. Everyone at different moments slides in and out of audience-performer.

From the drama perspective unlike theatre, we know "our turn" is coming. For this reason we become integrated into the process we are watching. As observers we are not passive, as in theatre, but witnesses, producers, directors. For this reason the leader guides the audience, as much as she guides the participants, by giving them something to do while watching. "Watch for _____. Did they find it? Why did you look over there?" By directing their focus she reemphasizes what the process has been about. (These directives are spread throughout both the exercises and the dramas.)

However, the value of the performer's expertise is not considered: Was it honest? Did it move you? Could you believe in him? The art of acting in a theatrical sense is not the focus of this text; for this reason the audience factor as a critical evaluator is not significant. Although the dramas are teacher directed, they allow for much student input within a structure, and the audience is a definite part of the structure.

As Viola Spolin pointed out, the audience is as important a part of the activity as the player in contributing to the event. Depending upon room space not all of the activities can be done in unison. To be directly involved those who make up the audience need to be connected to the ongoing activity as contributors through the leader's narration, **sidecoaching**, and questioning. Her directives become two-pronged, guiding the participants at the same time as she directs the audience's eye by drawing attention to the moment. In each situation she needs to adapt and use the beginning negotiation process as a contractual bridge so the children understand what is expected of them.

Borrowing the term of **give-and-take** from Viola Spolin we can appreciate the acute interchange between players and audience as the leader calls group numbers. She reinforces their taking or giving of space when she calls out a group's number because when one group's number is called, they instantly begin and TAKE the space by moving and speaking, as the previous performing group GIVES it up. Or, they GIVE the space up by stopping, as the other group TAKES it by moving and speaking.

Some of the most exciting moments of this use of sidecoaching have been when the leader no longer needs to lead, and the groups have become autonomous givers and receivers. Their awareness of each other and their own needs seem to become instinctive, and the process of giving and receiving begins to flow. The leader stands to the side to sidecoach by calling the groups' numbers, until the groups can GIVE and TAKE on their own.

Both Dorothy Heathcote and Viola Spolin have said that it is a proud moment when they don't need us any longer, and they are on their own. Like parenthood, if only this same dynamic process of guiding, watching, learning, and growing could be transferred onto the world!

Chapter 3

Creating Your Own Dramas

The beginning motivation for the development of a drama is usually an area of need or interest. The nub of an idea and a few echoes of color and form are enough to get the creative process going. A drama can begin and be carried out in a variety of ways in response to an idea, subject or theme and is most often given definition by the personality of the leader.

I first began teaching in a self-contained classroom. The school administration thought drama was a frivolous activity only to be used for producing a school play at the end of the year or during holidays just before cupcakes were served. I could only use dramatic devices to find a way of bringing the child more inside the experiences presented in textbooks.

I was trying to teach about the five senses using a book that avoided anything specific, anything that the reader could get hold of and say, "So that's the way we hear, or that's how sound travels."

I thought, "How can I make sense out of statements that are so simplistic and indirect as to become meaningless?" and "How can I get the children emotionally hooked, so they'll retain the information?" It was that desire, first felt so long ago, to make learning meaningful, related to life, and memorable, that is the motivation for this book. Since that time I have done extensive research into brain function, learning modes and teaching methodology, and have practiced what I've learned with children and young adults and with teacher candidates. That research and practical experience has resulted in this guide for the use of Educational Drama in the classroom.

All those years ago, when I had only my own impulses to lead me, I remember telling the students about Helen Keller. This was during the late 50's, early 60's, and the play, *The Miracle Worker* had not yet been written. After telling a 4-5 minute story about Helen Keller, I asked the children to try to imagine what it would be like to be as cut off from the worlds of sight and sound as she had been. They willingly closed their eyes while I walked around the front and sides of the cramped classroom, varying the sound of my steps. I asked the children to tell me where I had walked and generally what they had heard. Next, they put their fingers in their ears while I did a 15 second lecture. They were well into experimenting with the "what

"Look for a lovely thing and you will find it."
-Sara Teasdale

if" of no hearing and no sight, when the answer came to them: TOUCH. I told them the story of her teacher, Anne Sullivan, signing the word for water into her hand as she put her other hand under the dripping spout.

Later we were studying how cities develop or can be planned. This text was better and contained a few good pictures. I put a grid on the blackboard and had them make decisions about placing on it all the necessary items needed in a city. The children soon realized that nothing can be substituted for a lack of city planning. It was visually real for them.

Upon another occasion I remember that history and war seemed synonymous. Even though it was the early sixties and Viet Nam had begun, there was no mention of it in the text and only a brief comment about Korea. I started to deal with the concept, "Why war?" and decided to center on greed, since it suited the two wars mentioned in the text, the First and Second World Wars.

After placing the names of all the countries involved in the two world wars on the board and showing how alliances shifted around between the wars, I asked for two volunteers to come up in front of the class. I had collected things from around the room and began to hold up one item at a time for each to choose as their own. They were both cooperating by taking turns in selecting until I held up a baseball mitt. Then the war began, and they were working from their own feelings of, in this case, greed. After a discussion on greed, the explanation of the two world wars went smoothly and held some interest because the children had become motivated to see a picture larger than facts in a book.

I first began teaching in a room in which desks were "nailed down" and creativity, according to the principal, was a "dirty word." Drills, repetition and facts were the trend. I quickly saw that any change in this monotony brought rapt attention and seemingly instant learning and understanding. The smallest deviation from the monotony seemed to shift the classroom from a dreary, plain, antiseptic laboratory into a container of magical interaction and insight. Doing something as simple as rubbing a balloon on the wall in order to line up electrons and magically show the effects of electricity became an exciting experience.

In many places the classroom environment has changed, becoming more humane, but there are still many places where fear obstructs memory channels and children are filled with anxiety.

As Jerome Bruner wrote years ago in *The Process of Education,* dramatizing devices need to be used to enable the child "to identify more closely with a phenomena or an idea. Undoubtedly, this aid in teaching can best be exemplified by the drama-creating personality of a teacher. But there are many additional dramatic aids upon which teachers can and do call—and one wonders whether they are called upon often enough."[1]

Many teachers do not feel they can instantly assume a "dramatic personality." This text offers strategies that will help even the most timid; using a hand with a sock on it, using a mascot or a toy to address the class, or letting a mannequin take on a role, are some of the strategies offered. Even small dramatic additions help build an atmosphere of trust within which children can feel absorbed and contained.

It is this feeling of being inside the information, of being at the core of one's own learning that captures interest and enthusiasm. To create that kind of an environment is our challenge as teachers.

What the leader must ask is: How can I get the attention of each child, hold his attention and include him in such a way that this experience will change his life for the better? This question is not as presumptuous as it sounds if we understand that one's life is changed constantly, not always for the good. Some of the components of change are security, trust, interest, attention, challenge, imaginative thinking, expression, interaction, identification, sensitivity, invention, empathy, and commitment. All of these experiences are fair game for development during a drama session. They are largely components of the right hemisphere.

Why Drama?

A fundamental basis for drama is identification with the hero. This identification allows the heroic emotions to become one's own. Young children feel an especially strong identification with the hero who is helpless and needy. Perhaps it is their own feelings of helplessness and vulnerability which speak to them. Both the hero's quest to succeed and the realization of human need channel the child's emotions to grow toward an objective and to remember our deep connection with the less fortunate.

It is during the pre-adolescent years that the child feels a need to satisfy his own desire for knowledge and personal definition. Both the curiosity for knowledge and the identification with human need are implicit in the dramas presented. These two areas speak for the cognitive and the affective camps, represented by the left and right hemispheres, respectively.

The reason why drama works well to fold in curriculum areas is because drama is an imitation of life. People **do** discover, invent, work everyday, and children have participated in dramatic play up to the time they enter school. The generic exercises are reminders that what children already do can become an effective bridge into learning.

For people who have had a vivid, sensory-rich childhood, childhood remains alive in memory. Stimulation of sensory perceptions helps the brain develop many more mental associations and this connecting builds intelligence in many ways. Unfortunately, many children entering school do not come from a stimulating environment. The parent or parents are barely able to cope, much less provide mental stimulation. The responsibility of the schools increases in response to the child whose need for stimulation is so apparent. If the parent defaults, for whatever reason, it behooves the schools to provide some means whereby the child can become connected to the society.

We know how difficult it is for the teenager to gain identity without guidance and direction. In the earliest grades the teacher's use of role, affective questions, and a more personalized approach using the drama medium can help the child develop the inner resources necessary to cope with the world. We know that by the time children are approaching puberty there comes a cynical greyness out of which they can be lifted with the right tools.

There is a trend among psychologists and thinkers to emphasize the need for turning inward. They say that to balance the confusing elements of the external world, we need to be assured of the sense of who we are. The only true education is "know thyself" or "the unexamined life is not worth living" and in some ways this theme speaks for those right hemisphere qualities that are needed to balance the worldly confusion. The inner world of each one of us is represented by the "bowl" or right hemisphere which needs to be the

container of the whole (See Chapter 1). In contrast, specific products such as technological advances and subject matter areas are represented by the precise yet disconnected pieces of fruit as shown in the diagram below . (Also recall the chart on p. 12.)

The process used in this text penetrates into the inner realms and promises continued growth in awareness and a connectedness with each of our life journeys. These techniques speak to the child in a personal and individual voice, helping him to feel significant in a world in which he could otherwise become lost.

When attempting to teach something to children, it is useless to tell them, "You need to know this for your future." Just telling them doesn't provide the incentive that translates into an enthusiasm for learning.

Cognitive and Affective Objectives

The best criteria for the formulation of objectives are the cognitive and affective.

It is possible to choose the factual information to be taught first, thus satisfying the need for cognitive objectives. The human elements can then be considered and woven around the cognitive area, until both pairs of objectives begin to synchronize meaningfully. There is a dialectic relationship between the affective and cognitive objectives due to their interaction within the brain, but it is not easy to neatly distinguish one domain from the other when it comes to learning and experiencing new material. At the end of the lesson the teacher can pursue the children's learnings through questions to evaluate the drama. Questions are asked to deepen understanding. About half the questions are rhetorical (leaving the question to steep in the right hemisphere) while others will require response and give the teacher a way to check on the learning.

Myth and Fact Together

A drama in which the cognitive and affective domains are integrated is a good example of how to begin and follow through in one lesson. In Betty Jane Wagner's book, *Dorothy Heathcote, Drama as a Learning Medium*, we read about Dorothy Heathcote teaching young primary aged children in Hawaii about holes. She ranges from tooth cavities to volcanoes in her explanations, both very important to these children. She uses the blackboard, carrying out the lesson in true teaching form. The children have complained about the volcano's high degree of heat. During the break, Dorothy writes messages from the children to the Goddess Pele who is the primordial being in charge of the volcano. The messages accuse the goddess of causing the high degree of heat and choosing to stifle the inhabitants whenever she wishes to erupt.

As soon as the lesson resumes, a person in role enters carrying the messages, robed in a collection of burnt rags with singed marks showing on her body. She is enraged at the children for their accusations and continues a harangue about the difficulties involved in living in such an environment. "You don't know what it's like down there...how would you like to live in 500 degrees of heat all the time?" One must fall back on his own imaginative perceptions to appreciate how these children may have come to view life. On the one hand they've understood the academic explanation concerning holes; now they've been bombarded by a completely different view regarding explanations and causes.

In the first instance the logical, geological, academic answer is given; in the second, the mythological, anthropological answers that reach back thousands of years before scientific knowledge. Imagine the stretched perceptions of those children, receiving two diverse explanations, both true. Imagine the exhilaration a child would experience given two such opposite views. As one tunes into the children's thoughts, it is possible to see their understanding crystallize when they are truly engaged. Many vital thought processes are by-passed in the typical factual lecture. In the above lesson we can appreciate the factual as representing the cognitive domain, while the mythological, represents the affective domain. It is important that both areas are acknowledged in order to provide this type of exhilarating thought process. What is education about? If it is about gaining factual information which changes, facts which may not be important in a few years, they will know this intuitively. However, if education is about exploring, weighing, considering, wondering, theorizing, in short, thinking, we will enable them to be open to learning for the rest of their lives.

Analogy

Analogy is extremely useful in drama for many reasons. A single detail can suddenly expand into a universal statement because metaphorical use of language takes us there. A simile illustrates its value: It is like throwing a pebble into water and watching the ripples that result.

Another appropriate example is one that further serves the direction of this text toward the necessary recognition of our bond with nature: When a frog jumps into boiling water it quickly jumps out. But when it's in cold water which is brought slowly to a boil, the frog dies.

The language of analogy is not linear but spirals. It is "essence", poetic. This makes assessment of the arts difficult. One cannot test in the arts which are implicit, self-contained, and symbolic using the methods of the sciences which are linear, exact, and numerical. However, we can evaluate the impact of the arts; use of analogy is one way.

A common example of the use of analogy in drama is the play about rival street gangs, *West Side Story*. Many people, seeing this play, didn't know they were also experiencing a universal condition of romantic love being tested by loyalties between rival forces. Suddenly *Romeo and Juliet* can be revealed to them, as well as the troubadours of the Dark and Middle Ages; and the spiral goes on into balladry, poetry, a musical folk heritage, revealing not only a historical tradition, but a universal situation of passions and tenderness.

Drama serves as an analogy when the leader conceives of a concept and follows it up by asking <u>final questions</u> which shift the concept to make a more universal connection. Some examples from Chapter 10 illustrate this.

In the *Toys* drama the child has developed self-esteem in a very controlled manner. A natural follow-up could be the leader's suggestion that the toy become a real person. By giving him this opening, he's empowered to decide his own future. It is using the symbol of Pinocchio, yet unlike Pinocchio, he will be more autonomous, not adrift and vulnerable to the evil powers of society, a theme applicable to teenagers as well.

In *Taking Care of Pets*, the child begins to care for the environment by first becoming responsible through his own empathetic need to care for something that depends upon him.

The exercises can also be a single action that becomes layered through analogy; for example, the exercise *Waiting* (Exercise 40 in the Character Section) is a funnel through which not only the Dust Bowl but perhaps the history of our ancestors and the future is viewed.

Most would think it silly for people to be fighting over a book or even food because they are free to think and have never been hungry. In the dramas dealing with oppression it becomes the teacher's task to insure, through the negotiation process, that the children "sign a contract" to shift into the metaphor that says: for the majority, much of history is oppression. In a sense the learner's own affective needs to survive as a species are used as a hook to connect with a broader and more planetary need that enables everyone to survive. Once the connection has been reinforced by reliving it in a drama, real learning follows; names and dates are learned and given an underpinning and though they change and some are forgotten, the main thrust will continue to spiral because it was once given birth in the child's own need to survive and transform. Drama is an analogy, an imitation of life.

In the same way that analogies stand for a comparison between things, anything can be a symbol. For example, the soldier is a symbol for all soldiers and can be used by the leader to represent the personal and subjective side of war.

The leader may use any of the dramas to stand for a particular aspect of human nature: *The Forest*, disrespect and abuse of nature; *The Gold Rush*, greed; *Immigration*, alienation. In this way she can direct her thinking before the drama to become multi-layered, guiding her questioning and approach to role.

Psychomotor and Aesthetic Objectives

Two other important objectives are the aesthetic and psychomotor. With young children the aesthetic is experienced when they are directed in a journey using images. The psychomotor domain is linked directly with movement.

The use of the aesthetic objective is directed toward a consideration of beauty and form. Even though a psychomotor activity is not a part of every drama, aesthetics is, for it speaks to the need to keep children within the world of the drama.

In the drama *Ecology and the Ocean*, the journey proceeds smoothly toward the objective of finding out more about pollution, while maintaining a delicate balance between fear and excitement to keep the chiuldren focused. The leader narrates a series of images and surrounds them with the feeling of the beauty of the ocean. In her narration she chooses images that both titillate and inform the children by including narration about the currents, changes in color due to light and luminescence, changes in temperature, the plant and animal life.

Brainstorming an Idea

The leader will know what she wants to do a drama about. I want them to know about endangered species...children like animals...what animal shall I use?... will the animal be present?... if so, how will I show it?   It makes no difference what choices the leader makes, as long as it meets her needs and resources.

After the means for handling role is determined, she needs to continually ask herself: What will the children be doing? What will they see? How will they feel about this? How can I keep them interested? What materials will I need?

So far she has chosen her main idea which translates into a **through-line of action** such as endangered species and wanting to save them. She obviously would want the children to express this need in some form, letters to a congressman, news articles, fictionalized accounts. However, they may wish to invent their own way of saving the animals so they design a trap in order to tag them and find them later on, study them for medical reasons, explore a new geographical area where they won't be endangered, etc.

Some Ways of Beginning

The teacher knows what she wants to teach—holes, layers of atmosphere, geography of the plains states, subject/predicates, etc. Perhaps thoughts on a particular subject area have been circling through her mind, and she has jotted down ideas. These ideas together with any research that is necessary can be looked at as the material she wishes the children to learn. Using an intrapersonal approach, these ideas may be turned into a **monolog** which the main character speaks, delivering the factual material in a casual though deliberate way. The *Medicine Person* drama is organized in this manner. The same material can be used as a **soliloquy** that is spoken as if no one else is present. The Indian child in *The Forest* drama uses an example of this approach. Of course, the children are overhearing the ideas, and as soon as they are recognized by the role, they would then be acknowledged as part of the drama. The focus would become even more intense, since the children's presence isn't obvious until recognized by the role.

Similarly, the same material could be used in a more interpersonal approach such as a dialogue. If there is another person available, the dialogue would be shared. If not, the dialogue could either be shared with a mannequin or spoken as if another person were sharing the conversation. This person would exist as a kind of empty set, but given focus. Often, the simple placement of a chair is enough to indicate identity. The children would be acknowledged after the ideas had been presented.

If the leader knows of a particular story she wants to employ, she chooses the major problem and action following the problem. Lifting these out, she presents the problem to the children and, after getting their answers, selects tasks, either physical or mental, for the children to work on.   As they work, she may introduce other complications in the form of interventions or announcements. She may even decide to enter the drama as an **antagonist**.

Most plays move toward rising action, a climax point, falling action, a denouement and conclusion.   After the climax has been reached, children rarely care about the falling action.

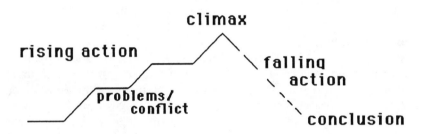

When the leader has decided on the kinds of questions she will ask to introduce the subject (see Chapter 5, Questioning), how she will cover the factual material, both the academic-cognitive and the experiential-affective, how she will depict the role (see Chapter 4, The Teacher in Role), she may begin to understand what can serve as a climax point in the drama. Though it isn't always necessary to reach a climax, it is necessary for the "playwright" to begin to see the drama as a whole to understand how the children will perceive it.

It becomes possible for the leader to see the drama not as an assembly-line production, but as a train climbing up a mountain, yet stopping to refuel along the way to insure the greatest mixture of new passengers, new complications, and perhaps reaching the last pinnacle of action or the climax before asking the final questions.

Components of The Dramas

While dramas can be infinitely different and serve a broad variety of purposes in the classroom, there are certain components that are common to them all. These components are exposition, off-stage action, identification with the role, emotions, dynamics and rhythm, and slowness.

Exposition

In theatre vocabulary the term **exposition** is used to stand for any factual information which must be known by the audience for the play's action to move forward. In Educational Drama exposition includes any information either about the topic or the drama which children need to know to keep the drama moving forward. Exposition is used throughout the drama. Both left hemisphere-factual material and right hemisphere-human material are co-ordinated and represented by exposition. The leader includes it in the narration, in the role, as a catalyst who mediates for the role, in a document carried by the one in role, and/or by means of other written materials such as letters, diaries, maps, journals, news reports, etc.

Off-Stage Action

Anything that is referred to on stage which is going to happen or has happened can embellish the present tension or conflict. In dramas dealing with war, for example, off-stage action can be the determiner of how the drama acquires complications. A war or large-scale activity of any kind cannot take place on stage, but takes place within the minds of the participants and within the world of the drama. In this way the war can become much bigger in the children's minds. Even in Shakespearian dramas we see sword fights depicting WAR. Next, a messenger runs in making announcements and bringing greater tension. As soon as the drama starts the war becomes a specific significant incident, and any reference to it re-establishes the conflict in the drama, so belief is emphasized. Much information and exposition can be introduced in this form through roles, written material, and/or stepping out of the drama to inform, once the belief is secured.

Identification with Role

The most important aspect of depicting the main role is the children's own identification with both the problem situation and the role. It is the absence of identification that dangerously effects many children in school today. They do not identify and so don't care. Their capacity for caring by identifying with another caring person has been so thwarted that they grow sullen and become detached from the larger realm of society, people, truth, a way of behaving, and with what is stereotypically called, what is right. As a result they drift, trying to formulate their own truth, while their consciousness becomes more and more narcissistic, detached, and at odds until nothing matters.

Once the child's caring has been alerted, it can become re-nourished, practiced, instilled, and made permanent. We can care for others and the world to the degree that we can interject our caring spontaneously until it includes even ourselves.

It is during the beginning negotiation process when the teacher moves from questions about the topic to questions about the drama, that significant numbers of primary aged children are drawn in. It takes the introduction of the main role to satisfy the intermediate ages. It is often at this level that a conflict between future and past becomes felt. The "we must, but we can't" is reiterated, and the sudden emergence of will to prove, "we can" takes root. It is this drive toward the drama's work or context that the teacher wants to influence. Hence, from the seed of an idea she chooses questions and develops a beginning by deciding how to introduce the role and the problem. (In some dramas, identification with the problem or situation may precede role.)

Some dramas begin casually. The leader is arguing, the children become interested in the argument, and the only resolution is that the children must help. Once the drama has begun, the teacher needs to know what she will include to keep it going by having devised a mental check list. How am I going to insure that their identification with the role or problem grows?

Next, the constant questions that are asked are those questions dealing with how the children are involved. What will keep them involved? Where will they be focused?

Emotions

Teachers are often afraid of extreme emotions, yet instilling emotional depth makes the drama work, and the extreme emotions are contained within the frame of the drama. They do not spill out into the math lesson or the cafeteria. Helping the children to feel emotionally involved comes through their ability to identify with the human situation. Human weakness is basic to the quality of vulnerability needed at some point in the drama to build the empathy necessary to insure change. The teacher must decide how she will encourage their identity. For example, the child will not care about the eagle and its demise unless he has enjoyed first the feeling of freedom during the eagle's flight. As a fact by itself, it is outside his area of experience. In short, "How will I help them to FEEL the needs of this role and, in turn, of society?" A generic visualization exercise or journey-type experience where the children soar with an eagle will facilitate their identity later with the eagle role.

Within this right hemisphere area the level at which the problem is acknowledged—receiving, responding, valuing, organization, characterization —will determine its depth. Bloom's affective levels are helpful and show that the drama has required at least some manner of responding. It is necessary, however, to reach the next layer, that of valuing, whereby a child will take it home with him. In this way the experience will become part of his life as will the factual knowledge.

The leader needs to be aware of the area of concern normal to the children. In essence the degree of pain the children feel needs to be equated with the opportunity to elicit their help through questions. In the dramas about pollution, most children care about the environment in reference to the degree they care to become involved in their roles. When their degree of caring reaches a stage in which they feel pained, their caring will increase, and their participation in the world will carry over as it's given direction. Few adults reach the stage of characterization whereby they are willing to make sacrifices for an idea. It is the commitment area that is called forth, or the last stage in the area of the affective domain which Bloom calls Weltanschauung, ones view of the universe or one's philosophy of life, or the final stage in moral development. A certain degree of maturity needs to be reached whereby a child's degree of empathy and awareness find equilibrium.

When the leader decides the climax or moment of highest tension has been reached and reacted to verbally, she suggests that the drama be concluded and sits with the children in a group so that together they can evaluate their learning.

This is a very delicate step, for many children may still exist in the realm of the drama. Final questions, as seen in the section on questions, help the children to reflect on their own creation, their own "orchestrated painting" of life and to stand back as if once removed looking at life being lived. As Emily said in *Our Town*, "Do any human beings ever realize life while they live it, every, every minute...That's all human beings are, just blind people." Can we satisfy Emily's concern? Perhaps we can imagine what it would be like to go through our life always being in both camps, the one of personal play (the child's own play involvement) and the other, projected play (the child watching play while he is participating in it imaginatively). We can imagine what life would be like if we really did reflect upon each thing that happens as if it were projected upon a movie screen. It could be equated with being conscious of the larger expanse of human history. Judgement is suspended as awareness grows, allowing for a broader viewpoint to be adopted or a different truth which becomes universal and common to all.

In *Left Brain, Right Brain,* Springer and Deutsch say, "...consciousness depends on linguistic processes and the creation of an internal, metaphorical 'I.' Consciousness is a smaller part of our mental life than we have assumed. A great deal of our mental activity is not conscious but automatic—we don't think about it. This is one reason why it should not be so difficult to imagine ancient humans going through life without the self-consciousness we have developed. They may not have been able to view themselves at a distance or to imagine themselves doing something in the future."[2]

J. Jaynes, in his article "Reflections on the Dawn of Consciousness," says that "Consciousness is learned on the basis of language and taught to others. It is a cultural invention rather than a biological necessity. . . We know now that the brain is more plastic, more capable of being organized by the environment than we previously supposed....We can assume that the neurology of consciousness is plastic enough to allow the change from the bicameral mind to consciousness to be made largely on the basis of learning and culture."[3]

It is this attempt to evaluate our life in common with universal principles that can be seen surrounding all the other ideas in the drama. The new insights give the children a new underpinning that helps them transform and mature both mentally and emotionally.

Dynamics or Rhythms   (see Slowness,p. 54; Distancing, p. 92; Rhythm, p. 94)

We turn to the theatre world and to the word *dynamic*—a word meaning change—which insures that there will be a rhythm in the drama. The leader never wants the rhythm, movements, or changes to become static. A new **beat** is introduced, adding tension and eliciting interest. In the theatre, whenever a new character is introduced, a messenger reports off-stage action, or where any new aspect of the situation is reported or occurs, it is a new beat and serves to increase the pressure toward gaining a resolution. Not only are the animals hungry in the forest, but there is the increasing danger of poachers. We can give this family a citation for being irresponsible and having caused a fire, but what do we do about poachers? And suddenly we are plunged into a national crisis dealing with those people who only think of immediate gain, and re-echo that they "don't care."

So far, the drama has built toward a satisfactory point of tension, or conflict, leading toward the climax. It is this presence of the on-going demands of life which the leader brings into the drama. The leader works as a playwright to introduce these situations into the drama. These activities grow out of the need to keep the drama going in the children's minds, keeping them connected to the drama physically, psychologically, emotionally, and socially. After they have lived in the world of the drama by doing tasks related to it, they have experienced a shift in their own knowledge. The inclusion of these incidents, tasks, complications, or problem solving situations has also contributed to a plot structure (refer to the diagram on p. 51). If the reader glances at the diagram and reads it, she can begin to hear the accompaniment of sound designating the different climatic peaks or high points of tension. She can appreciate a rhythm, working consistently toward a climax, with a single beat to represent the conclusion.

It is this rhythm which analogously represents any action from the smallest rivulet on the beach to the pulse of city-life. Even in the silence, there is the rhythm of a heartbeat, or an intermittent breeze. Whenever a new complication is introduced by the leader, the regularity of occurrences is interrupted by a much stronger accent or beat: da—da—da—DA—dum, dum. Aesthetically, we are momentarily surprised, take a new breath, and are temporarily exhilarated while we attend to this new issue. We elude boredom, restlessness, wandering of attention. As soon as the leader hears these signs, she introduces something into the drama space—a thought, question, new idea. The rhythm doesn't need to move more rapidly, but the moment needs significance. The leader must make the most of the moment. If necessary supplies are forgotten by a crew member, as captain of the ship she gets angry, and with a 15 to 20 second beat the tension is magnified. If it is diluted, the effect on the children will be like static and will not carry.

A meaningful rate of slowness sustains attention because it is compelling, not hurried in an effort to get through. It is this same quality of dynamic tension the leader uses to guide the drama.

Slowness (see also Journeys,p. 28; Visualization, p. 29, Narration, p. 27 ; Chapter 4, Teacher in Role and Chapter 5, Questioning)
    Children always prefer action and are more interested in what comes next than in the present moment. In order to keep them connected to the drama so they can experience it fully and deeply, the leader needs to slow it down. She needs to work against their natural inclination toward action. Whether she takes a role or not, she can intercept the drama at any time. She is always guiding it by using all of the means mentioned. She is always holding on to moments

which can be slowed by her own ability to narrate, provide **transitions** through narration, stop to question through role or out of role, make statements which invite questions, build anticipation, project a presence of being unsure about the protagonist's future, all of which will increase their interest and provide **tension** (see p. 91). A **transitional narrative** combines narration with tension by compressing the moment to show the passage of time. For instance, in *The Island* drama they are taken from a sinking submarine to an island during a transitional narrative (see p. 200). Whenever she works as a **catalyst** between the person in role and the children, she is able to control the speed of the drama (see Chapter 4, Teacher in Role).

During rituals and ceremonies a drumbeat and/or chanting or narration in monotone help to create a tranquil mood just as journeys can be slowed down by music accompanied by narration contributing to an aesthetic richness.

Whenever an object is used to represent a **symbol**, all the many layers of meaning can be considered as the children react to the object. In a drama about Eskimos, the activity of passing a candle and envisioning the whale's eye looking back and speaking to each child is an example of slowing and at the same time deepening the moment for each child. "The spirit of the whale will speak, if you wish it to speak." It is important that the leader designate specific places in the lesson to slow down either using narration, a transitional narrative, universal "musing" or wondering questions (see Chapter 5, Questioning), asking for the student's own contributions in a ritual or reactions to be delivered in a ritualistic manner. This concern will enable the drama's theme to become part of the memory, thinking, and life of the children.

When a teacher tells children, "Let's all become flowers" and two little boys decide to become a horse and a carrot, she knows she has expected product instantly without going through process. Before each drama begins the leader informs the children through the negotiation process, beginning questioning, and prepares them so that they know what their action is and should be. At this time she also sets up signals through narration, "When we hear the bird's call, then we know that we're..."

Management

The main difficulty in guiding these dramas will be when the leader herself goes into role. Her changing into role can take place in front of them or out of their view, but they must be prepared for it, unless shock is required by the drama. She may or may not warn them that she'll be taking on a role, but she must be careful not to break the feeling that has contained them thus far. The teacher may go from one role into another as simply as taking one step to the side to provide a transition(see Chapter 4, The Teacher in Role, Role Transition).

By the middle grades, she may ask a child to be in role. In many dramas, she will need a few monitors to provide light or sound cues, if she can't manage these herself. Using a battery-powered, hand-carried tape recorder to provide instant sound cues will keep the drama flowing.

When children are involved in presenting scenes in groups, as in *The Forest* drama, everyone works at the same time until they are ready to begin. Most teachers will be pleasantly surprised at how readily children can accept role and adapt to its conventions. When everyone, leader and children alike, have some practice at exercises and dramas, more and more occasions will present opportunity for drama and hence more and more occasions for deepening the child's emotional involvement in learning.

Noise Level

If the leader needs the children to be quiet, she must invent a reason which suits the demands of the drama event: for example, "We need to be quiet or the spirit will be afraid" (inside the drama). "If you cannot listen then I cannot take you" (outside the drama). If children have had little training or discipline in adhering to a form, I often use a sports analogy like, "What are the rules of the game?" and/or give them a signal like, "When you see the room lights blink or hear the drum, etc....then freeze." Such changes are intriguing to children, giving them a license to transform. Use of a control device such as a tambourine, drum, or music is always effective. "As soon as you hear this (beat on the drum twice) then you know it's time."

The Generic Plan for the Drama

There is not one single plan that consistently covers all lessons. The following list might help guide your thinking as you begin to create your own dramas:

Objectives
cognitive (factual and conceptual)
affective (experiential and emotional, related to life)
aesthetic (beauty and form)
psychomotor (movement)

Teacher's own thinking (brainstorming):
   What subject area should I use?
   What will I need to use as materials?
   What beginning questions should I ask to link them with the
      drama and to find out what they know?
   How will I depict the role?
   What tasks will the children be doing?
   What will they see?
   What feeling level will be produced?
   How will I keep them focused throughout the drama?
      (through role, pictures, sound, complications, questions)
   What conflict is being resolved? Or what is the "crisis
      question"? (See Chapter 5, Questioning)
   What are possible outcomes?
   What final questions shall I ask to help them reflect upon
      their new understandings and responsibilities?

Readiness for the Drama
   After the leader has gone through the negotiation process of
determining the children's understanding and commitment to the
drama (see Chapter 2, section on Negotiation) by asking questions
and holding an informal discussion, she introduces or defines the
topic.
   "Today we're going to..."
   "Have you heard of....?"
   "Does anyone know of...?"
   "They say that...,"
   "What about...?"
   "A long time ago they..."
   "I have also heard that..."
   At this point she shows them pictures, brings out objects or
displays any memorabilia which helps to bring the topic closer to
their understanding. It is during this phase that the leader begins to
feel and see their potential interest which she can enlarge upon by
using all the main ideas she wishes to extend into the drama.
   "Are we ready, then, for the drama to begin?"
   "Let's see if we can find out how_____works."
   "We have a lot of ideas."
   "I certainly hope we'll be able to_____in our drama."

Transition into the drama

There are decisions regarding given circumstances which the leader needs to make beforehand, but some decisions she can ask the children to make. Any decisions which are related to emotional depth and timing cannot be made by the children because these determine the overall effectiveness of the drama. In setting up the drama the leader may lead with either her major decisions and/or the children's minor decisions.

"Today is the day for_____" (major decision)

"What would you be doing?" (minor decision)

"They have told us to find_____"(major decision)

"Where would you be so they won't see you as easily?" (minor decision).

Often dramas begin with someone in role, either the leader, "I'm going over here and when I turn around the drama will begin..," or someone else in role, "He will be here any minute..." or, the leader may bring in a mannequin or introduce an adult or child as the one in role.

The Drama

The sections which follow indicate a rough approximation of the length of time to spend on various parts of the drama. Time limits are variable; depth can be achieved within seconds through the use of role (see Chapter 4, The Teacher in Role).

Ten Minutes (Entering in role)

"How do you do...Is this the group who...?"

"I've heard that all of you are..."

"I've seen the...coming from across the valley."

From this point on the role instructs them, appoints them to a task, gives them needed background to build a fence, plan their attack, determine questions, needed lists, design buildings, map treasure, rehearse a method, all of which can be done in smaller groups, unless children are in grades K-1 and often 2.

Two Minutes

In the midst of the groups' involvement, the role may intervene, leading the group into the main body of the lesson. The whole group may be reconvened to hear or witness each others' decisions, or they may be led in some activity such as those illustrated in the exercises. Several of the children may be called upon to speak. New roles may be needed amongst the children.

Ten-twelve minutes (Main body of the drama)

At any point during the drama, the leader can call upon all to stop. She may either be within the drama in role and wish to stop to have participants talk to each other, or she may stop the drama to come out of role. If she does this, the drama becomes like an on-going tapestry to which the participants can refer (see Chapter 6, Distancing, p. 92). She may question them about their decisions in a complimentary fashion, and at the same time, introduce a new complication, or ask them a question by which a new slant is suggested.

"What are we going to do about...?"

"Do you think we can...?"

"Do you want the people to become...?"

At this point she may decide to introduce an activity which has been chosen by the group, an exercise from the generic list, or one from the regular exercise section, or she may wish to announce a situation leading to the climax.

"I have just found out..."

"The orders have arrived, and we will..."

She may be either outside or within the drama directing this segment.

Outside: "Let's stop the drama for a minute. Do you think...?"

            "We need to..."

Inside: "I see them in the distance."

            "Today is the day for..."

The leader's decision to conclude is based upon many factors, depending on various circumstances such as time limitations and/or the children's responses.

Five minutes (Final Questions)

Finally, she will stop the drama and bring them all together to ask the final questions in order to lead toward **reflection**. Through the process of reflection we become our own teachers. Children need some adult guidance to accomplish this.

This last activity is the second most important step in the drama(the first being the negotiation). By asking a few pointed questions, the leader can cause the children to mentally conceive of themselves in a new way.

"Do you think this will happen again? How? How do you think it will be different if it happens again?"

(These questions can match the beginning questions with the difference that now they can be answered.)

"Why is it important to...?"
"How did you help in this...?"

Universal questions
    Although these questions can be asked at any time during the drama, as final questions they have greater impact and resonance, relating participants to the larger world perspective and the human condition.
    "How are these _____ like those of today?"
    "Why hasn't this always been the case?"
    "How do you think these _____ have changed?"
    "Is it important to change?"
    "How will its affects make long-range changes?"
    "Do you think children in other parts of the world have responsibilities?
    "I wonder why we feel so small when we see the ocean?"

    The whole drama as suggested above should take about 60 minutes total.

Creating a Drama from an Exercise (an example)

                    Title of Drama: Poetry Writing
Objectives
    1. Cognitive: To understand that words are used and chosen to express special qualities as a result of their sound.
    2. Affective, psychomotor, aesthetic: To move to the sound tone a word or image suggests, interchanging and reacting to the partner's interpretation.
    3. Cognitive and affective: to express a concept using a poetic form.

The Drama
    Using exercises 1 and 2 in Chapter 8, the leader asks the children to get into even numbered circles so that the person standing opposite becomes their partner. After the children are paired up and numbered off, the leader calls out color words, emotion words, and/or onomatopoeic words, and then the pair's number. The children take on the qualities of the words and interact as they move into the circle and either back to their original places or exchange places with their partner.

Next, the students sit in a large circle on the floor and close their eyes. The leader places objects in each child's hand. The child thinks about the object and brings to mind an association (not one that is literal). These objects are passed in the same direction so that each child has one and until all object have gone around the circle once. All the objects are collected while children still have their eyes closed. A discussion about metaphors is held (see Chapter 8, Exercise 3). As the children give their associations, the leader pulls out the prop that may have been a stimulus for the association. A list of these metaphors is placed on the board.

Finally, the leader gives each group a picture that she feels will evoke images from the students. While the students look at the pictures they entitle their poem to correspond with the subject of the picture, and each child offers a metaphorical phrase to complete it.

This old ship...
...is a boulder covered by moss in which a cave is hidden...
...creeps silently while waving her hair ofseaweed...
...is a monster in the deep...

After about twelves miniutes of writing the students are asked to combine and express their ideas in movement.

Creating a Drama from an Exercise (another example)

Title of Drama: Conservation and Recycling

Objectives:
1) Cognitive: To understand how to recycle so the waste products can be reused.
2) Affective: To empathize with the street person.

Drama:
In a drama the students were given cards with different situations on them: 1) wasting food; 2) wasting energy by leaving water, light, and electricity on; 3) wasting gas by making several trips to the store; 4) throwing away old clothes while doing spring cleaning.

These scenes are enacted while the rest of the children who are not in the scene become the television audience.

The last scene is enacted by the leader who may have introduced these scenes. At this point she gives instructions to one of the children to announce: "Now we wish to take our TV camera out on the streets to see how people are coping with this problem of waste."

The leader enters as an old person who goes through the trash endowing it with special significance by carefully placing the different items into piles labeled: recyclable, biodegradable, non-biodegradable. The streetperson may be interviewed during the show, or the reporter can bring the show to a conclusion and take the streetperson into the "TV Studio" where the interview can take place (see Chapter 9, Character, Exercise 29). In either case the street person should have a biographical sketch; any questions from the children are answered by the streetperson as she draws from this biography of her life.

The following lists may help with beginning decision and lead into dramas.

Some Ideas for Role

A cowboy teaching about branding

A foreigner asking the children for help in an area they've just learned about

A seafarer who explains myths about the sea

An explorer who explains his/her trek

A dietician teaching about the food groups (see *Nutrition* drama)

An environmentalist who explains the need for maintaining a balanced ecology

A historical person who represents his/her era and can be interviewed by the children

A toy manufacturer who listens to children's suggestions and studies their designs and movements (see *Toy* drama)

An author of children's stories who takes suggestions from children which they then can turn into their own stories (see Exercise 7)

A veterinarian or animal-trainer who gives information about animal care, treatment, and training (see *Taking Care of Pets* drama)

A person who has any problem that the class can help with, such as: rejection, prejudice, firing, illiteracy, dishonesty, homelife, finding a job, bad manners, rudeness

The "devil's advocate" role may be played by any of the above, bringing out even more layers of thought.

Task possibilities
   Daily work:

chop wood	pick fruit	plant crops
harvest crops	cook	serve
wash	paint	haul water
prepare food, drink	man boats	take care of animals
weed	mow lawn	build boats, houses
fish	hunt	carry heavy objects
shop	eat	prepare for a storm
in line at store	plant gardens	collect and sort trash

   Professions:

pioneering	exploring	office work
construction	carpentry	assembly-line
cutting and labeling	circus performer	buying and selling
restaurant work	demonstrating and presenting	
forester checking trees for disease		

   Recreation

fly a kite	play in orchestra	conduct an orchestra
walk a dog	train an animal	make a sandcastle
mime sports		

   Drawing

charts of gardens	maps	imaginary pictures
ideas	house design	toys
machines	a particular environment	

   Planning

rituals	harvest	burial
trips	exploring	fixing up a park
planting	building and working	

   Writing (see Chapter 8)

newspaper articles	letters	reports
reviews	summaries	diaries
journals	stories	scenes
histories	logs	documents

NOTES for CHAPTER 3. For complete citation see Bibliography.
Listed below are authors and page numbers.

1   Bruner, p. 82
2   Spring and Deutsch, p. 259
3   Jaynes, p. 58

Chapter 4

The Teacher in Role

(Several of the roles included are the result of my having studied with Dorothy Heathcote and are mentioned in B.J. Wagner's book, *Dorothy Heathcote, Drama As a Learning Medium*).

The teacher in role

The intention of this text is to explore some fundamental ideas on drama for the teaching situation. When the teacher takes on a role for the purpose of developing a drama, she need never 'act.' Nor do any of the children who take on roles need to become 'actors.' Though the terms teacher/actor can overlap, and I will use the term actor throughout this section, *stepping into role* is a natural process. Stepping into role is a means of suspending disbelief, and if the teacher/actor first suspends her disbelief by assuming a persona, the children will more easily suspend their own disbelief and become more deeply involved.

The teacher tells a story—"I was walking down the street and there in the distance I saw..."— and by doing so creates an involving situation.

When the child first begins to talk, he is reporting what he sees and does. From here on he becomes a reporter, telling what the movie was about, what the trip was like, or verbalizing adventures that he wishes to pass on. His natural inclination is to become an actor in his own story. Within the story framework, the actor can inform, instruct, explain and pass on information. Unlike the lecturer, the actor is within the story, making the event more personal and enabling the listener to immediately empathize through his own emotions.

"They say that once a year a white horse can be heard neighing and galloping outside on the heath. It raises its hooves as though to warn..." or..."I could hear the beating of hooves coming closer until the horse rose up and neighed..." In the first version the actor is telling the story and distancing herself from the action, while in the second she's a participant in the story and directly related to the action.

The teacher casts a net of ideas, feelings and images to attract and include the child. Using role enables her to impart not only information, but a quality of feeling related to the information that the child would not receive from other methods. Belief in a situation is sustained as long as the teacher wishes to indulge this belief through her eye contact, vocal changes and personal interest. Through role she can protect the child by pressuring him to channel his own emotional response (see Chapter 2, p. 32). The use of role puts the teacher on a continuum somewhere between her teaching self and herself as actor.

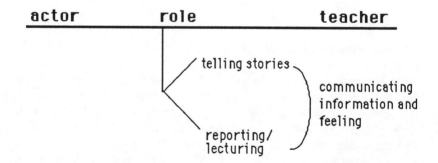

There are many levels or types of role that the teacher might employ.

The Authoritative Role

The authoritative persona is much like the teacher's daily role of lecturer, yet she has made a slight shift by using her voice differently to help the children develop an inner attitude. This slight shift from the teacher's ordinary personality is very much like a teacher changing her voice to take on a character when reading expressive literature. If the teacher feels comfortable in this particular stance, then she adopts the role of the one who knows. She may decide to adopt any degree of knowledge or status necessary to her objectives.

An advantage of this role is that it satisfies her own need to direct the children's activities and to inform them—"And this is how the Indian children were taught to walk... ." But though she retains control, she is not outside the action, but inside, and gently, through the beginning questioning and activities, she's enabling the children to get a sense of being inside it too.

She may impel the children to react to a situation which may be new to them, as in the drama *Homeless Children*. In this drama two authorities are included, the real estate lady and a landlady. The leader quickly exchanges costume pieces from a silk scarf to an old apron, becoming first one and then the other character in the drama. What's important to the children is not that their teacher is acting like a crazy person, but that the drama moves forward.

Another gradation of this stance is the role of **devil's advocate** which the teacher uses to challenge the group and surprise them into a reaction. In some cases she may turn the children against her and cause them to argue amongst themselves. In the drama *Medicine Person*, she works to turn the group against the antagonist. At any point in the drama, she may 'stand to the side,' (sidecoaching) only coming into the drama as needed to re-direct the activity, to take it further, hold it in place, or stop it to reflect. Her role is now so firmly in place in the minds of the children that she is free to use the flexibility of moving in and out of the drama to keep the children working from the inside.

Mid-Authority Role

A person fully in charge can defer to someone above her in rank. She can suggest to the children that they are all like pawns in the system. *The Island* drama builds on the fact that the second in charge is incompetent, and the children have to make up for this by their own assertiveness. Tension and pressure on the children can occur quickly when the teacher steps out from behind her chair of power and knowledge. As soon as she mentions, "The President will now speak to you," and turns on the tape recorder to hear the president's message, she has taken on this role. It is a good role for "passing the buck." "I don't know; it's the order from above."

Shadowy Role

Using shadowy role the teacher casts herself in a non-determined role. She is superficially in and out of role, not noticeably in any one role. She is not an authoritative teacher; she is a teacher who is cheering the group on by being on the side lines guiding and directing. This type of role offers a great deal of flexibility, encourages versatility, and yet enables her to stay one beat ahead of the class. Instead of being directly forceful, the leader supplies more indirect guidance, allowing the children to seem more in charge. "I don't know...maybe you should...what do you think...?" In some sense she becomes the task master, the director. She may spontaneously warn, cajole, question, provide narration, whatever verbal directive is useful to keep the children pressured within the net of the drama.

Catalyst

When the teacher becomes a catalyst she connects the person in full role with the children by questions and other verbal directives.

This type of shadowy role is extremely important when the **protagonist** or main character remains non-verbal for a long time as in a drama using full role (see next section). As catalyst she protects the role and retains it as an image or symbol. Due to the distance between the role and the children, the role retains a quality of awe, capturing and sustaining belief as long as the drama lasts. If the person in role remains silent, this awe translates into a state of wonder which can grow into a real caring attitude. However, the leader must continually keep the children's focus on the role by watching the children's responses, intervening with verbal directives and questions. Since the children's focus upon the one in role is assured, the teacher is free to interact with the children and the person in role who is locked in his own world. The teacher leads the children through that world by the use of questions and generally controls the drama's direction by using verbal comments (see Chapter 5, p. 84).

Full Role

In full role, another person is brought into the classroom to play the role, and they remain in role throughout the drama. The advantage of this technique is that the teacher is freer to insure that tension is created between the role and the children. By remaining mute, the full role increases the children's natural curiosity. In such dramas as the *The Soldier* and *Addiction* a single person is trapped into the lifestyle of the role. Metaphorically, these roles are like a painting which comes to life. The role is set apart from the immediate surroundings. The children can be watching for as long as an hour if the teacher keeps their focus connected to the role through verbal directives. The person in full-role is often helpless, vulnerable, a know-nothing. The children feel needed, are curious and don't know what is going to happen next. As the children watch, the teacher is outside the drama, a third party (catalyst) attempting to illuminate the role's condition through reflective questions. "I wonder why he looks so sad?" She can watch the children's facial expressions and physical intensity, interjecting a new thought whenever it seems appropriate. She becomes a catalyst between the role and the children, intervening to keep them connected to and also respectful of the role.

Another example of full role was used by a teacher who had invited a robot into her classroom. The person in role as the robot was there as a specialist in environmental concerns, and so had to begin talking on whatever subject the children asked about. As experts (see **When children speak for themselves, p. 75**), they were given the task of testing the robot. In this case, the children were in 3rd grade; the person in role was an adult and could give answers that were general enough to pass the test. If no second person is available, the teacher could become the robot and become her own catalyst. This would require a firm negotiation process. In many dramas such as *The Soldier* drama the teacher would not be in role, but a child could at ages ten or above, depending on the type of drama, its level of seriousness, the maturity of the children, and their psychological comfort in drama. The *Addiction* drama would require a more mature child, 12 years or older.

Secondary Role

Secondary role is suggested by something other than a person. It is some object which may or may not be present, but stands for and represents a person. A candle may symbolize the eye of a whale that is passed to the children by an Eskimo woman; or a letter may represent the person who wrote it. Through the use of an object a character is present.

The advantages of secondary role are that it helps to expand the drama in time and depth and contributes to greater complexity. Using the strategies of theatre, anything the teacher says about another character is used to build the drama. A spotlight in place can be used to represent a god-like person from Greek mythology. A valet, or old-fashioned suit hanger hung with a costume piece might represent a person.

"This is our people's land," says the Old Medicine Person, referring to a map, and suddenly the emergence of a tribe thousands of years old is revealed by the map. Secondary role offers many different layers for identification.

The Mannequin

In some cases the leader may wish to use a mannequin to stand for the role. Mannequin comes from the French meaning a dummy or model. It can be represented in many different ways and used for different levels of authority. Almost any of the roles discussed above can be used in combination with the mannequin depending on the teacher's feeling of ease in making transitions. Since the mannequin can't speak the leader must act as go-between, taking questions from the children, reinterpreting them for the mannequin and dubbing in the mannequin's responses.

The mannequin is an object that stands for an individual identity that, for whatever reason, the leader does not or cannot supply in herself. Especially useful for a leader who has difficulty turning on her dramatic personality and stepping directly into role, it can be anything from a large puppet to a sock, to a drawing on butcher paper fortified on cardboard; represented by a toy and placed on a stand; a stuffed doll created especially as a mascot; or simply a glove puppet worn on the teacher's hand. As a type of puppet it can provide protection for the teacher as she moves the story forward, just as it provides protection for the child when he uses it, and it seems to speak for him. The mannequin becomes an independent extension of the teacher's personality.

To speak for the mannequin she adopts different voices becoming like the catalyst needed in full-role, protecting the mannequin's role as go-between, taking questions from the children, reinterpreting them, and dubbing in the mannequin's responses. She will keep the **aesthetic distance** (a comfortable distance to insure belief, see p. __) between the mannequin and the children if she thinks they might show their loss of respect and so, loss of belief.

In any of the dramas using another person in role besides the teacher, a mannequin can be substituted in order to give the teacher more flexibility. It enhances her versatility and enlarges her repertoire. The price of an increase in flexibility is having to make more decisions about options. The teacher must ask herself: How many different roles do I want to handle in one drama? How will I change roles and remain in charge of the children? These questions are addressed in Chapter Three, Creating Your Own Lesson Plan. The use of a mannequin is referred to in Chapter Seven, Cooperative Learning; Chapter Eight, Writing and Drama; and in Chapter Ten, Dramas.

Whether or not the teacher is in role, brings in an outsider in role, uses a mannequin or an object in secondary role, or uses a child, it is often necessary for her to become a catalyst or go-between connecting the role and the children. In all of the forms described above when using a mannequin, she becomes a catalyst, the interceder between the role and the group by going into a shadowy role. As catalyst she continually works to insure that the connection between the role and the children is maintained. To provide this pressure, she continually asks questions of the children. She is tied to the drama and must constantly be thinking on her feet, even though she may be within a sequential structure.

I Don't Know Role

This is perhaps one of the most utilitarian uses of role the leader can adopt, particularly with young children. It puts the leader at the service of the children. The leader becomes a reflective storehouse of their needs and right hemisphere knowledge. This role stance can be combined with any of the above roles or used independently. At one point the leader's attitude simply says, "What do you think?...I don't know what I should do? Can you help me?"

Invisible Role

This convention is often used with young children because it is what they do in their own play. The invisible person is referred to and in this way is given existence.

It is commonly used with older age groups as an acceptable device in improvisation. In formal acting , when the actor is giving a soliloquy (see *The Soldier*, *Addiction*, *Westward Journey*, in Chapter 10) his thoughts are overheard by the audience; whereas, when giving a monologue, he is heard by the other actors.

To avoid confusion when using this role, the one speaking must keep his focus precisely glancing at the space the other (invisible) actor is occupying. This role is very useful for the leader, offering many variations in presentation (see diagram, p. 68).

The invisible role

Taking Role

"When I turn back around I'll be____." During this moment of suspense the children are riveted in the mystery of the moment, their focus is assured and their attention is arrested. In *Three Looms Waiting*, a film showing children working in role, Dorothy Heathcote says with determined wisdom, "You've got to arrest their attention." By practicing skills in using role the teacher will find that she more often arrests the attention of the children and hence need demand their attention less.

At this time the teacher can also put on a costume piece or take up a prop. She can take as much time as she wishes, prolonging the children's suspense and state of wonder. They begin to experience that drama is timeless, even as it always remains in the immediacy of the moment. Within this moment she can take them anywhere and into any time, past, present or future. If one were keeping the rhythmic oscillating pattern in mind (see diagram on p. 28), this moment would look like an arrow going up. As soon as she begins to speak, the 'spell' is broken and the declimax begins which looks like an arrow going up, turning, and then going down. Holding onto these moments as long as is necessary stretches the child emotionally and mentally and prolongs his suspense.

Another way to enter role is using **twilight role**. The twilight is the first or the last glimmering of daylight, and in twilight role, the teacher approaches role gradually, by tiny gradations so that within a few seconds she has shifted her stance without alarming the children by any sudden transformation. In the twilight role the teacher begins by informing and questioning about factual background for the drama. She continues to inform the children but slowly begins to invent specifics and in about 10 seconds has made a transition from her authoritative "teacher" stance to a non-specific character who may be suggested by a different attitude, voice, or stance to represent the role. The combination of this character's demeanor with specific given circumstances leads the children into the drama. She then directs the children so that they know right away what tasks they need to perform and what is expected of them. The whole process may take about seven minutes. From here she can proceed into a shadowy role (while they carry out a task), reclaiming any authority when necessary.

Role Transitions

When the teacher makes the transition from one role to another within the drama she may choose different styles. When needed, the individual dramas themselves address this topic. There are many possibilities for making transitions in role within the drama. For example, in *Endangered Species*, she may have the children prepare for the moment by closing their eyes while she leaves to find the eagle. During this time she then puts on the cap and wings becoming the eagle.

The choice of transitions will become part of the leader's personal style as well as being determined by the goals of the drama. If the children have never before participated in a drama, she simply needs to set up her intentions in the negotiation process, telling them what to expect, unless she wishes to surprise them. However, once they have participated and become involved, they will trust the process, even to the degree that she can become both the main character in full role and also her own catalyst by vocally stepping in and out of character. "When I go over here," or "When I sit in this chair, I'm in role." Along with this there may only be a slight change in stance, attitude and/or voice. They, of course, will know it's their teacher, but they are involved, and anticipating the next moment.

Voice of the Role

Of the three different voices used in fiction, 1st, 3rd, and omniscient, the last is least used in drama. It can be said to hold up a panoramic view of life, a kind of Carl Sagan quality of speaking of eons and eons. It is appropriately applied to the mannequin in the role of an author. As the teacher manipulates and dubs in this voice, it speaks for a panorama that introduces an era as a backdrop against which separate scenes are played out or a larger universe is called upon.

Charles Dickens opens *A Tale of Two Cities* with, "It was the best of times; it was the worst of times..." and gradually we are guided from the heavens into a city, a street, a door, and a personal situation with which we begin to identify. When using the omniscient voice, a character can speak on a Sagan-like level, and in the same breath can talk about a single subject, scene or character. This strategy has been used to engage children with epic works and mythology. The teacher may wish to introduce, finish, or review particular stories as the author or a character. The mannequin can become like the author who knows only so much and then begins to need the children's help. Slowly we begin to see the author's authority diminish and his need for information grow. As he becomes more vulnerable, the children's immediate response is to fill in the empty space. In role the leader can fill this space by asking the children questions and by allowing them time to think and reply.

As children mature, they will wait longer in accordance with the depth of their thinking. The responsibility of the teacher as catalyst is just as necessary, and the use of the varieties of vocal approaches is greater. An older child will be more attuned to the subtleties of meaning in accordance with the situation.

The figures of Abe Lincoln, Paul Revere, Emily Dickinson, and Sacajawea were presented in full role as in a wax museum or as tableaus to 5th graders who knew a little about them. (We found them in a haunted house since we were doing the drama near Halloween). They were played by adults who remained remote from the children by denying direct eye-contact. They used a classical tone to maintain the children's belief, and they switched between first person, third person and omniscient points of view. When Abe Lincoln was asked how many pairs of gloves his wife had, his answer was purposefully vague, for at the time the nation was being divided by war. When Sacajawea was asked about retracing the route that Lewis and Clark took on the map, she chose to speak from her Indian mind which did not know a map, but knew very well the path that followed the way the rivers ran. In this way the role may deflect questions with factual answers, perserving mood and involvement.

Classical speech (see Leader in Role, p. 293) as distinct from domestic, everyday speech, offers a type of language which is typical of the character's time and/or background. "Thanks a lot," is spoken every day by most people, but "it is a pleasure to conceive of," or " 'em sure much pleased," represent a different way of saying the same thing. Any unique quality befitting a character's background suggests much about life-style and challenges the belief level of the children.

What is most useful in any of these presentations is the quality of awesomeness that surrounds the role, a quality very necessary to learning. It is the right-hemisphere approach and answer to the pressures for left hemisphere accuracy of factual information. Through role the teacher can continue to KNOW yet shift her powerhouse onto a role: moving naturally in or out of role; into a monolog; speaking in 1st or 3rd person with or without dialogue. She may also use these same speaking approaches with a mannequin.

Never talk down to children by using overly simple language or an indulgent tone. Children are sponges, actively and instantly absorbing complex thoughts when placed in an appropriate context.

When children speak for themselves

Dramatic play refers to children's beginning play, when they first take on characters. It has been used by psychologists for the last 50 years as a means whereby children's emotional and psychological problems can be diagnosed. In *The Island* dramas, children between 6 and 12 create their own island on paper and begin to function within the imaginative guidelines they construct for themselves. They take their maps and walk across the room toward a closet filled with P.E. equipment, but instead find a cave filled with hunting equipment. This transference of reality is a step taken quite naturally.

If the child has no severe learning problems and has been able to develop normal language flow, the step where the child becomes an **expert** in role follows. As an expert he may know a great deal about something or imagine that he does; it is the latter belief that the drama rests on. The child's state of innocence protects him from the pride of having either too much or too little knowledge, and so he will know as much as he wishes and as much as he feels able to explain according to his role. No biographical data sheet like those created by an actor is needed. Often the teacher gives the children role cards, but they are brief, at most containing a name, profession and a sentence or two defining attitude. For example, a card might contain the following:

Ms. Ticky-Tacky   gift store owner

"I'll pay my taxes as long as we are sure to have tourists; I don't want to donate to a bunch of free-loaders. Tourism is important for my business."

In addition, she encourages the child to speak as he feels the need in relation to the topic of the drama. By taking this step, all of the child's knowledge coalesces and he reaches a synthesis when thoughts become words which are based upon feeling. When the child begins to speak for himself, expressing his emotions through the character's facade, knowledge and feeling come together.

If children are older and new to drama
The diagram on the next page suggests that the older a child is before becoming involved in drama activities, the more reticent he will be. Generic exercises and improvised scenes are a valuable beginning place because they require concentration upon what Stanislavsky called "given circumstances."
In the process of children taking role or role playing, they are guided to select one aspect of a character quality which permits the level of concentration they are then capable of. When approaching role, particularly with older children, it is essential to show and explain how possession of an attitude/emotion (see Chapter Two, Improvisation) is important. As children mature, thought and feeling come together less spontaneously.

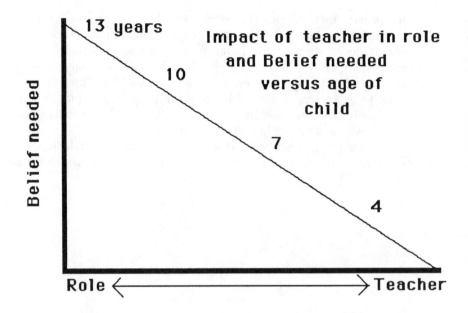

The change when a child takes on role can be accommodated by using generic exercises and simple improvisations. In this way it is possible to help them ease into a drama with the teacher in role. Town meeting dramas work well for 5th to 8th grade children who have never been involved in drama before. As well, skit type dramas which follow a theme, especially one of interest (making commercials; hard times) or attached to the curriculum, work well with this age. Besides seeing its connection to their learning, the teacher uses a few volunteers in a model which the others can pattern in small groups or pairs. The generic exercises can be used just before a drama as a pre-drama activity to get the children involved imaginatively or to direct their energy into the drama using a specific topic.

When the role speaks for himself
If playing in full role   (see p. 71) it is important that the actor has filled in a **biographical data sheet** which answers many of the questions posed in the section on improvisation, especially, "Who am I?"

For example, the child knows the *Soldier* has a family life when he takes out a picture of his wife and children. Small details begin to color in the human qualities of this otherwise semi-conscious, wounded, lost pawn. The educational actor cannot share his repertoire or daily workouts with the professional actor, but can share the creation of the biographical data sheet which answers whatever questions he wishes to ask of himself. Not only "Who am I?" but "What symbol or image stands for me?" are questions that need to be answered; the soldier's use of props can depict this area. Gradually the role fills in specifics dealing with his background and slowly begins to imbue his own personality.

When using other roles, the more information a child has, be it history, literature, etc., the more spontaneity and ease he will have in his delivery.

Chapter 5

Questioning

Whenever children ask questions or are asked questions that engage their imaginations, an atmosphere of rapt absorption becomes apparent. The pursuit of the unknown produces a pause, a time for wonder, for concern over possibilities. Thoughts begin to burst forth into the imaginable sphere where serious prospects abound. Asking appropriate and timely questions is what makes teaching an art and places the teacher on a plane with the shaman, a wise and thoughtful person within the culture. Since the profession of teaching isn't extolled in Western cultures as it is in those of the East, we need to find models to help guide us. The Socratic method uses deductive questions to test a hypothesis. Scholars of religious orders, the Jesuit priests in particular, used similar methods.

If the leader questions, minds will open.

Seeing a child's attention suspended by an unanswered question is like seeing the mind traveling in search of an answer while the question lingers in the air. When children are questing for closure, their minds are open to learning. This quest begins in earnest around the age of two and continues to grow until they begin to ask the "why" questions at around three. When the teacher asks the questions the process is not reversed, but continues, instilling a quality of openness and expectancy.

A major difference between the right and left hemispheres of the brain is in the manner that each processes information. The type of question considered "left-hemisphere" requires facts and is based upon the backlog of knowledge collected over time. The left hemisphere analyzes factual material, makes a generalization, and after a step-by-step process, forms a new theory.

The right hemisphere goes through a different thinking process because attitudes and values are being shaped and feelings analyzed, motivating each new step until a personal philosophy is formed. Both right- and left-hemisphere processes develop cumulatively as the thinker takes steps to form a new theory or a personal philosophy of life. Both the "thinking" and "feeling" sides of the brain are used continuously to make decisions and cope with daily life.

When asking questions in a drama, more emphasis is placed on guiding the children's feelings than helping them to collect more facts. Yet facts are given a more solid underpinning through the drama experience than could be attained by factual input only. The brain is so complex that feelings and thoughts are constantly being woven together, and there cannot be an absolute distinction made between them.

Drama usually works in a collective, so there are lots of minds at work at once. Asking the proper questions becomes a way of guiding the group's thought processes and keeps the group working as a unit. The kinds of questions asked usually have no single answer and so are not dependent on facts alone. Answers are based upon personal insight, so each person has a chance to think and respond either verbally or silently. Silent reflection on a question may be the most valuable and important response of all. *The process of reflection is the silent and personal teacher of us all.*

The **hourglass** shape is a useful outline to follow during the questioning process. A general question is followed by a more specific

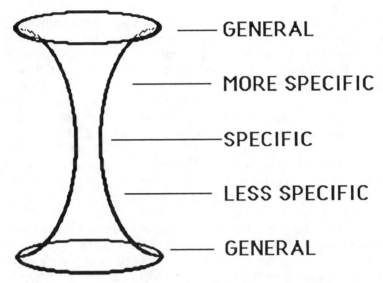

question, and so on until the waist is reached and then less specific and more general questions follow once more. This progression helps children focus in on the topic. There is always a curricular reason to take up a particular topic that is to become the subject for a drama. Questions give focus and form to this topic.

The top half of the hourglass form is used in activities like the Who exercise (p. 143) and when the catalyst attempts to connect the children to the person in full role. She is moving from general to specific, as a zoom lens would so that the child's connection becomes gradual and slow.

Affective Questions

Affective questions are those questions that inquire about ones personal life. They affect or excite emotion, draw upon ones inner resolve and inspire a deepening of the thought process. Affective questions can be asked at any time within the drama process, connecting the children to the material and uniting the group.

"Have you ever had a favorite place to play?" "Have you ever known children who haven't had a place to play?" These questions ask for a personal response that has its basis in emotion. They are affective questions, and they prepare the child for questions that lead into the topic, questions such as, "I wonder why some children haven't?" "Does anybody know?" These follow the hourglass form.

Beginning Questions

Beginning questions are used to discover the current knowledge level of the children, their degree of interest, and to feed in new information in preparation for the topic. The teacher wants to motivate the children by broadening their understanding of the topic and by planting questions that will be referred to later in the drama.

In a drama about taking care of pets (see drama *Taking Care of Pets*), the teacher might ask, "How many of you have any animals or pets to care for? Have any of you had a pet that died? Did you get another pet? I wonder why pets die? Are animals like people? Do they need the same things we need?" The first beginning question, an affective question, is general, followed by two specifics, and back to three more general ones which are universal, as well. We have established a basis for the drama.

With older children, the level of factual information already held by the children needs to be discovered, so a general question is asked on the topic, in this case, Indians. "Do you think there's much difference between how the white man and the Indian lived, say 50 years ago?" By the fourth grade most children have studied about Indians, so the introductory question brings the children closer to the topic. The questions continue, "How was Indian life different from that of the white man 100 years ago?" "Are they still living like this?" "Why not?" "Do we have something to learn from them?" "Can we think of ways in which nature is important to them?" The first two questions are general, the third and fourth more specific, followed by a fifth which is general. To gain a particular focus, it is necessary to ask more specific questions. After the children relate the value Indians place upon nature, the leader might bring up the topic for the drama dealing with animals. "What about the Indian's feelings toward animals?" At this point the children's level of knowledge is clear, and according to their non-verbal signals, the leader gauges their interest and attention span. This class knew some facts on how Indians were related to the environment, but little about their religion and legends. Here the teacher needs to introduce and develop the concept of spirit or soul. The questions continue to be specific until she finds the limit of their knowledge and then introduces the information needed to carry out the drama. She might feed the information through texts or use a storytelling mode, spending as much time on images and details as she thinks would both interest them and help them in their drama.

It is usually at this point that the children's belief begins to really take hold. They have already invested knowledge into the process; when the teacher adds on information, it is almost as if it is part of them already.

Questions, together with information, story background, preparatory exercises (see Chapter 9) and more questions are all preparation for the concept that is to become internalized and deepened. It is during the beginning questioning in all dramas that the teacher provides the underpinning for what is to follow.

Preparation Questions

If the topic of the drama is particularly powerful, either because it carries so much affective emotional weight or because it might excite the children into misbehavior, the teacher might decide to increase preparation time to avoid problems before they begin. In *The Soldier* drama, the subject of war needs careful preparation so that the children can empathize with the soldier. "Have you ever felt worried or sad?" "How would you like people to treat you when you feel that way?" "Would you laugh at a person who felt badly?" "Have you ever known anyone who fought in a war?" "The person you are going to meet today will need your help because he's been through a lot." These questions request information the teacher needs to know in order to determine the children's background and consequently their ability to meet the drama half-way. Whenever the teacher needs the children to behave in a certain way, but is not sure they'll be able to because of their limited background, she needs to validate this point by pulling the situation out in the form of questions as evidenced in *The Soldier* drama.

Events such as Halloween which are natural inspirations for drama are fraught with potential disaster. If the leader initiates the drama with a question like "What do you want to do on Halloween?" she might well get a response like,"Throw rotten eggs at Mr. Magillicuddy's house." In such a drama she knows they'll be excited and may sabotage their own experience, so she prepares for this by saying, "What would you like to have happen to you on Halloween?" In this way she's undercutting their natural inclination to "throw rotten eggs." Having deflected them into thoughts of what they would like to have happen to them, she can say, "You'll need to listen carefully to hear the sounds which will lead us to the spirit, otherwise she may be afraid to call us. Do you think you can be observant?" Any questioning of their abilities to be able to carry through and maintain a consistent level of responsibility strikes at their own self-image and challenges them. Anything she makes up will work as long as she reinforces it by getting the children's commitment. If there's the least infraction within the drama, she can use her role to focus on the misbehavior and curb it.

Specific Questions

After the beginning questioning has taken place in *The Soldier* drama, the children are introduced to the person in role as the soldier. The soldier is 'unconscious' and they watch him until he gradually comes to. Even though nothing has happened or has been said during this time, the process of internalization is taking place. Questions are planned to keep the drama going in a single direction and become cues for the person in role. "I wonder what's the matter with him?" "I wonder what he thinks and feels?" "Can you see what he's carrying?" "What do you think he's reading?" The funnel becomes more specific because the person in role is right in front of them. When he "overhears" us talking about the letter he is holding, he begins to focus on it. It acts as a secondary role (see Chapter 4) since it represents his wife and includes pictures of his children. Now the questions reverberate from general to specific, until the leader, as catalyst, encourages the children to ask those same questions of the soldier, especially how they can help him

The hourglass figure can be kept in mind as a relative pattern for questioning. When beginning a drama it is difficult to know about the children's right-hemisphere experiences which correspond with their inner values and emotions, so very direct questions need to be asked at first in order to prepare them for the topic. It is delicate ground, yet it needs to be understood clearly for the drama to be successful.

Questions during the drama

Questions are asked during the drama to keep the children connected to both the actual drama and to the drama going on in the children's minds. Questions like, "Do you think the trees you've planted will grow all right without our watching them?" help keep the children's focus concentrated and fights the tendency to lapse into a stupor of restlessness and unease, a familiar demeanor in the age of television.

Final Questions

Often these questions are an amplification of beginning questions, but after the course of the drama, their answers are more imminent. The teacher brings the drama to an end by asking final questions;

otherwise there is no official ending.

Following the *Homeless Children* drama, final questions such as these might be asked. "I wonder if there are many children like this?" "Do you know any people who have adopted refugee children?" "Does anyone know why these children don't have places to live?" "I wonder if there are many?" "For every picture I showed you, I've heard there are many thousands." "If everyone did what you just did, do you think that maybe all the orphans in the world would have places to stay?" "It's very good to know that there are people like you who would look after these children." These questions are universal, except for the last two which are affective. They provide closure and a way for children to own their experience in the drama.

The child is now at the evaluation stage in the cognitive domain. Asking questions based upon the drama, the teacher blends the children's emotions with vital factual information, integrating the two hemispheres. By bringing in the affective, right hemisphere area, she revitalizes the conceptual area and enables the children to create their world of the drama, offering a synthesis of newly created meaning. After the creation has been formed, the evaluative stage is reached. Instead of talking about the created world of the drama, however, they are asked questions about the actual problem area which served as a basis for the drama and their connection with it.

Universal Questions

Like the affective question, the universal question can be asked at any time during the lesson as well as at the end. Examples are: "I wonder what kind of life this person has had?" "I wonder what a person in this situation thinks about?" Those asked to support the beginning objectives of the lesson using *The Soldier* drama help children to empathize and identify with a person who's suffered in a war and to realize war is not an answer to problems. Follow-up or final questions insure that the objectives have been met. "What can he tell his wife?" "Do you think we'll always have wars?" "What will we have to do not to have wars?" "Do people always win?" "What do they win?" The last four are classified as universal

Universal questions take stock of the child's right hemisphere as well as left hemisphere and attempt to provide understanding about the commonness between people. In many ways it answers the question of 'why' people act as they do. Instead of seeing the outside differences which seem obvious, emphasis is placed on how people from different cultures are alike, what all people need to live, which behaviors or conditions are inevitable and which are in our power to effect. Even though the questions need not be answered, perhaps can only be answered superficially, the questions must be asked, for these kinds of questions help develop insight, creative thinking and concern, and may lead to long-term answers to problems that the present generation hasn't solved. So we cast it out and hope it will reverberate as the children become more aware and more socially conscious.

Crisis Questions

A crisis question is a question the leader asks herself when she prepares the drama. It is implicit in the problem the drama is about. It is a question which lingers over the drama, particularly if the tension is strong. "How can we cure the plague? And if we don't, what is the worst that can happen?" The leader must be aware of the question and choose the moment to ask it carefully. If the question is asked too soon it may hamper the children's efforts; if not asked at all the children may not realize the seriousness of their tasks. Generally it is best to ask it at the end of the beginning questioning or at the end of the final questions.

Statement Questions

A statement question is not a direct question; it is indirect, a query. The teacher states it to challenge the children to think, leaving the question to hang in the air and draw the attention of the participants.

Example of a statement question: We know that when white settlers first came to America, the Indians were relatively peaceful and became more war-like later because we pushed separate tribes closer together. Some say the different tribes may have gradually wiped each other out. I guess we'll never know. ("What do you think?" is implied here as an indirect question. The teacher is casting a net of concern.)

Chapter 6

Drama Elements

The terms theatre and drama are often confused or used synony-mously. The root of the word drama means a deed done, and original-ly the term drama was thought to be inclusive of theatre. Though the beginnings of drama are shrouded in antiquity, the deed done was possibly based upon a current war, a need to revive some soul from death through sacrifice or a need to make atonement, linking drama forever with the human need to survive and make life meaningful. A theatre is a place where one sees, views, witnesses or receives.

In trying to understand the terms theatre and drama, we come to the old war between process and product. Drama has appealed to the human condition because it demands that we feel our way, search, explore, wonder, become confused, understand, misunderstand. In doing so, the processes of living life out and interpreting the human condition are given priority. No props, sets, costumes or theater accoutrements need to be used to do that. As a result, Educational Drama depends less on external elements to suggest the dynamics of change and more on the child's internal resources to accept change and continually become refocused.

In Educational Drama, the gulf between drama and theatre depends upon the way we view the child. If we expect the child to get up before a group of people and begin to display his emotional experience in verbal and physical form, then we adhere to the concept of product. This product can take the form of a play or event with a spectator audience. If we expect the child to come gradually forward, introverting, absorbing, acknowledging and stepping out ever so slowly until he bursts out with something his own, then we expect process. Whatever we expect of the child, we are the ones to guide him, and we cannot expect of him any more than we can do ourselves.

Educational Drama has been confused by definition and usage, principally because there has always been a strong need for children to continue some form of "acting out" or "imaginative play." This agreement to make believe without an audience, to become involved in unreality, in fantasy, is the 'big lie'. Unlike the other fine arts used in schools, theatre rests on a consensus that promotes belief; without the belief that we are creating something connected with life, the 'big lie' could not exist.

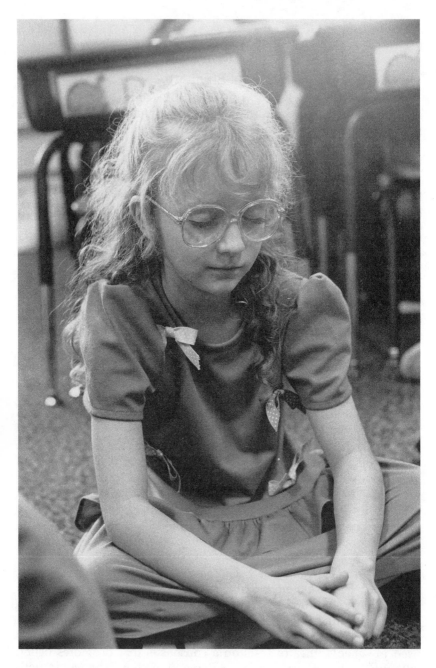

Let us imagine.

The goal of Educational Drama is never the performance, indeed there rarely is any audience outside the participating group. The biggest factor in Educational Drama is the fact that the children need to get up and use the space. Teachers need to enable them to do this by demonstrating their own experience, by demonstrating a willingness to talk about the extremes of life. The teacher needs to motivate concern and interest, and involve children so that they will be able to think, feel, and speak in the drama experience.

Resting on the 'big lie' of unreality is the 'magic if' of the willingness to imagine. A question is asked. "What if...?" The question acts as if the fantasy were real. It offers a way to go, a frame through which to view a new occurrence and anticipate a reaction to it. Often it re-echoes the crisis questions (see Chapter 4).

If there is a fire tomorrow, what will we do? What if I get a bad grade on this report? What if a light comes out of the forest and takes me to a different world? All of these "what if" questions provide material for drama simply because we ask the question. When a question is asked, the need to know the answer provides an accompanying tension. Often we play out situations in our mind's eye in order to mentally rehearse what may be more traumatic otherwise.

In drama, we know we are moving through time, we are in charge of choreographing these movements, changes, tensions. Teachers say, "let us imagine," and by this are constantly inventing ways to circumvent our human limitations in order to affect perceptions and bring about more depth in learning.

The child enters the classroom with real happenings stored up in him. The teacher asks him to fantasize about the borders of far off countries, about number systems which at the time seem irrelevant and remote, about grammatical patterns that must seem arbitrary or whimsical. For a child, school can seem like a fantasy world filled with useless information. Unless there is strong motivation for him to participate, he escapes into his own realm. A local fifth grade teacher said, "We try to make school an island of safety and comfort in an otherwise troubled community." It would seem, then, that Educational Drama would be most at home in the school since it appeals to the imagination. Here are some of the many reasons why drama is **not** in the schools.

There is little tradition of theater in the schools except for the occasional school play performed for parents. Unfortunately, this works against the spontaneity necessary for truly Educational Drama, because it demands all the accoutrements of theater and approaches a script largely through memorization.

Most teachers have not had the opportunity to be trained in the techniques of Educational Drama.

Teachers as well as children must exploit and explore their own experience, but neither teachers nor children have a tradition of practicing these arts and are often inhibited by fear and apprehension.

Unlike most other forms of art, drama demands that the participant be inside the experience. One doesn't have to be inside a painting to be emotionally involved nor does a player in an orchestra have to become part of all the other players' thought processes to keep the concert going. But in Educational Drama the degree of individual involvement in the group experience is intense. Even if a few children are up before the others who become an audience, the latter become witnesses for a reason. The leader can make the drama event run smoothly for the children if the beginning negotiation, questions and motivating exercises precede the actual drama. They, then, begin the process of belief so that the players gradually enter their roles and the responsibilities that the roles require. Teachers are often afraid of dealing with emotions, yet within the drama all is safe. (See beginning exercises in Character section.)

Focus

Dorothy Heathcote, dealing with the concept of focus, says, "I knew I had to arrest their attention and let them know very quickly, what's up." Teachers do this unknowingly all the time as they try to get and hold the children's attention. Telling a brief incident, writing on the board, showing an object, a picture, a drawing, taking them through some process related to the senses, in short, keeping them inside the learning situation is the teacher's task. The teacher and theatre director are allied in this way.

In theatre each time a different person speaks, or an actor enters or exits, or the lights change, there is a predicted response in the viewer. Everything is planned to manipulate focus so the mind is continually challenged and intrigued.

The teacher must ask herself, "Once focus is established, how often do new points of focus need to be provided in order to maintain interest and attention? How does one keep the child inside the lesson? What is there implicit in this material that will speak to them on their own emotional level?" The answers to these questions will determine the rhythm of the lesson.

Tension

The concept of tension deals with time and expectation, and asks the question, "What's going to happen next?" Tension and focus are interconnected and collaborate so that where there is focus, tension follows. Both are based upon a coalescing of energy that is directed and fixed.

In a drama called *Medicine Person,*we are told that "they are coming, and to get ready we must..." Tension results from anticipation and the imperative need to prepare in too little time.

Having too little space is a problem that creates tension in the *Immigration* and *Missions* dramas. "...there is nowhere for us, but to stand tightly bunched together."

In *The Island* dramas the tension creating problem involves both time and space. When looking at what human beings need to survive, the fundamental tension occurs when these human needs aren't met. If they are met for only a percentage of people, these people might not care about the others, creating tension between the haves and have-nots.

In the *Save the Dinosaur* drama tension is created by having to choose between two unpleasant choices. The dinosaur must be caged before it gets any larger. But once it's caged, they'll kill it.

The drama can be stopped at any time during its course, enabling the children to reflect on their actions. Stopping also holds them in one place, and is an immensely helpful step toward allowing them to own their work. "What have we done these past few minutes? Can you comment on how you see these issues?" Whatever is implicit in the drama that challenges our basic rights of survival, our right to living space and the essentials of existence, or a specific problem that keeps us from going on when the need to proceed is great, can cause tension. Also, any limitations the teacher can make at the beginning of the drama, as well as intervening in or out of role to hold and entrap their energies, creates tension.

The teacher may introduce tensions and focus points by getting the children to make a decision during the negotiation process at the beginning of the drama, "What would you like to have happen to you?" "We'll need to explore this region and map it out. Do you have the knowledge necessary?" If not, a disaster is implied, causing tension. Or she can introduce new tension while in role during the drama. "Remember the Indian ways so you can pass them on to your children. I am old, and I am the last one who can teach you." In other words, without me, your spirit will not transpire.

In some dramas there is the initial tension of the unknown,

compounded by having to make decisions along the way and the overriding tension of knowing that this is a matter of life and death. Questions which ask the children to reflect upon what they have experienced can be asked at any time, holding the drama in one place and not allowing the players to move forward in the action. All of these instances press the children to stretch themselves within their own roles as special people who have to be concerned with matters that determine their ability to grow and succeed.

Distancing

Whatever is distanced automatically earns tension because it can't be brought nearer. When a thing is distanced it can not be immediately acted upon. Because it does not allow immediate active response, distancing encourages reflection and prompts thinking in depth.

In the drama *War and Conflict* the tension is caused because the actual war is distanced from the children, yet the pressure of trying to find the culprit becomes their immediate concern. In Educational Drama, wars are never fought on stage. They are distanced. We know that the war exists, but its beginning and ending are merely announced on stage. The hero gains stature while he is distanced; people talk about him, bring messages, and if the hero dies, his stature becomes even greater. Our imaginations have been nurtured to see the hero as even more heroic than he may be in reality. Distancing is comparable to off-stage action (see p. 50).

Theatrical examples of this off-stage action are many. In *The Master Builder* by Henrik Ibsen, the master builder is off stage, putting a wreath upon a high church tower. We need only hear "Oh, oh, no,---no" to know that he has fallen to his death. In *Antigone* by Sophocles, we hear about Antigone being walled up and slowly murdered, but do not see it. Through distancing the drama is slowed. The leader holds back the movement of events, increasing the depth of emotion the children will experience.

Each drama approaches tension and focus in different ways depending upon the subject, but in general, conflict of tension is created by holding the children in one place while they are continually being invaded by messengers, phones, letters, orders, announcements of natural disasters, darkness, a previous decision, a question from the teacher suggesting concern and wonderment, or the information about a particular incident which changes the course of action. All this affects them emotionally, yet they cannot "fight back" which increases tension through distancing.

Aesthetic Conditions

Aesthetic conditions are the medium of theatre. The term aesthetic refers to beauty, significance and harmony to which value and meaning are tied.

Unlike a regular play in which tension and focus are built in, a drama requires that the leader be aware of the need for keeping the children inside the drama. While inside the event they become audience members as well as members concerned with the tasks connected to their roles. Even though they are kept in one space, conditions around them change.

The leader is always working on a continuum between having nothing occur to having too much happening. Below is a chart illustrating the range of aesthetic conditions. (The following chart is taken from Betty Jean Wagner's, *Dorothy Heathcote, Drama as a Learning Medium.*)

stillness . . . . movement
darkness . . . . light
silence . . . . sound

Notice that in the left column nothing is happening, but when you move toward the right side, too much may be occurring. Some choices need to be made. For example, in *The Sacrifice* drama, the leader asks the children to become little animals who are hibernating. All is still and silent, until the leader becomes a hunter who is trying to find them and begins speaking in a gruff manner, moving from stillness to movement and silence to sound. After the hunter leaves, she narrates for the children to appear and follow the imaginary bird who will guide them, moving from darkness to light. By illuminating the bird, "Let us follow the bird," we momentarily move into the metaphor of light. By focusing upon anything that the leader singles out for the group's attention, we are shining an imaginary spotlight on the object. Having the children close their eyes before something is revealed and opening them on the thing revealed is also causing something specific to be brought into focus, figuratively moving from darkness to light.

Aesthetic distance is a term meaning the distance needed to insure maximum effect, belief, and communication. If children can count the hair follicles of the person in role or can't see the person in role because other are in front of him, the distance is not aesthetic and limits belief.

Rhythm

There is a rhythm to a drama. (see also Rhythm, p. 53 and Slowness, p. 54). For a serious drama to work and maintain a profound impact, it needs a slow rhythm; comedies are based upon a fast sequence of action. This text emphasizes serious dramas. There is also a rhythm in the leader's introduction of new aspects of the drama as she orchestrates the movement between silence and sound, darkness and light, stillness and movement. The rate of movement between the six elements will largely be determined by the kind of drama it is and the kind of depth required and discussed in the negotiation process. "In order for this drama to work I need you all to think of yourselves as race car drivers," implies a very different rhythm than if she asked the children to imagine themselves as deep sea divers.

Unlike the slow rhythm of the deeper dramas, acting exercises tend to be more rapid, and the leader would be trying to "keep up the pace." A general rule is that the drama is dependent on a certain depth resulting from the objectives. The leader must make her judgment of how much she needs to pressure the children through manipulating the ingredients of role, questions, and narration that will enable her to use these elements. The leader uses all these techniques to slow the drama, countering the children's natural inclination toward fast action.

Dramas dealing with oppression (last part of Chapter 10) need to take place slowly, so the children can feel the tensions within the experience. Most of the dramas in which the teacher is in role are of this kind, and the quality of the drama is determined by the presence and authority of the leader. Once this is in place, she then gauges how often it is necessary to change activities in order to re-create focus and tension, introduce new elements, and use questions to either assert a provident authority or to emphasize the roles of the children. Or, she may be at the side of the drama, interfering only in 'shadowy' role as needed, but keeping the rhythm going, intervening as director/actor when it seems appropriate.

Style

Classical style (see p. 75) most often describes dramas requiring depth. Descriptions of classical dramas contain words like ageless, enduring, authoritative, heroic. *The Sacrifice* drama and the *Medicine Person* drama are classical. Each movement is deliberate, based upon tradition and therefore we are not rushed because, "we have been and always will be—forever, as long as the rivers run—."

The leader's role may seem exaggerated, much broader, as though speaking for the whole cosmos. In the classical style, the leader has complete authority, she moves slowly because she is in full charge of her world in the drama.

The melodramatic and cartoon styles are discovered accidently by children to hide their self-consciousness when they make up their own material, like scenes of a fractured fairy tale (p. 140). Neither style would be used in the dramas in Chapter 10 because the loss of seriousness built into the objectives would keep the dramas from working.

Exaggeration applies to the **melodramatic** style. This style is somewhere between comedy and tragedy. Words like superficial, sensational, sentimental all describe the melodramatic style.

The **cartoon** style is also exaggerated. Fast movement is interchanged with sudden freezes; slapstick, colorful, bouncy, are all adjectives used to describe this style. The best examples are the cartoons the children have already watched on television. Like melodrama, this style would be useful in certain designated situations dealing with skits or scenes that the children would make up themselves. It is a choice the teacher can suggest.

The concept of being able to go from a very small here and now identity into any time period or space location and become any type of being presents an enormous range of possibilities. And though there are a few rules which must be laid down, the price is small in comparison to the possibilities for entering this world in which space, time and identity can be in constant flux.

Self-esteem and assimilation go hand in hand.

Chapter 7

Cooperative Learning

Cooperative learning or **student team learning**[1] is a teaching strategy that has gained great credibility in recent years. It is reminiscent of the one-room schools in which older children helped younger children. As distinguished from the controlled learning strategies of competitive learning and individualized learning, cooperative learning offers children the opportunity to engage in heterogeneous interactions that promote a positive learning environment for each child simultaneously. Individualized and competitive learning stimulates only those 10% of students whose interest and hard work are continually repaid because their efforts prove successful.

In cooperative learning the class is divided into small groups, each child has a definite contribution to make to the other members of the group, and the whole group is involved in some aspect of learning together. The teacher monitors the groups' progress according to expectations established in the beginning. The children help themselves by helping each other. A socialization process is also taking place which may be the most important contribution that the school environment will make in the long run.

As William Glasser emphasizes in his text, *Control Theory in the Classroom*, 50% of the children now in classrooms don't receive any satisfaction from their tenure and so give up. Glasser bases his theory upon the fact that in the post-twentieth century, human beings do only what is most satisfying to them, since basic day to day survival is insured. He delineates these satisfactions as wanting to belong, have power, have fun, and be free. Cooperative learning maximizes the general level of learning so that all will achieve something. If we hold to the theory that the very bright will learn quickly, the next level will learn with some study, and the next will need still more study or help to reinforce their otherwise superficial knowledge, then it is possible to understand how the repetition and repartee of the group's human dynamic should make a difference to those who would otherwise find themselves on the bottom. As Glasser points out, the goals of learning are remote to the lower 50%. These children don't carry a 'picture in their heads' or an image of themselves that is related to succeeding with the skills they are having to artificially practice. As a result, they won't lend that extra bit of study to something which is remote.

Learning and the practices that lead to learning are less remote when undertaken by a small group. Peers who do carry the 'picture in their heads' provide valuable input to those who don't, and they gain new teaching and interviewing skills. The others, who wouldn't raise their hands in a large group, find that the small group of which they are an essential part is interested in them and in their contribution. They receive praise and encouragement and the satisfaction of contributing to the success of their group.

At the end of each learning segment, the group may be stopped for five minutes while each member reviews the significant learning. Student team learning, another name for cooperative learning, replaces boring drill work, helps those students who are in the lower 50% to feel less frustrated and more accepted as persons, and provides direct feedback through a vehicle of public recognition. The grading system reflects both the team's score, and the individual's score, but usually the latter is compared to his usual level of performance and not some arbitrary standard. In student team learning all students must do their best to achieve a high score.

These techniques have been researched and tested showing that students who have used team-learning score well above the average in such areas as math, language arts, reading and social studies.

Teams are organized into groups of four, usually. Nothing above six is recommended in order to insure maximum interaction and reception. Teams are balanced racially and sexually, reflecting the percentages of the class. The next step is for the groups to master the material presented by the teacher. Students study together. All members must know the material and to accomplish this, they drill and explain concepts to each other. Teams usually remain together for 6 weeks to insure that positive interrelationships are formed, then reorganize. Some types of cooperative learning emphasize skill subjects such as reading and math, others emphasize deeper understanding of concepts and their relationship with life.

Cooperative learning strategies lead beautifully into dramas, and vice versa, because children work in groups when doing drama. Since they're already building loyalty in their groups, the teacher can assign each group a specific task or specific readings leading into and connected to the drama. Because children's attention is focused upon each other, the teacher is freer, her flexibility is increased, and she is able to come and go in or out of role. Each team member is responsible for helping the members of his group understand the material. She convenes all team leaders and instructs them, in or out of role, as experts. They, in turn, return to their groups to help team members understand. A mass of material is comprehended and is ready to be shared among the groups. The benefits are clear: increased learning of academic materials and basic skills, increased concern and care of other's learning, increased positive relationships between different races and ethnic backgrounds. Most important to building both the futures of the students and the social fabric that keeps the country healthy, is the news that this strategy also significantly increases self-esteem.

Apart from the actual academic work, each child may be given a separate task that is integral to the group's progress. Those tasks might be: checking (asking to verify), summarizing (capturing main ideas), encouraging (stimulating other members of the group with praise), and observing (watching with awareness). The individual teacher can use any other tasks that seem to be appropriate to the particular lesson or subject. If the teacher is introducing a topic to be dramatized, individual tasks may include: spokesperson for the group; questioner; director; researcher, or supplier of information; observer/reviewer; scribe or note taker.

Imagine a unit on Indians. As additional source material the teacher might have materials like the following ready to use: pictures depicting a lifestyle; simple objects like two sticks which are bound together with reeds, which the groups can examine deductively to determine their probable use; combinations of wood, stones and reeds that can be used as musical instruments; material for mapping. Through the reading of source material, the reporting of team experts and the handling of artifacts, the children become "expert" anthropologists.

The teacher enters to tell the children that today they are going to explore the "secret valley" a place which very few anthropologists know anything about because it has been protected by mountains and dense rain forests for centuries. As soon as we hear the sound of the grackle bird, we'll know we're in the approximate location. The teacher can explain the way by drawing a map on the board with a legend to accompany it and referring to the maps each group has, finished or not, depending on whether or not mapping skills are to be emphasized. While the children check their anthropological equipment, she transforms herself into role. Besides working in groups, the second advantage in using cooperative learning with drama is that the children's focus can be shifted momentarily onto their plans while the teacher makes her transition into role.

"We'll begin our journey. Please pay careful attention to the kinds of plant life, soil quality, anything unexpected, or anything you may find which you think would tell you something about this region." (The journey can be taken as a visualization process.) She simulates the environment by narrating images. Toward the end of this introduction to the drama she can introduce the selected sounds including the bird's singing she has spoken about.   "We have arrived." During this time the teacher has darkened the room and made any changes that would enhance the room quality. She has placed artifact-like objects around the room. The child in each group who is the researcher/supplier of information takes charge of this item. "We don't know how these may have been used, but it is the task for each group to deduce the possibilities and report back to us. Careful scientific methods are important because each group will share its findings, and we will write a final report to send to the Smithsonian Institute in Washington D.C."

To extend the drama, the leader can enter in role or with the mannequin in role as one of the native inhabitants of the valley who will answer the questions the groups develop. A ritual is explained by the role and re-enacted. A final report is written and maps or drawings are provided.

From here, many tasks can proceed: mapping, rituals, story writing or telling, myth making, many kinds of artistic expressions, or a deeper academic investigation into how primitive peoples lived, all the time answering the questions of the past by imitating the processes anthropologists use to imagine the past with accuracy.

A curricular unit that incorporates cooperative learning and drama is exciting to children. It engages both sides of the brain, requires large and small motor movement, involves many academic skill areas, teaches responsibility and discipline and fosters group harmony. What is learned is retained.

NOTE for CHAPTER 7.

1 Johnson, Roger and Johnson, David, see Bibliography

Chapter 8

Writing and Drama

Drama and writing are natural companions. Just as drama enhances other areas of the curriculum, it supports and enriches the writing program. Children's writing improves when the topics and content they deal with are given shape before they begin to write, when they experience in their bodies the ideas to be given written form, when they share and expand their ideas with peers, in short when they can explore the possibilities before they put pen to paper.

Children speak with their bodies. From movement comes feeling, from feeling, thought. Today's experiences are tomorrow's ideas. Movement involvement in drama generates a feeling connection that stimulates the need for expression. The language arts progression has its foundation in movement. Children are word players organically, if their language flow is encouraged.

While playing, movement turns into sound; sound becomes speech; speech evolves into writing and reading.[1] In play the child's toys are extensions of his own body at first; he speaks through them moving between first and third person, gradually becoming conscious of his own separateness. This early language flow depends upon the safety and stimulus of his early environment. Upon several occasions after having told my five year old son stories at bedtime he would continue the story during school art sessions. These retellings seemed to occur when the art medium required slow physical action like working in clay. Teaching at the same school, I would be privy to this information. Through the teacher's description of the instance I could see that as the clay began to live in his hands, he put words to it, the words from the story he had heard the night before. And slowly this large country school kindergarten of thirty plus children would grow quiet and hear the scenes emerge and become activated by the movement of the clay. In kindergarten and first grade, the lack of ego development allows for this spontaneity in children.

After I've finished doing dramas with children, teachers have had them draw and often use captions identifying their scenes. Spontaneously some will write dialogue in bubbles over the character's heads. If a drama extends over a week, the teacher or I ask the children to write a letter to the main character to reassure him or give advice. Through their identity with the character a strong emotional tie motivates the child to become very wise. When

From movement to sound, from sound to speech,
from speech to reading and writing.

given an outlet such wisdom seems to emerge without effort, and the writing task becomes a pleasurable personal experience. After several weeks a drama about going West brought forth diaries and journals that became personal detailed accounts that matched any historian's rendition. Similarly, in a debate that followed a drama on bio-engineering, ten- and eleven-year-old children wrote from a first person account as rats who had developed the intelligence level of humans. Because the children's identity had shifted into becoming rats, they were freed to expand into the writing task with more energy. The result was an enthusiasm to use words that carried them into the realm of synthesis, or 'original' thought, **the focus of this text.**

The following exercises may be new to many children. The leader needs to demonstrate them in order to provide security for the shy as well as for the extroverted.

Exercise 1   Vocabulary development

The sounds of some words suggest their meaning. Onomatopoeic words provide both sensory and mental images enhancing the meaning when children physicalize them through movement. Children can also invent words like these, exploring sound and its connection with letter combinations. Thus their spelling abilities are embellished since these words tend to be phonetic.

Onomatopoeic words

rustle	craggy	clump
tassel	limpid	bumpy
whirl	whoosh	jiggle
bumble	tumble	rumble
crumble	twinkle	crackle
crinkle	grumble	lumpy
stumble	blurb	swirl
grumpy	topple	slug

Words like these can be acted out by the group to create a movement poem. Freezes are used at different points to punctuate and frame them, thus providing discipline within the form.

The children are organized in circles of 4, 6, or 8 so that each has a partner standing in the circle directly opposite him. Each couple has a number which the teacher calls. After she calls the couple's number, she calls out the word, "rustle," etc. The designated couple has been alerted, and they step into the circle and respond physically to both the word and each other's interpretation of the word, using their bodies fully and exploring different levels. She must play a drum or tamborine consistently tapping out a synchronistic rhythm. This serves as a foundation, motivating their responses. Following the teacher's lead as they move to her drumbeat seems to happen simultaneously at first until they gain more assurance and the teacher follows their lead.

When they have interacted for about fifteen to twenty seconds, she signals them with two hard hand taps on the tamborine to return to the circle.

Variation: Gather poems which are highly onomatopoeic. Either the teacher in role or the mannequin is used to introduce Ms. Onomatopoeia who has a few of her poems to read for us.

Ms. Onomatopoeia: "As I recite these poems I want you to close your eyes and use all your senses to both feel and imagine these images. Oh, dear, I'm so nervous. You're the first people to hear my poems. Oh, I hope you like them. In order to really know what they mean you have to see the images or pictures in the poems and receive feelings from the images."

A few poems can be presented in this manner to get the children's minds working before group work; discussion can proceed about the images they experienced. The teacher may wish to give the children some context before poetry writing occurs in groups or singly. (See Kenneth Koch, *Wishes, Lies, and Dreams.*)

Exercise 2   Poetry Writing (see Koch, above)
Color words and emotion words suggest movement qualities.

The leader uses the same physical configuration as in Exercise 1 and the same method but instead calls out color words or emotion words. (Color words work better with primary grades; emotion words with intermediate grades.)

Variation: With older children it is wise to begin with a color orchestra before doing the movement. Each child vocally intones his own chosen color, or the leader sets up a specific arrangement like a rainbow. The children must watch her as she conducts their voices, raising and lowering her hands determines loudness, and moving her hands horizontally means "cut."

A few child volunteers help to demonstrate, at first. It is best if they stand as a chorus before the class. They should be encouraged to physically move in place so the vocal quality will be richer. From here, the leader presents a loosely adhered-to poetic form, for example favorites such as **haiku** or **cinquain** (a five line poem), or by popular children's writers like Dr. Seuss or Shel Silverstein; the children begin to respond on paper with words and phrases to a theme they choose.

Emotion words such as anger, joy, satisfaction, etc. can be brainstormed so words flood the board as reminders.

The next step is the creation of images. If performed outside, a game structure is used, such as **Who Stole the Bacon.** If not done outside, Exercise 1 will suffice for preparation. The 'bacon' is represented by anything which is placed in the center of two numerically even lines which face each other. Players are paired so that when one through eight number off, they are facing each other, running toward each other from the greatest distance.

After the game is played several times, the 'bacon' is removed, and the leader calls out the number of a couple as before, but adds directives such as color words, emotion words, or images. The following images have been used successfully:

airplane and fog	cork and ocean	bird and storm
pea and fork	soap and hand	marshmallow and fork
spoon and jello	kite and child	peanut butter and knife
fish and fisherman	frisbee and player	balloon and child
yoyo and child	bull and bull fighter	

For more than two people: sun rising above the desert; big bang theory; eclipse of the moon; life under the ocean; even more abstract concepts can be used.

Note: The give-and-take is spontaneous and moment to moment since there is no preparation. One person gradually takes on one of the forms and while using peripheral vision, each one automatically reacts to the other character. After one or two jumbles, children will be guided intuitively. The teacher provides encouragement with a series of beats like a drum roll on a tambourine or like instrument.

After this absorption in images, poetry writing can follow.

Exercise 3   Thinking in Metaphorical Language

A phrase from a childhood poem reminds me, "my bed is a boat," and sleeping becomes an adventure. Within this experience many adventures unfold. So it is when words are used to free the imagination and inanimate objects begin to reveal their possibilities for humanness.

Have the children look at possibilities available in the room. Present them with chosen objects and begin to describe them by saying, 'it is like a—' or 'it is a—'

Using a metaphor as an example, the teacher's desk becomes, 'a cave from which forest creatures appear—.' Using a simile, 'a thermos bottle is like a vial of elixir offering curative treatment.' During brainstorming, phrases are written on the board, and the teacher may either assign provocative words such as, mirror, spider, chair, etc. or let students choose their own words. In groups or as individuals, brainstorming over phrases begins and a poem is written. Improvisation follows.

Exercise 4 Having a Point of View

Setting up an activity or improvisation serves as a stimulus. For example, slow motion movements between several players are observed by all. The movements can be a combination of spontaneous, realistic gestures and need to be slow. Whether this activity is carried out inside or outside, children need to be placed at many various positions relative to the scene. Each one is given or chooses a role in relation to the scene and views the scene accordingly; e. g. a relative of one of the players, a reporter, a painter, a manager, etc. From these points of view many approaches to writing are encouraged.

Variations: Family scenes, arguments, any topic connected with the curriculum.

In the following exercises a mannequin can be used to represent the author.

Exercise 5 Endings for Stories

An author, either the leader in role or a guest, enters. She has been having problems finding endings to her stories. Any ethnic or folk tale can be told until the ending is reached at which point the children can finish it, in groups or as a class. It doesn't matter if the children are familiar with the stories, their endings will always be different from the known ending and from each other's endings.

Exercise 6 Making up Stories

The author doesn't have any ideas. In the **Ideas Game** (from Peter Slade, *Experiences and Spontaneity*) the children brainstorm around an agreed-upon theme; sharing, borrowing, repaying, for example. Questions are asked dealing with these words and are arranged in a network or cluster on the board. Children act out scenes to see what works best until a completed group story is agreed upon and writing begins.

Exercise 7 The Author Has Ideas But Can't Put Them Together
The leader, in role as author, scatters ideas over the board in single words and phrases. These ideas might have some central theme known only to the author, but in role she is confused and needs the children's help to make sense of it. In dialogue with the children the theme is discovered. Through the author's questions, she can elicit more phrases to be placed on the board, encourage an ordering of what is there or bring the discussion to a conclusion and challenge the children to begin writing.

Exercise 8 Objects Carry Meaning
Many books in children's literature have an object as their centerpiece. Objects from a book are brought in by the "author" or a "character." In Doris Gates' book, *Blue Willow,* a blue willow plate was used like money to pay the doctor for his help in saving the mother's life. The teacher, in role as author, is interviewed by the children, or offers to interview a child volunteer about some object that is important to him, but may not be to someone else (see exercise 39, p. 146). Each child brings in an important object to serve as a centerpiece of a story (see Secondary Role in Chapter 4). Objects are combined to form a plot leading into writing. The variety of objects brought to school can lead into a discussion of **genre**, symbol and metaphor with ages 10 and above.

A variation of this includes a picture which is an original drawing made by the child, one the child brings in, or one the teacher selects. At some point the children can reconstruct the picture as a tableau or series of tableaus (see Exercise 29, p. 136), bringing the picture to life as they move into their improvisation.

Exercise 9 Using a Newspaper Article, Advertisement, Cartoon, or Picture
Any of these may serve as a stimulus and centerpiece for the child's writing. An improvised scene containing dialogue as well as many modes of written expression are produced from the child's natural ability to imitate. Choosing a character and situation (the five w's, see Improvisation in Chapter 2) to elaborate upon can be narrowed down by the teacher's curriculum requirements.

Exercise 10 Reviewing a Book

If the teacher wishes a book or story to be reviewed by the class, she or the mannequin enters in role as the author, as one of the characters, as an inanimate object from the book, or as a critic.

Questions asked, e.g.: What happened and what effect did it have? Why did things happen as they did? How do events cause us to change and direct us to make new discoveries? Are we challenged to understand new meanings?

Conclusion

Any of these exercises lead directly into improvisations for the whole class to watch.

In this way the public media such as radio, television, motion pictures, theatre are all available as a way to frame the assignment.

These ideas are of a dramatic nature; that is, they utilize the leader in role; they involve rhythm or movement; or they ask the child to assume a character. It should be remembered that, not only will drama inspire a wealth of new writing modes, those activities stimulating writing will improve writing skills when drama becomes a part of the curriculum. Writing, even in its most academic forms, is a means of personal expression. Drama helps children access their own expressive natures and reach the levels of emotional involvement that truly illuminate ideas.

Opening this text to almost any exercise or drama can give the teacher ideas for writing prompts, vocabulary development, story starters, research directives

Chapter 9

Additional Exercises

Introduction

In Chapter 9, Additional Exercises, and Chapter 10, Dramas, the narration of the leader will be in **bold sans serif type.**

This Chapter contains simple beginning exercises which can be extended into longer dramas (see p. 61). Most of the dramas invite writing assignments. (See the list of possibilities extending into writing p. 63.)

A descriptive breakdown of activities from easy to more difficult is shown here so the leader can choose to begin at the level which is the most suitable to her own development:

1. The generic exercises are included in the exercise section; these are about 20 exercises that always work, being an outgrowth of children's daily play. At the end of some dramas, generic exercises may be recommended for extensions.

2. The main exercise section contains exercises under the following sub-headings: senses, space, imagination, plot, character, and speech; these exercises can be applied to most areas of the curriculum: LA, Language Arts; Lit, Literature; Soc Stud, Social Studies; Geog, Geography; Hist, History; Sci, Science; PE, Physical Education. This symbol system accompanies each exercise, and the exercises are ordered in a progression from beginning to advanced. Those which contain journeys are accompanied by the following abbreviations: Jp means journey preparation; Js, a journey which requires horizontal movement in space; Jin, a journey which can be done in place.

3. The next step is for the teacher to try her wings by:
   (a) reading an Aesop's Fable, or a similar short piece from life, in order to get the feeling of how it can be broken down into playable action (see Plots, p. 134),
   (b) telling it in her own words,
   (c) taking up a puppet or object to talk through,
   (d) working on presentational techniques such as those suggested in Chapter 2,
   (e) choosing any role she feels comfortable in for a short presentation to the children such as telling them a story using a role (see Chapter 4): for example, a short repetitive piece from children's literature,

"We have tomorrow
Bright before us
Like a flame."
-Langston Hughes

(f) telling her story and using it as an assignment for the children (see Chapter 8),

(g) using 'starters in role' together with 'tasks' (see pp. 62, 63), and using the mannequin (see p. 70),

(h) something the leader chooses herself that will coordinate with a curriculum topic

(i) practice doing this as many times as seems necessary until she can extend it by applying either her own ideas or any of the exercises in order to make a longer drama

4. Finally, she may feel she can use any of the dramas included in the text as guides for developing her own dramas (see Chapter 10)

5. Consult Chapter Three for ways to organize an original drama

This Chapter contains the following sections:

Senses

Much of who we are and what we will become is based upon what we remember. According to recent psychological theory, those childhood memories which we recall as pictures or images but were experienced through all of our senses--visual, auditory, kinesthetic, olfactory, tactile, thermal and even gustatory--are not stored in the memory as images; what is stored is the process by which the image was initially perceived.[1] Images from the past are immensely important; they help us continually redefine our own meaning. I can still retrieve many moments of childhood through visual imagery, but the single one which is most vivid for me occurred when I was very young. I remember thinking: "I will look at that red lacquer dish on the antique table and really see it so that I can save this moment forever." Even now when I recall that red lacquer dish all kinds of settled and peaceful feelings engulf me. That moment becomes a foundation for what was otherwise a fairly turbulent childhood.

The use of sensory awareness encourages use of the imagination and encourages an internalized response. Relaxing exercises enable children to become more perceptive and hence more able to continue drama activities in other school subjects. Although sensory awareness begins in the very earliest years of a child's life, it is too often not encouraged. Instead, it is soon replaced by other, more competitive activities and further development of sensory awareness is neglected.

A conscious use of the senses is fascinating for almost any age child. Using the senses enables children to bridge the gap between themselves and their environment through use of their own faculties. Performing the exercises which follow helps children to be alert and responsive. This, in turn, helps them in all academic areas and to be more unified when working on a group problem.

Nurturing of experiences through visual recall may seem a conscious act, but the memory of bodily feelings, tastes, odors and touch are more prevalent, and these come to us from the unconscious, unasked for. It is clear to me that a period of three years in China during my formative years is made real through my olfactory senses. A whole civilization is re-experienced through odors of Asia experienced over a half century ago. Similarly, a memory of a woman singing, an impression of a beam of sunlight and a kinesthetic memory of small arms on a crib frame recreate moments from childhood which would otherwise be forgotten. Because painful experiences are often repressed in this culture and many sensory pleasures are not socially acknowledged, the memories associated with these experiences may be less easy to reconstruct.[2]

Clear visual images known as **eidetic imagery** are not common to the majority of adults. About one child in ten cannot close his eyes and mentally see an image from the present moment based upon my own samplings. The majority of those who could not form these eidetic images were children who excelled in math and otherwise quantitative skills. And children demonstrate better eidetic memory than do adults. If ninety percent of us cannot recall an immediate visual memory, what must that say about what we have lost of our rich visual past?[3]

Developing eidetic memory, though it may seem difficult, is an important skill, well worth the time devoted to it. Many exercises in this chapter deal with visual memory. Try this one to get an idea of what eidetic memory is: Make a black dot 1/2" in diameter and place it on a brightly colored surface. Focus your attention on it while keeping yourself in a state of relaxed detachment. Now close your eyes and you may still see the after-image from the retina. This exercise will help to give the viewer an experience of what a mental picture is like. Albert Einstein described the important role of polysensory (visual-spacial and kinesthetic) imagination in his own extremely abstract thinking: "The words or the language, as they are written and spoken, do not seem to play any role in my mechanism of thought. The psychical entities which seem to serve as elements in thought are certain signs and more or less clear images which can be voluntarily reproduced and combined...the above mentioned elements are, in my case, of visual and some of muscular type."[4]

According to Robert McKim in *Experiences in Visual Thinking* this ability can be developed in adults through practice and exercise. For those who are not as able to restore eidetic images, other senses can be brought into play. The memory of eating a peach, hearing a familiar musical strain or the touch of a fabric might spark a deep memory from the past.

The majority of exercises that follow will contain a "Jp," standing for journey preparation. When the leader conducts children in a journey by narrating images, she moves at the same time while delivering the narration (see Chapter 2). For many beginners it is difficult to move and speak at the same time. It is also difficult for children to be guided if they haven't undergone any inner mental imagery preparation. The leader simply needs to practice while the children need some mental preparation (see Chapter 2). A journey exercise is one in which the group is conducted through space moving in relation to the images the leader narrates. Many journey narrations are handled in this text. Some journeys are "in-place" and others are traveling. The following exercises assist in journey preparation, Jp. In later exercises I will use "Js" for journey through space and "Jin" for journey in-place.

Exercise 11 Seeing It (visual) (generic exercise) (Jp)
Helps reinforce concentration in any subject area.
Instructions: Hold an object in front of you. Really see and experience it with as many of your senses as possible. Now, either with your eyes open or closed, restore the memory of it in a dimensional way by tasting it, hearing and feeling it. If your attention is really rapt, you will be able to repeat this exercise in future from memory and without difficulty.

Exercise 12 Tingling Limbs (kinesthetic) (generic exercise) (Jp) (LA)
When working with children in movement, kinesthetic imagery is most basic.
Instructions: After any combination of movements have been explored, ask them to close their eyes and feel their muscles still tingling. This is a sensation children find fascinating.
After some repetition the challenge to retrieve the experience with closed eyes is easily repeated. From here have them all move in and out of five or fewer different poses that are characteristic of their own personal way of moving. A healthy correspondence between the feelings of controlled abandonment and energetic experimentation will motivate them. Besides, children enjoy movement for its own sake. Having them close their eyes between positions in order to become aware of how their body feels will emotionally inform, deepen, and preserve **emotion-memory.**
Follow-up: reinforce otherwise abstract concepts like drawing numbers and letters in the air.

Exercise 13 Mood Music (aural) (generic exercise) (Jp) (LA)
Extending the imagination by listening to music also strengthens imagination and memory.
Instructions: After listening to music, have them respond to questions about feelings and images.
Classical music is most appropriate, containing the depth and thematic value which invites concentration. It is music which draws

ones own attention from within. Listening to music with a conscious awareness of the images evoked is always a good sense experience, as well as an effective relaxation technique. Other exercises in this book expand on the possibilities.

Follow-up: drawing a scene and adding written expression.

Exercise 14 Aura (kinesthetic) (generic exercise)

Concentration and the quality of perceptual awareness is induced.

Instructions: First demonstrate with a volunteer. The volunteer A closes his eyes and B moves her hand about 2" away from A's body over one spot, moving back and forth, up and down and covering an area of about 9" square. Neither clothes, hair, nor face should be touched. Keep the hand away from the hair and eyes for even with the eyes closed the changing patterns of light can be sensed.

The importance of this exercise is to allow the children to be in a state of deep concentration. The goal is not to guess where the person is working, but to provide an incentive toward concentration. However, when conducting the exercise, the objective can be: "See if you can sense where the person is working." About 50% can, in the same way we turn to see someone who is staring at us.

This exercise has been used in some of the dramas included in this text. In Indian dramas it has been used to re-echo the kinds of perceptions Indian children have developed which are in keeping with their closeness to nature.

Variation: A draws a specific form on B's back; B identifies it. Reverse.

Exercise 15 Listening for Relationships (aural) (Jp) (LA)

Students extend their curiosity with the suggestion that people and objects affect their environment.

Instructions: Make some sounds by using the voice, percussion instruments, and/or movement of objects. Make these sounds while the students close their eyes and listen. Student's imaginations can be stretched by suggesting that the sounds are occurring in some environment, a cave, a forest or a fair, for example. Sounds may be used as stimuli for a story that they relate or amplify to their classmates.

Variations: With practice sounds alone can form the sections of a fairly complex plot. Vocal sounds and music can be added. The listening activity can begin in a large group and be carried out by smaller groups into improvisations suggested by the sounds. For example: A cave becomes the setting, with bats, spiders, leaky walls, and unexpected obstacles. The cave comes to life, two trespassers enter for adventure, and a surprise ending occurs. All groups may be rehearsing at the same time and perform separately before the entire class. Children may become the cave, bats, other obstacles, as well as journeyers. Sounds have been the jingle of keys, tapping of fingers on a drum, closing a book suddenly, clicking the tongue against the roof of the mouth, and a plaintive calling of "hello-lo-lo-lo-lo". The students begin to get the idea and want to participate in the mood that has been created. The leader needs to remember to keep a low vocal tone, resonate, and not too far away from a monotone. Just plunge in, let your own imagination run. Success will inspire you.

Follow-up: inspires story ideas.

Exercise 16 Visual Recall/Memory (visual) (generic exercise)

Tableaus or still pictures are quickly and easily assembled with a few volunteers. This technique may be applied to social studies, historical incidents, science, scenes from literature, etc., suchas: seeing the first rocket off which went to the moon; tired, Civil War soldiers returning from battle; depictions of famous paintings, etc. Aesthetic skills are brought into use as the children ask themselves questions about balance, composition, relationship, and line, as if they are looking at a painting.

Space

Having enough space is as important to children as is being close. As they develop their space relationships with others, they develop an internal self concept. As they develop feelings of power over inner space through visualizations and the practice of other exercises (see Senses), they gain power over outside space.

Everyone moves inside his bubble.

In their first attempts at dramatic improvisation, children form a small circle, much the same way our ancestors did during early rituals. This shape is protective—it includes them all. From this point, they are encouraged to move about, yet retain their own individual circle of space. At first, little conscious exchange takes place between these personal spaces, and yet these individual circles become diffused and overlap. The more opportunity a child is given to move freely in his own space, the less need he will have to take space from someone else.

Stimulating a child to expand his vision to include imaginary objects in space, as suggested by the first few exercises in this section, gives a more concrete, three-dimensional quality to this space. If the concept of each child taking responsibility for filling his own space is built from the first session, and is consistently repeated by the leader in the suggestion, "Find your space," aggressive behavior will be greatly curtailed.

Drama is not an outlet for aggressive behavior; it's a channel for personality growth. The leader can redirect the child's energy by suggesting different weights and rhythms, by helping the child take on a variety of forms and within these forms, promoting interaction with the environment. Not only is aggression limited, but shyness is forgotten because the ego is not under scrutiny. Instead, objectives absorb the attention. In addition to general loosening and focusing of attention, the exercise can lead into almost any lesson, enhancing curriculum acquisition by refining focus.

The child's inner resources are affected in direct proportion to the way in which he uses his personal space and progresses to work with larger groups. Peter Slade's book *Child Drama*, written in the 30's, confirms the groupings which are natural for children: The circle is a natural shape for children because everyone is sharing space equally in relation to others. Next, a few courageous ones will run through, breaking the circle formation and begin filling the circle in. This stage is called obtaining **equidistance**. This progression is very much like adults who enter a room of strangers. Usually people begin by standing at the sides, until there is gradually more familiarity and the room (circle) is filled in. Finally, small groups begin to congregate together, and the "gang" stage has started. This continues all through one's life—we change groups as we change roles.

What all this means is that when we involve a group of children in improvisational drama we usually keep them in one large group during and up until about age 7, because in most cases they haven't developed the self-discipline to organize themselves and work in small groups without the aid of an adult. For older children, small groups accomplish more, encouraging leadership qualities in the shy as well as the more extroverted (see Chapter 8, Cooperative Learning).

Drama and dance are both performance oriented; the concept of "finding your space" is essential to prevent unnecessary chaos and achieve a freedom of movement within a structure of narrated images. The child is being invited to explore his own individuality and be responsible for it.

The following expands upon the metaphor of the child as a primitive in his beginning play. The primitive ritual utilized the circle as does the open theatre or arena stage. It is the most natural kind of playing space and the most easily used by a director and actor because it is so flexible. The Greek and Roman theatres, which were the first theatres in Western Civilization, became the amphitheaters that are still used today in Greece and have been copied throughout time. The next main theatre shape was the Elizabethan theatre, a versatile three-sided or thrust stage, which, for the first time offered a place for entrances and exits. In the evolution of the stage and the audience, the next phase saw the front part of the lower stage level become an apron, and the actors were moved back behind the proscenium arch. This type of arrangement came about during the Restoration period in England, a period of theatre development in which people sat in boxes close to the stage and often, if they were among the upper class, right on the stage. Finally came the proscenium theatre that we know today. It can be thought of as comparable to looking through a keyhole and seeing a life being lived. Stanislavsky, the Russian director, called this type of staging "public solitude." All of these theatre spaces are in use today. Children's ability to go from the security of the circle to the proscenium space where they stand alone parallels the evolution of the stage and re-echoes the need to prepare them by using these processes.

Besides providing an outlet for aggression, another apprehension expressed by teachers working in the performing arts is that the children will get out of control. Doubtless everyone working with children has had this experience. Being nice and charming is often the last thing to work. I've found that using an oscillating rhythmic pattern in voice and movement keeps pace with their energy level, especially in grades K-3. The leader's narration causes them to either intensify their action or to slow it down. For example, "Let's follow this pathway. You see that hedge a few feet away? Each one of you needs to run one at a time, to hide behind it—one at a time—to make sure no one sees us. Now, we've all made it but wait, I hear something —I think it's a sound coming from the old house. Wait, be very still. Let's follow—be very still." Before this type of narrated journey I always plan moments to bring the group's energy down and hold it there for a few seconds, maybe as many as 10 or 15. During this time I talk to them about facts connected with the background of the journey we're taking. For older ages the oscillation between crescendos and decrescendos becomes less extreme. And by about grade five or six the oscillating pattern can be compared more with the overall energy pattern of adults. As I narrate, I move and mime with the children, doing everything I expect them to do which helps to kinesthetically guide their movement. If music seems appropriate a small battery operated tape recorder is easy to carry along. (see pg. 18, narration)

Pacing is the concept that treats a segment of movement in relation to speed. When children are older than eight both space and specific motivation is needed. The leader's pacing with young children is faster than with older children, yet the leader must be aware of the type of pacing which is suitable for the needs of the class as a whole. Pacing needs to consider the children's ability to focus and concentrate. If they are slow but focused there is no need to force them to speed up. If they are erratic and unfocused, they need to be calmed first, and pacing may well be speeded up.

Exercise 17 Breathing (PE)

Basic to this idea is the concept related to proper breathing. Since many adults do not breathe properly, it is possible that their false start began as children.

Instructions: Children are asked to pay attention to what happens to their bodies when they breathe. The teacher uses a balloon to demonstrate expansion and contraction. The children might place their hands on their chests to feel the expansion caused by breathing.

Questions: What happens when I blow up this balloon? What happens when you breathe? Oxygen is conducted to the lungs which expand so that the diaphragm muscles also expand and the lungs becomes blown up like the balloon, and when you let the balloon go, it collapses, just like your lungs. The analogy to the balloon and rocket is applied in the following exercise.

Exercise 18 Open-light, Closed-heavy (kinesthetic) (Jp) (Jin) (Sci)

Students become acquainted with the space which surrounds them.

Instructions: (This can be done as a visualization exercise.) With as much space around your body as you need for stretching, imagine that you are resting on that space and that your body feels very light. With lightness you become larger and larger, as if you were a balloon being blown up. You sail away, walking through the clouds. A bird flies up, pecks at you and you begin to fall. All the air in the balloon gradually escapes and you fall gradually to the ground.

If the instructor is dealing with an older group, less literal terms than "bird" and "balloon" may be suitable. The instructor may then wish to ask how it would be to float and sink in air and water.

Questions: Why do balloons rise sometimes? Can you show what happens in a drawing? Can you draw a picture of the air inside the balloon before it rose, and after it rose? Blow up the balloon and without tying it, let it go. How is this like a rocket? A similar line of questions dealing with floating objects can be explored. Let's make a big circle and be like the light object that floats. What would we do to be like the heavy object that sinks?

Exercise 19 Balloon Journey (spacial/kinesthetic) (generic exercise) (Js) (Geog, Soc Stud)

Students become acquainted with their own space.

Instructions: One of the first ways I begin a drama session with young children (K-1) is to have them spread out in the room and show each other their individual "bubble" or "balloon." How high, how wide? Gradually we begin to travel in it, to music and/or narration. For children who are older, the image of a box or bottle can be used, if the bubble seems too oriented toward fantasy. Also, the space which the older child explores around his body will be more contained, and his movements will be more "in place" due to his size and maturity. Within this form, shapes and patterns of movement are expanded and yet contained within the form. There is the sense that the child is within his own realm as far as he can reach.

Narration: **This is your space. See how far you can reach. Up, down, to the sides, and now see if you can turn slowly around. Did you bring your balloon? Take out your balloon and, that's right, you want to stretch it before blowing it up. Now blow it up. Bigger, bigger, more air. We want it so big that you can walk right into the middle of it and feel it all around your body. Show how big it is and now you begin to walk, being careful not to interfere in some one else's space. From here we step off into a journey—and a breeze comes up and we feel ourselves being blown gently upward until we're in the air—going over the playground and we can see farther and farther so we can see the hills, rivers and we're floating along very gently when a bird comes by. We're carried away by it—it takes us through the air so much faster—we come to a rainbow and go through it—it has all the colors—see the yellow and the blue? There's the place we want. Follow** me. Now make a little pinprick in your bubble/balloon so you gradually come down. Now we are here.

Exercise 20 The Path to the Mountain (Jp) (Geog, Soc Stud, LA)
   Relaxation and space orientation.
   Instructions: Speak very slowly so the children have time to experience each facet of the relaxation exercise. Background music can be used to set the tone or mood.
   Narration: Lie down or sit in a relaxed position and let all the tension go right through the floor. Check yourself out to be sure. Your ankles are flopping over, knee joints, thigh muscles, buttocks, pelvis are relaxed. Feel your abdomen move up and down as your breathing becomes deeper and deeper. Your stomach muscles are also relaxed, and you can feel the oxygen filling your body. Your breathing is easy and unhurried. Your shoulders, back, neck are all relaxed, let all the tension flow out through the floor. Even your jaw is loosened, forehead, mouth and all the places where you tend to hold on to tension, you let go of. Go inside your brain and sweep out all the thoughts and just listen as I hum. You're completely relaxed. You feel very light even though you're relaxed. Your body feels as though you are floating. Each part of you is being held up by a draft of air that supports your whole body, as it glides across space. Currents of air allow you to fall and rise. You feel as though you could go anywhere. You drift through the air, looking down on miles and miles of landscape. As you view the scene below you see a spot to land upon and gently float down into a green meadow. Stay there a moment feeling the earth underneath your body and supporting you. You may remember having walked here before. You can feel the softness of grass and soil underneath your body, and catch the odor of freshness while feeling the stillness in the air and hearing a bird call from far away. Feel and see this place. Make it a pleasant place. A place that is important to you. You sense yourself getting up and standing. A kind of excitement begins in you. You feel your body being warmed by the sun and you stretch upward and inhale. At the same time as you do this, the tiny flame of your breath begins to flicker and expand. You sense this expansion. And

although you're lying on the ground or seated, a strong will pulls you slowly up. Your breath calmly reminds you of the little flame that is coursing through your body bringing energy. A bird is flying around you. You inhale and pull yourself up to follow the bird. The bird flies on, as though to beckon you. You feel that impulse inside your stomach acting like a strong will that's becoming more and more energetic with the good breaths you're taking in. As you walk, you feel your body being pulled as though by a magnet. You find you're on a pathway. The pathway leads toward a mountain. You look toward the mountain and continue to feel that strength inside guide you as you follow the path toward the mountain. Now close your eyes and know this strength which you feel being produced by your breath. Stay with this sense of your own breath helping you to feel energy and a sense of strength through your will.

I have included a great deal of narration above. You will want to shorten or lengthen it in response to the attention span of the group.

Discussions afterward need to be very casual so as not to interfere in whatever gains have been made. "Did any of you begin to climb the mountain? Were you able to, at least, begin to get the sense of your own will being strengthened through your breath?" This center, (at the stomach) is referred to in Yoga books as the power center, but children need to feel a sense of their own power and its effect over themselves. Developing control over our inner space helps us to control our outer space.

Exercise 21 Small to Mature (generic exercise) (Jin) (Sci)

The analogy of plant life is used with human growth.

Instructions: Provide music which is lyrical, calming, and steady. As the leader speaks, she also gets into a ball shape with chin between knees and chest up against thighs.

Narration: I want you to get into this shape and also to tuck your head in. Imagine you're a little seed moving deep down in the earth. It's very comfortable here. A little tiny sprout begins to break out of the seed and like your finger, it moves gradually upward through the rich earth towards the warmth of the sun. It breaks through the earth, being drawn by the sun's rays. Slowly cells begin to add more and more fiber to the stem, and it is strengthened. More buds form and leaves appear. The

cells take on a bark like appearance and the plant rises, fed by the moisture of condensation and the minerals from the soil and sun's rays. Slowly, **it becomes full and beautiful as it is gently blown by the breezes carrying new seeds to pollinate its little flowers.** And now we expand **and grow taking in the oxygen we need, just as the plant needs carbon dioxide and gives off oxygen.** We work in **harmony with it.**

Exercise 22 Follow-the-Leader (spacial/kinesthetic) (generic exercise) (Jp) (Jin) (Js)

Conducting children through space while introducing rhythm, freezes, and narrated images.

Instructions: After the children have had many experiences following the adult leader through movement exercises and realize the possibilities, they can experience leading the group themselves. Appoint a leader to direct the action in each group. As he moves, he leads the members of his group in an action, activity, or pattern. At successive signals, other leaders may be chosen to lead a group as they become motivated.

Variations of the above exercises include having the groups give and take movements like questions-answer relationships or moving two groups in mirror relationships, in place. A single leader can be chosen for both groups. Setting any of these patterns into a thematic structure becomes the choice of the group. Themes may range from literal ideas, such as seasonal change, work rhythms, rituals, to a more symbolic process, such as creation and destruction.

Imagination

We carry rich resources within us. In the belief that knowledge is deepened when the imagination is engaged, one of the aims of an improvisational drama program is the development of the imagination. Keeping or holding an image in the mind enhances and develops the imagination; and concentration and absorption are particularly essential to developing imaginative skills. Absorption furnishes the condition in which the imagination can travel, spiral, and leap. It requires a maximum of energy, yet furnishes energy as well. Absorption also provides shelter, and with this comes trust and a condition of safety and peace in which the imagination can grow.

We carry rich resources within us.

Like his span of attention for other tasks, the time a child can successfully spend in passive imagination exercises may be short. A child's need for physical release often blocks his receptivity. In the exercises that follow, his energy can be utilized so that both imaginative and physical needs are met, providing the active learning that research has proven so successful. Engaging the experience level also involves the student in many sensory ways and solidifies memorable events.

Children need much direction when they are moving their bodies. They cannot be left to move imaginatively if their imaginations haven't been developed, and the development of the imagination, especially combined with movement, is rare in schools. In beginning sessions, students frequently move erratically and without form, and will feel embarrassed and inhibited. Giving them an image on which to concentrate helps their bodies to think. Such techniques as freezing, using music, slow motion, or **mirrors** will not only guide, but will place controls on the movement. Their energy will not be dissipated into embarrassed giggling or talking. Sudden transitions help to take them by surprise, and their quick energy can be absorbed when the instructions keep coming. Lack of transition does not bother children. Lack of movement does.

There are two major objectives to the movement/imagination exercises that follow: to enhance physical motion so that the imagination can be extended through movement; and to give as wide a variety of movement alternatives as possible.

Inventors, scientists and artists have always relied on images from their sensory systems to prompt their vision. No one sat them down and told them they had to develop photography, the internal combustion engine, the refrigerator. So why did they? How did they? Whatever the urge and will, they were undoubtedly accompanied by many overlapping psychic strata; their right and left hemispheres were working together.

"The essential achievement of free will," writes William James, "is to attend to a difficult object and hold it fast before the mind." We can help children attend, to hold an idea in the mind and expand the whole world through their visions.

Guided imagery and exercises that develop imaginative powers have a definite place in the classroom. Many elementary school teachers have used visual imagery for years to help students recall information, relax, relieve fears and uncertainty as a preliminary to movement exercises. It is known that the best spellers are those who can recall a stored visual image of the word.

In sports, too, visual imagery can be used to increase skill and concentration. Timothy Gallwey in *The Inner Game of Tennis* points out how people may be trained to play tennis through repeated work with inner imagery "with something like a forty-percent increase in efficiency." According to Neuro-Linguistic Programming good spellers are those who can recall a stored visual image of the word.[5]

I know of a college professor in Business and Economics who uses guided fantasies in the beginning of each class to help students recall important items of their reading before a quiz.

We all use our imaginations on a daily basis, mainly to produce fantasies. We have the internal equipment necessary to transport ourselves to other realms. Used as a technique to increase learning, visualization is an easy and efficient way to get inside of the material and exploit our natural ability for fantasy to enhance our learning, but it takes practice.

Exercise 23   **Image Yourself**   (spacial/kinesthetic) (Jp) (LA)
    Instills self-concept; relaxation.
    Instructions: Have the students lie down or sit. Take them through a relaxation process.
    Questions/Narration: **You're lying on the beach. You can hear the power of the surf and the rise and fall of the waves pounding the shore. The gulls call. You inhale and receive the odor of salt. You see yourself getting up** (this has been done as a spacial/kinesthetic exercise by incorporating movement at this point) **and running in slow motion along the wet sand. Your body feels light, almost weightless. Each time you put your foot down your body feels lighter and soon your arms grow lighter, become weightless and turn into wings. You become a bird, and as you hold your wings out you are carried aloft and upward. Just as easily, you descend toward the ocean, letting the powerful draft of air carry you over the great sea swells. Again you hear the forceful roar and receive the spray. As you're carried through the mist you become the mist, rolling over and through a pulse of wind currents. You descend into a wave and are thrown down on the hard sea floor. You let your body be carried up onto the sand, and like one of the pebbles bouncing upon the shore, you land. Seeing your body lying there, you get up and walk toward your blanket.**

Exercise 24 Looking for an object   (Jp, Js) (LA)

Searching for a small object becomes your objective for being involved.

Instructions: Concentrate on searching for and finding several small designated objects which have been planted and are obvious. When you have found all of them, leave them there and sit down. After all have completed this search talk about how each felt. Self-conscious? If not, why? Compare this to the way one would feel if "on stage" without having an objective. Imagine that you are looking for a specific thing and half of you watch the other half. Notice if the object is found, if the person is outside or inside, if the object is big or small, and how the person feels about looking for it. Reverse. Next, do the same exercise to music, having listened briefly to the music first before deciding on the object. Reverse. Talk about feelings in reference to being watched and feeling or not feeling self-conscious. Why does the actor need to have an objective?

Exercise 25 Body Language   (kinesthetic/spacial) (generic exercise) (LA, Soc Stud, Geog, Sci)

Find out how our bodies work when we become other things.

Instructions: Provide background music to aid the children in moving to the spoken scenario.

Narration: **You are very heavy. Your body is being pulled to the ground and you lie there all bunched up like a sponge full of water. Gradually the tide goes out and you are exposed to the sun. The water evaporates and your body becomes warm and dry. Show what happens to your body. You expand and open until your arms and legs can be seen. One part of your body becomes heavy. You are like a puppet operated by strings. You can drop and raise your head. Your hands. Arms. Elbow. What's the difference between being open and walking along, and being closed as if someone just dropped your strings? Let's try being open. Closed. Can you show, just by standing in one place with one simple movement how you would look if you're being forced to go someplace that you don't want to go?** (closed) **Show how you would look if you were going somewhere exciting!** (open).

Extension: Now let's make a list on the board of places and feelings we have about these places. From their suggestions, the leader forms a list on the blackboard. An example might be:

Places	Feelings
beach	happy
graveyard	scared
dentist	awful
circus	excited

Divide the class into several groups of four or five. Each group chooses one of the places and one of the feelings. **Decide what you will see and what you will feel about going to these places. You have only 30 seconds to decide. When we start, each of you move as an individual, with everyone moving at the same time. Walk around the room as if you are walking to the place on the board that you have chosen. Remember how you feel about going there. What do you see? Walk and sit down as though you are there by yourself. Group one, Ready! Begin. Stop. Could the rest of you tell how they felt? Why? Where were they? What were they looking at? What about their use of space? Next group? Begin!** Continue using the groups. They will soon understand that body language may be conveyed by their stance and walk.

Further extension: Each group makes up a single line of dialogue from which its members build ideas for a sequence of actions. Lines that might instantly suggest tension include: "Let's get out of here; I think I hear them coming. I lost the key. We don't have much oxygen left. Be very quiet when you cross the creek. I see a light. Do you think we should go in?" Even better is when the dialogue continues spontaneously developing into a situation from a single line: "I don't know; it's awfully dark. I see a light inside. Yeah! I'm scared."

The same organization that has been used before when working with groups can be applied. The leader calls groups by number so that they give and take (see Improvisation, p. 36 and **give and take,** p.38) taking turns sharing the space while moving and speaking in intervals. At first each group continues for about ten seconds, until they become involved and intervals become longer.

After a few minutes of give and take ask them to bring their scene to a conclusion and end in a "freeze." If the leader feels the groups are confident, allow them to perform individually so that the conclusion may become more meaningful.

Exercise 26 Talking Hands (generic exercise) (LA, Hist, Sci)
Stimulate the imagination by using the hands to communicate.

Instructions: Have each participant decide on a subject (what), a character (who), a place (where).   Each child may become a character from a myth, fable, tale or some topic they've read in school. Any topic can become the subject for a dialogue. Nervousness may be eased if they imagine they're talking on the phone to each other at first. They may use simply their hands, a sock/glove or an object. Science concepts, social studies, anything can be presented.

For the whole class to participate as an audience, position a mattress box to be your puppet stage. Cut an opening in the center top about two and a half feet wide by two feet long. The players stand to the sides behind the box so they cannot be seen by the audience. The sides are adjusted in such a way as to be turned back away from the audience so the stage can stand up. Be sure the height is good for the average participant. It is soon realized that the mattress box isn't needed because the audience's attention is riveted to the hands. Gradually the children develop more security in front of the group. Besides individual hands, two hands or many people using both hands can also become actors in a scene.

Exercise 27   Movement "in place" (kinesthetic) (Jin) (all subjects)
A movement story where you remain in one place, referred to as an "in place" journey, a useful technique when space is lacking.

Instructions: When it's someone's birthday, it's timely to jump into a birthday cake-making   journey. The birthday person will feel special and all the children will feel as if they have given a gift. Begin moving your hips to mimic the mixer and accompany the following by miming each action.

Narration: **You're not sure what kind of cake you want to make. What kind shall we make? I heard more chocolates. We open the flour and measure it. One, two cups. Now the baking powder and a pinch of salt. Measure the sugar and margarine and cream together. Oh, I forgot. The chocolate needs to be melted. Open the chocolate, break a piece off, get out the pan and melt the chocolate. Careful not to let it stick. Pour the milk into the chocolate and mix. Now blend all ingredients together.** (Continue to move your body as a blender, like a mixer, or make stirring motions in front of yourself. Exaggerate every movement.) **Now we grease the pan, pour the mixture into** the pan. The oven's been heating up. We need to get under the pan to lift it up and someone needs to pull the oven door open. (Do this as a group) Everyone slide the pan in. Whew! Now to make the icing. Open the icing mix. Read the directions. Oh, yes. Pour the icing into a mixing bowl. Now blend in the margarine. Just a little water. Ready. Shh—sh—cake baking in progress. (Tiptoe while turning around in place in a circle stressing quietness.) Let's see if it's ready. Take a pot-holder and lift the pan out. Ta—da, the test! Stick the knife in and it's clean. Let it cool. Everyone take a big breath and blow on the cake to cool it. (Walk around again, stepping quietly, but in place.) We cut around the sides, turn the pan over and gently shake it out. Did we get the whole thing? Oh, dear. Well, just loosen that little bit and turn it over onto the main piece, wedging it into the little hole. Now, ice. And the next pan, cut around the sides and carefully loosen, turn over. Good, all of it came out. Now for the rest of the icing. Candles. Let's sing Happy Birthday. And we'll all get under the cake and carry it to the Birthday Person.

Follow-up: this is an extremely useful exercise with any topic, especially when space is hampered.

Exercise 28 Images to Music (kinesthetic, visual) (Jp)

Listening is accomplished by degrees, gradually allowing the environment to become integrated into the personality.

Instructions: Children need listening practice before they can develop situations fully enough to build a plot around them. Leader's questions will aid this development. Provide taped music or a record player. Music should be varied in pace, volume, etc. As the piece plays, the leader points out significant changes in the music, suggesting different actions.

Questions/Narration: Close your eyes and listen to the music. How does it make you feel? What do you think is happening? What happened first? What might have been the cause of that? What was the difference between the first and the second part? Let's do it again. What part could we act? Where would that take place? Would we run or move very slowly?

Kinesthetic reactions and visual images are more intense, and the environment, movement and character development are more powerful when the eyes are closed. If the children have suggestions, a simple journey with obstacles and actions may be narrated while the children move in place to both spoken directions and inner images sustained by the music (see Chapter 2, Narration).

Planning our fractured fairy tale.

Plots

The "well-made play," a play with a carefully wrought plot, did not occur historically in dramatic literature until the mid-19th century in Europe. Up until this time, prescribed plot forms such as boy meets girl, boy loses girl, boy finds girl, did not exist. Plots were more like boy meets girl and through a series of misadventures and subplots he either finds the girl again or doesn't. If it was a comedy, the girl was also trying to find him; if a tragedy, she didn't want to be found.

The pre-19th century type of play in which there are many little scenes weaving plot and subplot together is similar to the way children write. In creating a plot, children will instinctively create a sequence of actions which seem to flow from one incident to another. For children, action motivates character; from the stimulus of character a plot form may be developed. Otherwise, most children are not concerned with plot; they tend to become lost in numerous sequential happenings and get bogged down by them. The more story material to which they have been exposed, the more natural will be their imaginative flow.

It must be remembered that ancient storytellers rarely ended their sagas. Rather, a complete historic era might become a series of episodes like a journey. It is nevertheless possible and satisfying for young players to continue a series of fictional strands which branch out in all directions, beginning and ending anywhere.

Such questions as, "What makes a story exciting, meaningful or important?" can prompt a discussion about the components of a plot. A plot contains a problem, a conflict, a complication and a resolution, and an awareness of these concepts aids an investigation into plot construction. Other important elements of plot construction are tension, prolonging suspense and the climax.

The exercises which follow involve writing, either the teacher writing for the children as in the **experience story,** or the children themselves writing. As a general rule it is better if the drama exercise comes before the writing activity, because the activity deepens the experience from which the story comes, and so the written version will be more complete and thoroughly owned by the writer. If the children write first, they're too involved trying to remember each word and follow the "script" accurately, a stumbling block for the group since each one wants their version acted out. If they improvise first, they are not only freer, but find new ideas through interaction with each other. Of course, the scripts are never alike, and it is interesting for them to make comparisons with other members of their group. This procedure of dramatizing/improvising an idea first and then writing it down is used more and more by playwrights who are working in an educational setting with student actors. All of these plot exercises emphasize language arts activities.

The Experience Story

With younger children, the experience story can result from observations made during a field trip, riding on the bus, a science experiment, virtually anything that happens in school or outside of it. In the experience story, the drama or improvisation is discovered in the life children live. The teacher helps children relive the experience by drawing out its parts and writing them down with the whole group contributing. The story can be illustrated and read later. Specific, open-ended and affective questions will help the children make a complete story. What did you see on the journey? Did you find something that was important to you on the journey? What happened next? The experience story is not based upon what we think of as a plot. A tried and true reading instruction method, the experience story uses children's experience and their words; they are dictated by the children to the teacher who writes their ideas on the board. Though traditional plot elements may be discovered, they are not imposed.

Introducing Plot

A simple way to introduce plot is to show one action followed by another which conflicts with the first. For example, a person is eating something sticky, and the phone rings. Either the eater is successful in unsticking his fingers and reaches the phone in time or he isn't and has problems. If he has problems, we need to know his reaction. If it concerns him, then he will tell us. If it is tragic in tone, he would have let us know that he was expecting an important phone call, and then we might empathize with him. If this is a funny sketch without a lot of depth or comments on the nature of existence, the plot might be further complicated; the sticky substance glues his hands together or his mouth shut, or causes him to remove his false teeth and he can't get them back in, or he gets the uppers and lowers reversed. The possibilities are as vast as the imaginations of the participants. A comic sketch will result if an action is taken to its logical extreme and exaggerated on the way.

A simple way to define plot is to say that it is a story with a beginning, a middle and an end. The exercises which follow demonstrate that form.

Exercise 29   Three Freezes   (generic) (LA, Soc Stud, Hist)
Students create tableaus from action moments in a story.
Instructions: Choose any story to tell, and select three freeze positions that tell the story. Some easy examples for one actor are:
1. Grab something that looks good, freeze;
    drink it, freeze;
    hold your stomach, freeze.
2. Tie one shoe, freeze; tie the other, freeze;
    try to move, freeze;
    realize that both laces are tied together, freeze.

Exercise 30   Three Deeds   (LA)
A literary genre which adheres to this form is the folktale which often involves "three deeds."
Instructions: Share a folktale that utilizes the three deed form with the students. Ask for other examples. After a plot or two have been discussed it will be easy to see that folktales the children have known for years are organized in much the same way.
Ask for students to write brief outlines of events on the board from a folktale they remember. Have volunteers retell the story from the outline. After several outlines have been placed on the board, and you're sure that the class is familiar with them, erase a line cancelling out one main section of the story in each. Have each class member choose one of the outlines to re-write, using the crossed out section as an opportunity for elaboration and invention. The other sections can be a recollection of something they already know and feel some confidence in rewording. In this way they already have the spine of a story and in the deleted section can be as inventive and ridiculous as they wish while they improvise.
After sharing their stories, a discussion of these three main parts can take place. What other parts did this story have? How was the body or middle different from the beginning and end? How were the stories different from each other?
Over the years teachers have developed many inventive ways to help make creative writing an exciting adventure for children. To see and understand form, it is always useful to involve children in the creation of the form.

Exercise 31 The Fractured Fairytale/Folktale (generic) (LA)

Children practice writing through the use of fairy tales/folk tales, a type of story the children know well because it is part of the culture.

Instructions: Over the years I have used this approach with children but coupled it with dramatizing. Many children who don't feel enthusiastic about writing become much more eager when they see their ideas in action.

Together teacher and students fill in a chart like the one shown below. Begin by asking the children for the names of fairy tales they remember. List those on the left side of the chart. More questioning will fill in the chart.

Fairy Tale	Characters (Who)	Plot (What)	Environment (Where)
Red Riding Hood	herself, wolf mom, grandma hunter	goes to	forest grandma's house
Brementown Musicians	rooster, dog donkey, cat robbers	travels to city	robber's house
Three Bears	bears, Goldilocks	breaks into cottage, sits, eats, sleeps	forest, cottage
Jack & the Beanstalk	cow, mom Jack, giant	climbed stalk	country

After you've filled in the chart ask the class a "what if" question. What would happen if the three bears had climbed the beanstalk? Take the characters from one story, the plot from another and the environment from a third as you ask them "what if?" In this way elements from three different stories can be combined during the improvisation. Or a single story's ending can be fractured. For example, in the original story *The Princess and the Frog*, the frog turns into a prince. In the fractured version the princess turns into a frog. Any way the story is changed fractures it.

One basis of comedy is incongruence, a concept which matches two diverse thoughts or situations that do not naturally belong together.

My experience with elementary school children demonstrates their joy and seriousness in crafting complex plots based on fractured fairy tales. I found it easier to have them work in small groups. The groups study the chart, plan short scenes, act them out, and then write. The children realize how inventive they can be because there are no rules they must follow. Any complication can be introduced, any story combination can be successful, and they may make up whatever is needed.

When participants turn the dramatizations into written products they gain other useful skills. Each child's writing, even when working from the same plot outline and improvisation, will be unique; each will interpret the story in his own way, stressing different elements. Their stories will reflect the parts of the drama: introduction, body, and conclusion. They will use the conventions of dialog, quotation marks and paragraphing. And because their writing has its source in a playful, imaginative drama, their writing will be imaginative, too. This method acts to free them emotionally as well. I have watched children experiment with changing gender roles. The boys chose to play the princesses, girls' parts; the girls readily took on the boys' he-man and giant roles.

Exercise 32 Minimal Situations   (LA, Hist)

Minimal situations exploit the spirit of reporting and use four of the five w's: who, what, where, when. A minimal situation gets at exactly what happens—no descriptive language, detail, morals or interpretation—just the facts, Ma'am.

Instructions: A discussion in preparation for a drama might focus on action. What happens? Who does it happen to? Where does it happen? When does it happen? Minimal situations highlight the basic parts of the drama, the introduction, the body and the conclusion.

For example: (Introduction) The three pigs use recycled candy and pizza to build a house. (Body) The wolf chases Red Riding Hood through the forest. Hansel and Gretel and Goldilocks wander around lost, complaining about how hungry they are. They all end up at the recycled house. (Conclusion) They eat the house. The wolf dies of gluttony.

The more children write and repeat the process of language flow, especially in simple, manageable tasks like this one, the easier it will be for them to incorporate new learnings as they improvise. In this example, the noun-verb-object construction of the simple sentence, and the necessity of paragraph breaks to indicate new actions should be especially clear.

This same approach can be used with Aesop's Fables, Greek and Norse mythology, Indian legends, and literature which represents the ethnic background of the children.

Exercise 33 Episodes   (LA, Soc Stud, Hist)

Episodes are incidences or situations that are part of the main event, concept, or theme. They are not seen as sequential but rather synchronistic in relation to the other events. When using "episodes" a cross-over is made from literature to history and social studies. In this way they bring life and meaning to facts that would otherwise have been forgotten "after the test", never becoming part of their thinking or meaning for their own lives. There are several dramas included in this text using this approach. A major theme is chosen to stand for the through line, for example the *Gold Rush*. Supporting this theme, parallel events are chosen such as all the various groups of pioneers who traveled to the gold country: on the Oregon Trail; on the California Trail; around the Horn; climbing across Central America; and those who came across the Pacific Ocean. The children are still working within a partial fantasy realm because aside from the events, they are acknowledging vicarious experiences when they are interacting in an improvisation. Through the experience of improvisation, invention takes place, providing the cohesion whereby the facts gain an added level of depth.

Some dramas that involve episodic possibilities are those entitled: *Being Lost*, in which children begin caring for themselves; *The Island*, another land where they must survive, adjust, and find a way of being rescued; *Westward Journey*, to find a new land which they must make into their own.

As an example, the theme of *Westward Journey* presents many different groups of people, all seeking a better life. Traveling West in search of a better life continued on into the thirties after the soil had been overused and could provide no nutrients to crops. Indeed, people still travel West, as we can see by the continued growth of California's population. A dramatization of this period may include a number of "episodes" or parallel incidents. I have listed enough for a class of thirty children.

(1) A drifter, who is moving West, stops by a farmer's house to ask for food and finds the farmer has only enough to feed his own family.

(2) An eastern farmer and his family travel West to find homesteading land and must bury two of their children, who die from tuberculosis or malnutrition.

(3) A teacher and his family who have been sent to teach in the school are rounding up the children they find on the farms.

(4) A family is caught in a severe storm and must cope.

(5) A single parent with several small children, an older child who helps, and a grand parent are trying to preserve the farm. All except the grandmother realize the need to move on.

(6) A landlord comes to collect the rent but finds that he must accept some other payment, a treasured heirloom perhaps, in its place.

In other words, any situation elaborating upon the theme of specific people moving West and encountering all the problems of survival, summarizes and synthesizes the period in history from many viewpoints. For each, a situation is written on a card by the teacher and given to the children, or teacher and children together can choose scenes. Through discussion of text material in the middle and upper elementary grades the teacher's scene suggestions will become the class's scenes as a result of their elaborations. With the extension of their imaginations, the dramas and experiences become theirs and as true to history as the imagination of any historian could project. In this way, then, the experience will live in them along with the factual historical situation.

Character

When forming characters, children tend to create character types rather than the subtleties of an individual personality. Because drama works best when it takes advantage of the same kind of spontaneity found in children's play, complex, involved, and detailed character development is not commonly a part of early drama experiences.

Rangers getting prepared.

Children's play is at the heart of their development. As they play, children naturally talk to themselves, speaking in the first person for each doll or toy or plant. They enter into the object and endow it with character. They are like little deities in charge of their own worlds while becoming playwrights linking all their toys together. They imbue each object with an intent much in the way a dramatic personae would do. So revealing is this activity that it has been the method which clinicians have practiced with disturbed children.

Character development begins with the child's own development. He plays himself. Gradually children imitate those things and persons they have experienced in their own lives, including all the images presented by the media. They may take on the swagger of a policeman or the shrill tone of a wicked stepmother. Slowly, over time, a dramatics program can help children visualize and emulate far outside their own experiences. I can still see a first grader complain that his gianting skills had diminished over the years now that he was old, and upon giving his farewell speech to the world, he collapsed as dead, in character and very serious.

The exercises which follow help to channel energy and remove inhibitions. They are fun, and will often surprise and delight. When children are surprised, the spirit of play frequently overcomes the fear of appearing foolish in front of peers. One great advantage of these and many exercises in this book, is their versatility. The children will be growing, in control, and stimulated. They are simple enough to require no introductory preparation and flexible enough to fit into what is already going on in the classroom.

For example, a way to encourage oral language development among young children is to have them speak out loud to themselves as they are occupied carrying out a task. They may be working on an art project and as they work the teacher might encourage them to speak about what they are doing: "Now I'll take my scissors and cut this paper—before I do it again, I'll remember what I've done and repeat it—" The advantages of this are probably obvious to teachers of young children, but what if the teacher includes suggestions that teach elements of drama? "Oh, you're drawing a flower. Can you begin to speak for it as though you were becoming it? I wonder what this flower thinks and feels about being here?" These questions are like the questions teachers ask everyday, but as "Can you name the parts of the flower?" deals with left hemisphere functions, "Can you speak for the flower?" uses the right-hemisphere more as it teaches the child to become a character outside himself.

So important is this link to creative imagination that many

psychologists affirm it as primary to the child's mental, psychological and emotional health. Much potential identity is loosened and projected out onto these figures, just as it is when children use their hands as puppet extensions. The hand/puppet naturally speaks for an object as children do in their play. This natural play energy can continue into the writing of dialog as seen in the sections on writing and plots.

In the exercise *Inanimate Objects*, group characters are used that are either **conglomerate** or **tribal.** A conglomerate character is one in which the elements of a single character are inextricably connected, but each element is played by a separate person: for example, different parts of a tree with each part represented by a different person. A tribal character is one in which the elements are separate and yet are all part of a larger whole, such as a forest. In this case each tree would be a single voice, yet part of a larger tribe or forest.

If a child has had no previous training using drama techniques by the time he is nine, the following exercises can be performed in sequence enabling him to enter the drama experience with assurance and excitement.

Exercise 34 Drawing   (LA, Soc Stud, Hist, Sci)
Introducing character identification through art.

Instructions: During any curriculum project in which an individual picture or mural is created, whether to be used as a backdrop for a drama or not, children can be given the opportunity to immerse themselves in character.

Whatever is being drawn or painted can be spoken with. "Find out what its name is. You don't know? Then ask it. As soon as you know something about it, introduce it to your neighbor. Now, let's all come into a circle. Is there anyone who would like to introduce his new friend?"

Follow-up: Any idea in subject matter areas comes to life.

Exercise 35 The Who Game   (generic) (LA, Hist, Sci)
Appreciating the different qualities of people.

The Who Game is a guide into character that children will understand.

Instructions: Both versions of the Who Game are a bit like Charades or 20 Questions. A person volunteers to leave the room. The group decides who this person is to be. Choose a familiar or famous identity for the absent person so the group will already know many of his qualities. The person is called back into the room, and each comment or question addressed to him is expressed according to the given circumstances of the person's life and situation. He answers in kind until he understands his identity. He can continue to answer as long as he wants to before revealing his discovery.

An extension of the game is to have the chosen person enter as a character that he knows but the group doesn't. The group queries him until they discover his identity. In both cases, information needs to be given out gradually, both in questions and in clues, so questions need to follow the top half of the hourglass, (Chapter 5, Questioning) from general to specific. (Adapted from Neva Boyd's *Handbook of Games*.)

Exercise 36 A Knows, B Doesn't (generic) (LA, Soc Stud, Hist)
Discerning the situation while in the middle of it.

Often a demonstration by the leader with a child volunteer works best. The leader has the children give the volunteer suggestions covering at least two given circumstances: Who, (character), What (activity), Where (place) while she has kept her ears covered. She then "walks into" the scene, slowly extracting clues as she gets a sense of the scene. Clues should be given using the general to specific form (see Chapter 5, Questioning). Reverse.

Instructions: Children work in pairs. One child knows the situation either because he made it up or was given it by the leader. Situations might be written on cards and drawn by the students. A begins the dialogue. B takes up the cues as it progresses. For example, the following dialogue occurred after partner A was given the topic of two people discussing the outcome of a game of donkey baseball: A- Sorry to hear about the game. B- Oh, that's all right, I didn't think we'd win. A- It's hard to know what animals will do, I guess. B- (is baffled) Yea, especially when we don't have any. A- (tries to remain with topic) They said this breed had done well before. Well, I guess those watching had a lot of fun. B- (begins to get it) The other side did a lot of practicing with theirs cause their donkeys wanted to go to first base but didn't want to go to home base. A- Must be frustrating to have a good team with such stubborn donkeys.

Exercise 37 The Perfect Friend/Adult/ Parent (LA)
The student synthesizes the best he's known and/or wished for in a human relationship.

Instructions: Students may work in one large group at first, giving two volunteers their suggestions of qualities to be found in one of these relationships. They also decide the situation or conflict involved. It's played out. This is followed by brainstorming new situations. Children next work in pairs, one becoming the "perfect___" the other, the one with some kind of problem or complaint that he needs help with.

Exercise 38 Inanimate Objects (generic exercise) (LA, Soc Stud, Hist, Sci)

Internalizing an object and ascribing characteristics to it is a most versatile exercise at any age.

Instructions: Plot situations are written on cards. Small groups of children draw a card and extemporaneously act out its situation. Inanimate objects are sometimes left in a room by themselves without the presence of human characters. Plot information and suspense frequently can be provided in an improvisation through the relationship of these objects.

In many folk stories, objects become animate and provide conflict by dividing into groups. The following situations are examples of this.

* The articles in the wizard's cabinet are complaining that the wizard hasn't been ethical and they want to undo him.
* There are different kinds of trees talking in the forest. They are in disagreement over the various forms of magic each can use to save the situation.
* Articles in a junk store are talking to each other about being bought.
* Clothes waiting in the dryer at various stages of dryness talk about their owners' use and abuse.
* Medicines in a medicine chest comment on their uses and users.
* Objects in a deep freeze are beginning to thaw because the plug has been pulled.
* Cars and other vehicles in the garage are talking about their owner's qualities.

Whole environments may be created.
* A city containing tall buildings, trees, street performers, a fountain
* The inner workings of a machine, computer, television, an imaginary machine
* Underwater plants, fish, sunken ships and treasure
* All the refuse and buried material in a dump

Exercise 39 Character Study- interview   (generic exercise) (LA, Soc Stud, Hist, Sci)

The need for subjective identification with a character, through which the students can empathize, is important to accepting a role.

Instructions: Collect pictures of people in various situations. The instructor holds up a series of illustrations, asking questions about each. Close-ended questions are good because they are not difficult to answer, especially when dealing with an unformed character. The pictures provide only some of the information. The rest is up to the children to develop logically from the picture beginning.

Once each of several pictures has been discussed generally, line the pictures up on the chalk tray and encourage the children to choose one and develop that character more fully. The leader may still ask questions, but each child will respond privately, on paper perhaps. Does this person like sports? What are his hobbies? What is his occupation? Is he adventurous?

The questions the leader asks might be general or specific, whimsical or serious, but each one will help the child define his own character.

Begin to think about some possible questions you would ask of other characters about their background. What do you do in your spare time? What is your fondest memory?

When the children have developed their own character and thought of questions to ask of others, they can take turns responding to group questions on behalf of their own character using the biography they have written as a resource. This introduces the character to other members of the group. Members of the class take turns in the "hot seat," answering questions until the class can identify the picture from which the chosen character was drawn.

Variation: Have the newly developed character, played by his biographer, walk into the class, pose, and verbalize an attitude. The group tries to identify him as he answers questions. A second variation is to place several of the characters in a situation, perhaps escaping a fire or eating in a restaurant. The situations, in this case, must be quickly established. Have several groups of new characters participate in the same scenario. Interviews follow.

After some knowledge has been gleaned by the children, either the teacher or a child volunteer is introduced as Ishi, the only surviving member of the Yahi Indian tribe in California found and taken care of in 1911 by anthropologists. The children become experts in some field, such as anthropology, in order to question him. This is a convenient way for the teacher to give information. (See Authoritative Role in Chapter 4.)

Exercise 40 Waiting   (Lit, Soc Stud, Hist)
We can identify your character by how you feel and what you do. This also includes development of concentration and poise in front of a group and expression through body language.

Instructions: This may be done by a single individual, by a group of individuals all waiting for different things, or by a group all waiting for the same thing, a bus, for instance. If waiting for a person, each character needs to know specific given circumstances in order to reflect these to the audience. Dialogue follows.

Speech

If a child has been stimulated by a particular experience, the excitement of wanting to tell someone else about it is an outgrowth of natural emotion; verbal flow seems automatic. Factual information is often harder for children to convey because it lacks that experiential involvement, but there, too, the emotional desire to share is often motivation enough.

Human speech is an outgrowth of the most highly developed process levels of both the left and right hemispheres: synthesis and characterization. In synthesis as a left hemisphere function, all previous experiences have culminated and a sense of confluence is reached. (The term synthesis is used in this context in connection with both the left hemisphere and right hemisphere. In the left hemisphere it refers to the next to the last step, as a culmination of steps in the hierarchy. Synthesis in the right hemisphere is a term describing its overall gestalt function.) The development of characterization is the most highly developed category in the hierarchy of the right hemisphere and is the expression of ones philosophy of living.

From infancy to age five, when the child often has the undivided attention of his parents, speech growth is rapid. A child learns a whole language practically in its entirety. But still, developing verbal fluency is a long process; oral language development is a major focus of early childhood education and remains an important element of curriculum through college.

Helping the child make oral delivery more comfortable and natural is a job of the teacher.

With young children dialogue is often practiced through repetitive singing and movement games. These methods include antiphonal or question-answer chants. The leader engages them in dialogue as she narrates their "journey."

The tasks for older children can become more elaborate, utilizing their imaginative skills and broader experience of the world to give motivation and direction to activities that involve speech. Some of the exercises that follow put the children into improvised situations where they can draw on and extrapolate from their knowledge of the world and their knowledge of subject matter. Many of the exercises can be modified so that they extend into most curricular areas.

The prince and the fairy godmother made a pact.

Exercise 41 Teaching (generic exercise) (all subjects)

Instructions: Children work in triads. Each group member decides on a skill that he possesses and tells his group about it, in effect, teaching them the skill. Together the group figures out a way to combine all their skills to share them with the class. For example, if three of you have shared the skills of Japanese paper folding, washing the garage door and painting old furniture, you might use very large gestures to all fold a huge animal out of paper, wash it down with a hose and spray it with paint. Using this exaggerated form helps children to communicate with greater clarity and leads into humor. The teaching doesn't have to be demonstrated to the rest of the class, nor does it have to be physically demonstrable. Speech can be introduced in different ways. The leader can accompany the skill with speech, give a brief introduction, or narrate as the participants are working. Each group member can narrate his part of the activity. Or, the audience can call out guesses about the skills after the scene.

Exercise 42 Caught in the Act (LA)

Instructions: Working in small groups either draw a card on which some misbehavior has been written or decide together what you have done wrong. You are caught in the act. You try to explain your way out of it. One member of the group acts as the authority who has caught you. The act need only be known by those involved and need not be directly revealed. An example of this involves lying. You are caught and tell why you lied.

Exercise 43   Helper/Helped (any subject area)

Instructions: You are in a situation in which one of you is definitely an authority and the other needs help. For example, dentist-patient, teacher-student, librarian-student, mechanic-car owner, policeman-citizen, storeowner-buyer, street person-business man, hunter-animal, farmer-wealthy landowner, parent-child.

Variation: The situation is reversed so that the authority needs help.

Exercise 44 Viewpoints/Reporting   (generic exercise) (any subject area)

Instructions: Working in small groups decide upon a situation that all of you are watching and react as though it were right in front of you. The reactions need only be expressed so that those watching get clues from the **subtextual** conversation. It can be a ship in the distance, something valuable that has been lost, a plane in trouble, survivors in a mine disaster, a game, a TV show, a circus, men working in a sewer, archaeologists at a dig, a fight, someone putting out a fire, a quiz show, a soap opera, nursery school, a teenage dance, an animal act, a magician, a tight rope walker; scenes from history; a science phenomenon or experiment.

With middle/intermediate grades, a **monologue** is delivered in which the participants' thoughts are revealed about their situation: historical, present, or future

Exercise 45 Verbal/Non-verbal   (LA)

Instructions: Divide into couples. You are trying to show and teach something to a person with whom you have no common language. Slowly he begins to understand.

Suggestions: How to run a power mower, an airplane, a motorcycle; how to cook; exercise; feed a temperamental animal.

Exercise 46 I'm an Expert   (any subject area)

Instructions: Choose a simple character to be. You are all going to be on some kind of show on which you must answer questions. Decide what kind of show it is and who in your group will be the interviewer.

Suggestions: knowledge of the future, millionaires, the garbage dilemma, solving environmental problems.

Variation: To aid concentration, choose something to concentrate on while you are sitting there. This object serves to aid concentration; it need not be communicated and may remain ambiguous. For example: you have a physical irritation of some sort which bothers you and you cannot reveal what it is.

Follow-up: extend into an occupation.

NOTES for CHAPTER 9

1 McKim, p. 91
2 McKim, p. 92
3 McKim, p. 89
4 McKim, p. 9
5 Williams, p. 121

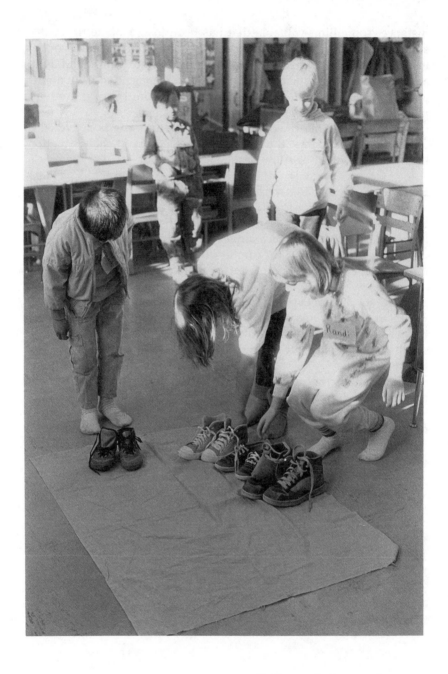

Getting ready for our adventure.

Chapter 10

The Dramas

We have seen how exercises can be extended into dramas. In this chapter, the exercises are used as extensions of many dramas. All of the dramas in this chapter have been tried and found to be successful in classes of various grades K to 8. Some authors call these dramas, lesson plans. I prefer to call them dramas to avoid confusion with the normal Lesson Plan form taught in many colleges of education. These dramas can be considered generic since each follows a similar outline (see Chapter 3) and all are flexible.

Each of the dramas takes about an hour to do. Extensions are included at the end so the theme can be carried on at a later time. Each drama falls into one of eight themes. The themes have been selected deliberately as analogous to the child's psychological needs with growing educational requirements. Each thematic section contains introductory notes which include information, particularly in the latter sections, adding to the teacher's background. The dramas contain (symbols) abbreviations standing for the following subject areas: LA, Language Arts; Lit, Literature; Soc Stud, Social Studies; Geog, Geography; Hist, History; Sci, Science, to designate their inclusion in a particular area of the curriculum, and numbers to indicate the grade levels they have been used with. Many dramas include movement, but are not classified under PE, physical education. Instead exercises are included or recommended. Those which contain journeys are accompanied by the following abbreviations: Jp, means journey preparation; Js, a journey which requires horizontal movement in space; Jin, a journey which can be done in place. A "generic" exercise is one which is a continuation of the child's natural growth process and is comfortable for him; thus, one which works easily without preparation, unlike the dramas. Single quotes ' ' are used around words which refer to specific concepts noted in the first few chapters.

Summary of the Drama Areas (see p. 47, Analogy)

Being Lost: the children help someone find his way, compensating for their own feelings of lostness by becoming more autonomous; in turn, they develop self-confidence.

Toys: a familiar and comfortable theme and a stimulus for children's acting out.

Animals: most children's human compassion rests upon their immediate identification with animals. This caring attitude is an important contribution for many social reasons and needs early acknowledgement. Includes three dramas: *The Fair, the Zoo, or the Circus; Taking Care of Pets; Save the Dinosaur,* developing the awareness of extinction.

The Old House: focuses upon the experience of having a secure place to be which is not taken for granted by many children. Includes the drama: *Homeless Children.*

The Island: the child has his own inner 'island' and in this drama he must survive and protect his new island within society, symbolizing his place within the social order. Includes two dramas: *Island-1, Island-2.*

Nature and the Environment: after having had a relationship from within his own sphere or island, he is given more of a task to care for his misunderstood planet. Includes four dramas: *The Sacrifice; Ocean Ecology; Endangered Species; The Forest.*

Human Nature: includes the human problems such as diet, death, fear, war, hunger, and addictions in which a person is in role with a problem the children help solve. Includes four dramas: *The Dead Bird; The Soldier; Nutrition; Addiction.*

History and Oppression: is a theme that runs through these dramas in order to help children in the middle grades become involved in thinking about and approaching solutions to many of the problems in the world today. Includes seven dramas: *The Gold Rush; California Missions; The First Thanksgiving; Westward Journey; Old Medicine Person; War and Conflict; Immigration.*

Drama sub-headings
Sub-headings accompanied by an asterisk (*) are not always included. Since every drama is different some will include other necessary headings.

Sub-headings less often used are: preparation; planning; movement activities. These assist the leader in getting the children ready to do the drama.

The dramas contain these sub-headings:

*Introduction: relevant background material

*Research: knowledge the teacher needs to lead the lesson

Objectives: rationale for doing the drama; includes both cognitive and affective goals

Materials: items needed to carry out the drama

Concept: the theoretical intent of the drama

Strategy: drama techniques the teacher uses

Story: a through-line of activities

Beginning or motivating questions: used both to gain their interest and to inform the teacher about the children's background

Drama: the actual process

Final questions: asked to complete the children's understanding
and to determine whether objectives have been met

Extensions: how the drama's theme can be carried out in future

*Narration: refers to the leader's communication of the scene to
the children, as well as to the reader.

*Transitions: refer to changes the leader makes when moving
from one character into another.

Drama Structures

The dramas illustrate the following structures, beginning with
simple and moving toward more complex structures.

1. The journey structure

The leader guides the children using a continuous series of
images which she narrates as all move and adhere to the images (see
Chapter 2).

2. The journey structure combined with the authoritative role.

In a drama such as *The Sacrifice*, the leader not only guides
the children with journey narration, but she steps out of this
ambiguous, "shadowy" role and takes on an "authoritative" role (see
Chapter 4). After she relinquishes this role she guides them back
using the shadowy role again. The drama *Homeless Children* is
similar; however, in this drama she employs two different
authorities.

After being in an authoritative role in *The Island* drama she
may decide to become the primitive, the pirate, or some role of her
own choice whom the children meet on the island. If, in these
dramas, the children are working in groups and focused, she may go in
and out of role more easily (see Chapter 8, Co-operative Learning).
Possibilities are described in the introductory notes of *The Island*
drama. The same structure is employed in the dramas *Ocean Ecology*,
and *Endangered Species*. In both she guides the children in a journey
after which she may become the creature (a mannequin has been used
here) or eagle. In the *Medicine Person*, the leader's role is also
authoritative as she confronts the children, coaching them into their
Indianness.

3. Town Meeting Dramas

In *Taking Care of Pets, Save the Dinosaur,* and *War and Conflict,* children are sitting and cooperating in a type of town meeting structure. Directives are given to them through the leader's role(s).

4. Full Role Dramas

Dramas in which the role remains intact throughout the drama are called full role dramas. *The Dead Bird, Nutrition, The Soldier,* and *Addictions* are all of this type. The focus is upon the role during the entire time. If the teacher herself assumes the role as in *Endangered Species,* then she has laid the ground work in the negotiation process, and she has insured the trust and the acceptance on the part of the child (see p.224 *Endangered Species* and Chapter 4, Role Transitions). As a catalyst the leader is needed to keep the children tied to the role through her comments and questions.

5. Small groups,   the leader as director, using shadowy-
   ambiguous role.

In *The Forest* and *Westward Journey* dramas some structure is provided before the actual drama begins. Since the children are older they can work in separate groups in order to prepare themselves to enter the drama. This frees the leader to go from group to group insuring each group of their objectives even before the beginning questions are asked. When the drama begins she becomes like a conductor who's in charge of the whole drama, bringing on each group as others remain involved, yet on the sidelines observing. They must remain observant in order to use any new exposition they learn from watching.

Bringing on different groups or highlighting groups by giving them focus is used in the drama *The Circus, Fair, or Zoo,* with the teacher in the role of a type of ambiguous barker. By age eight on, dramas such as the *Gold Rush* allow children to work in groups while the leader becomes an active media director, demanding, "quiet on the set." As well, *The First Thanksgiving* needs this same type of directorial management. The Indians and whites work within their own groups, until the leader acts as a catalyst to bring them together. With some changes, this drama has been used in grades K through six.

6. The Dramas of the Oppressed

The most difficult dramas to carry out are those in which the children choose to become oppressed. "If you want to know how it feels then you must allow yourself to take the kind of abuse that goes with it." If the leader has their commitment, then she uses her role to reinforce the quality of oppression. The *Immigration* drama and *Mission* drama uses this type of coercion.

If we can learn from her, she may help us.

Being Lost

(Geog) (K-3)

Introduction

Young children often experience a lack of trust upon going to school. This drama speaks to this emotional condition by solving the problem physically.

Research

Mapping skills are needed.

Objectives:

1. To learn strategies for ways to become familiar with the environment and guard against becoming lost.
2. To learn to become independent and resourceful by surviving in a foreign locality.
3. To understand the shallowness of first impressions.

Materials:

Paper and crayons for map making; aviator's hat and scarf; tape-recording of a plane landing; old clothes; a whistle, melodious (not strident)

Concept

Helping a 'lost person' compensates for ones own lost feelings.

Strategy

The leader takes on the role of aviator in the "I don't know" role, and during the transition, takes up the role of the fisherman in the "authoritative" role, unless other adults are available.

Story

The leader introduces the concept of map-making by beginning with the classroom and school environment. Direction, legends, scale and other cartographical concepts can be considered. While the children's focus is on mapping, she re-enters as an aviator who needs help because her plane has been forced down, and she's lost. The children share with her their understanding of direction. She takes them on a journey to validate the maps' findings. They make an emergency landing on an island. From here it is suggested that the leader follow her curriculum requirements.

Beginning questions:
    Have you ever been lost? How did you find your way? What can you do to keep from getting lost? If someone were lost in your neighborhood do you think you could help him find his way? How?
    The leader begins to take suggestions from the children while drawing a map on the board. Here's the school. What street is this? Block out as much of the community as the children know before specifying an open area where the plane can land. Beyond this area fill in whatever geographical features are appropriate.

Drama
    We hear a taped airplane engine and a landing. The person in role enters wearing an aviator's hat and scarf. She looks surprised and is somewhat unsure of her surroundings. **Where am I?** She looks at her map. **Oh, dear, I'm completely lost. Can you help me? I'm looking for a historical site.** This can be a redwood forest, the ocean or any particular landmark which has importance for the class. At this point the children are encouraged to help the aviator find whatever place she needs to locate by drawing a picture map of the historical site in small groups, directed by her description. In the meantime the aviator may search out pathways in mime, fix her engine, or intermingle with the children. After about 12 minutes of drawing the children share their maps with the whole class while enlightening the aviator.
    How would you like to come with me in the airplane? You must promise to follow all the rules of safety. Fasten your seatbelts. Practice breathing into your oxygen mask. Take your seat pillow and fasten it around your chest like this. In case we land at sea this will protect you from drowning. As we lift off you can see your school, then your house, and gradually we'll be up far enough so you can see the city. We're up now about 4,000, 5,000, 6,000 feet. Oh, oh, engine trouble. We're going to have to land. Be sure your seat belts are fastened because we're going to land on that island down there. It's an unexplored island. Your ears may start to pop but that's all right. Hang on! Whew! Made it! This is Captain Jackson, over. Made emergency landing, over. Need help, over. Oh, no. For some reason I can't get any response.

Transition I

A transition follows in which another role can be introduced. The role can be fashioned in accordance with the leader's teaching requirements. For example, a "bird" has spotted a fire which needs to be quelled; a native appears who aids the children in their attempt to survive, as in The Island drama; a "dolphin" can be played by using a puppet/mannequin who enters to take them down into the ocean, similar to the Ecology drama about pollution in the ocean. They meet a fisherman whose boat capsized; without a working radio he had no way of getting any help, re-enforcing the concept of being lost.

Transition II

(If the leader is doing the drama alone, she uses this transition to leave.) **Well, here we are. Don't know exactly where, but by this sextant** (can by mimed or made out of cardboard) **I think we're off the coast about 100 miles. I'm going to go look for help. I want each group to get busy because we may have to spend the night here. This group gathers berries; next, gathers leaves for beds; catches fish for dinner; for water, digs a well, if fresh water streams can't be found; and gathers wood to make a fire for cooking and warmth.** During this time, the children are engaged in dramatic play and a change is made by the leader into a fisherman by donning ragged clothing. The transition need not take more than thirty seconds and needs to be completed away from the children's gaze. To regain their focus, in the new role of fisherman she places herself in the middle of the room, watching the children. In order to eventually get everyone's attention, she blows on a type of whistle which is preferably melodious and not strident. The encounter with the children needs to be gradual, allowing for recognition and tension to build to the count of about 20 after almost all have been alerted. Both sides exchange stories; the fisherman explains that her radio wasn't working nor did she have any life-saving equipment. Her biography gradually unfolds, and she can teach a variety of techniques for survival: the use of the sextant for plotting direction, Morse code, how to fish, and how to fix the aircraft in which all will be returned to safety.

Final questions

What should you do so that you won't get lost? Were you afraid of the fisherman at first? Why? Have you ever met people who at first seem scary, but turn out to be very friendly? How can that be? Do you think that after you get to know people, they seem friendlier? But you still need to be careful of strangers, don't you? (Unfortunately, children are naturally very trusting and need some warning.)

Extensions

Aerial journeys (Js) in the exercise section on Space can be used as the leader combines other characters for extending this theme.

Who wants to be a toymaker? Who wants to be a toy?
What toy do you want to be?

Toys
(self-concept) (K-2, 3 see note in **Other Versions** at end of drama))

Introduction

Children's identification with toys is instinctive. Consequently, it is not unusual that they identify with them automatically.

Research

The leader must find out from someone involved in the toy business about toys that are currently popular in order to protect the drama from the kind of toy which "pops" ammunition and could cause the drama ultimately not to work as well. Trendy toys like Cabbage-Patch dolls are not effective because their movements are not interesting. This research helps the leader to gauge beforehand how to incorporate movement in the drama by knowing which toys offer the most possibilities. The leader could ask the children before the drama what kind of toy is their favorite and one that they'd want to include in a drama. However, the leader must guide the children to include toys she believes good and steer the children away from those which aren't as workable dramatically. If the less acceptable toys are still important to the children, they might still be included, although potentially their movement would not be as versatile. A point may need to be made about the negative uses of military force if this type of toy is included.

A **Casting question** is: Who wants to be a toy, a toymaker, or a customer buying the toy? Half the class as toys, a third as toymakers, and those remaining as customers, would be the best distribution for this drama. If the teacher does not get anything like this distribution, she can suggest that, in order to do the drama, it is necessary that we have a few more_____, and not so many_____. The ratio between toys and toymakers is variable, a few toymakers have been used with many toys.

Objectives

1. To develop concentration, cooperation and motor skills.
2. To enhance listening abilities.
3. To incorporate problem solving skills into a dramatic situation.

Materials
Tambourine or drum. The sound of a phone ringing is optional. It can be mouthed by the leader or played on a hand-carried, battery-powered tape-recorder.

Concept
Children are given an opportunity to practice what is familiar to them, gaining self-respect, trust, and discipline for form. An extension is suggested in Chapter 3, Analogy.

Strategies
1. Toys are used as an analogy to growing up
2. The leader remains in role as a toy store owner and directs the drama through the use of the "I don't know" and "invisible" role.

Story
Children become toys. The leader as a toy store owner will go bankrupt unless more toys are sold. All have a brief meeting in which toys realize they are unique and can accomplish what live children can accomplish, i. e., talk, move, etc. For a more sophisticated class, toys parade in front of a group of children who become buyers (see Extensions, p. 165).

Movement activities
The leader needs a list of the children's toys either in her head or on the board so she can take the children through a movement sequence to develop each toy's movements. The commonly accepted toys from the past can be used: teddy bear, rag doll, jack-in-the-box, ballerina, airplane, fire-engine, soldier. They hold some meaning for the children. Movement activities can be used as a warm-up. With young children, all move together to the leader's suggestions. After each question is asked, movement follows. <u>Introduce and model moving, then make two taps or some other sound as a signal for freezing</u>. **How does a teddy bear move? Umm, and maybe he sees some honey over there on the tree, umm. Yes, he wants to get the honey off his fingers. A rag doll? Loose and floppy. Kind of falling all over itself like this. A jack-in-the-box? Up and down. A ballerina or ballet dancer? Leaps and turns. How does a soldier walk? Stiffly? An airplane? Careful to keep to your flight pathway. A fire-engine?** etc.

Activities, planning
Where would we find these toys? How many toys do we have? How many toymakers? Customers? Will the customers draw the toys they would like to purchase? In this way one group is working to deepen their belief while the leader works with the other groups. **Will all the toys stand over here? I would like for the toymakers to be in charge of one or more of these toys.** Depending on the ratio, the leader can also pick up the slack in case there is not an even number on both sides. **Have a little talk with each other and find out about your toy. That's right, see if you can help each other out and find out how to move the toy. After you find out, please come over here with your toy and place him on this display shelf. Now, we want to get ready for the customers.** Miming readiness concerning dusting off toys, placement, and general fixing up is carried out as the leader speaks out loud about each thing. She can be directing at the same time.

Narration
These toys look so good all standing there on the shelf. Oh, here come some customers. I haven't sold anything for a week. I certainly hope they buy something. The customers (if needed the leader may use the invisible role in case no children become customers), who have been drawing, arrive and the leader goes through her sales routine and proudly shows off the toys' movements and any other special features which the toymakers come up with. They may buy some toys or not. After they leave she checks the mailbox and finds that the bank is going to foreclose unless she makes a payment on her loan within the week. **Second notice, oh, no. I'm going to lose my toy store and all these beautiful toys—$10,000! What am I going to do? Why don't we all relax and gather around. I know you're all very special** (refers to customers also) **more so than any other group of toys I've seen. And before I opened this toy store I went to many other toy stores to find out.** This break may not be necessary. In every drama I've been involved with the children all stood in character as their toys for, in some cases, over an hour. She asks the children what ideas they may have. She can incorporate any of their ideas and/or embellish these ideas with some of her own.

I've got an idea. It's just because you're special that this will work. Each one of you can do what no other toy

can do—can you think of some things—? The leader needs to continue to ask in order to get as many children thinking as possible and not just take the suggestions of the consistent talkers. **Yes— yes—and what else?** **And, I bet each of your toys has a uniquely different way of working just like each of your personalities are unique and different. What else is different about us? Talking. Are there toys that talk? What do they say? Can we all repeat that? Are there other sounds that toys make?** Individual children may wish to parade around demonstrating their uniqueness while the leader synchronizes their movements with a drum beat. **That's what I'm going to put in my advertisement. These toys are unique. They can move, talk, make sounds, read letters and words, read numbers and count.** She asks the children who have been drawing their toys to explain about their toys' unique traits to give ideas to the class. **Will the toymakers have a little talk with their toys to see what special things their toy wants to develop? Will the customers check their drawings to be sure they have nothing to add to their toy?** The leader waits to be sure all is understood before miming her phone conversation which will give the children further information. Be sure to get the children's attention by using a louder voice.

Hello, is this the newspaper's ad section? I'd like to run the following ad through this week. Yes, I'll wait. Oh, dear, I'm not sure exactly what to say. She hangs up and asks the children for help in writing the message on the board. **Toys for sale, unlike any others. Can talk, walk, what else—?** The message is completed. The leader continues to look pensive and asks children: **Can you think of anything else we can do?**

Extensions

Takes suggestions. Depending on what is mentioned, she asks them about calling in a reporter to do a special story on them. An outside person could come in briefly to represent the reporter and to take pictures. There is also the possibility that a child can represent a reporter, and the teacher can fill in with as much help as the child needs. **Could you say that again? Did you hear that? He asked—.**

Now we're going to—Oh, there's the phone. (response) **Yes, they are. The prices are the same as for other toys of this kind, but they may be going up because there's only a limited supply.** (Hangs up. Refers to customers.) **Let's practice**

with these new customers here. We can have a kind of rehearsal to be sure everything goes well before the others start arriving and before I call the paper again about the ad or reporter. From here on, as many skills can be presented by children as possible. And each time a new skill is introduced by one of the toys and toymakers, the other toys can practice this new skill, encouraging repetition which is not boring. Skills are practiced such as chewing, walking, bending, talking, blinking, smiling, saying their names and telling about themselves.

Besides skills of movement or speech, any academic area such as numbers, math combinations, colors, vocabulary, letters, new words, spelling, social studies and science information can be presented, learned, or reviewed by the toys.

The drama can be slanted towards Christmas by just mentioning the idea of Christmas.

For any kind of drama the toys can move independently whenever the leader's back is turned, but remain frozen whenever she turns back around towards them. **Oh, dear, I just don't know what to do. Oh, I remember that there was a special notice on the box when I opened it: THESE TOYS HAVE MANY TALENTS TO DEVELOP, BUT NO ADULT CAN BE WATCHING.   Do you think that if I turned around you could develop some of these special abilities?   What would they be?** It is important that she makes them think of possibilities and listen to each other for ideas since young children have difficulty organizing themselves. When she turns back around, they should be prepared to give some ideas. She could also leave to go to the bank or somewhere else giving them the time to develop themselves. <u>She could watch from the sidelines and come in to help them in case they are having some difficulty. She is outside the drama in "shadowy" role.</u> The same problem of bankruptcy can be included, and as she leaves to go to the bank, the toys with the help of their makers can be developing new talents to show her.

Children enjoy the game of inanimacy while being watched, but being fully active as long as the adult in charge is not watching…very much in the tradition of Hans Christian Andersen's folk tales.

She can disappear, leaving the toys on their best behavior or under the watchful eye of one of the children who will volunteer to be either a friend, a policeperson, or a member of her family, and she can reenter in another role as reporter or customer. The mannequin can be activated in order to serve any of these functions: as watcher, policeperson, reporter, or a magic caretaker with any desirable archetypal qualities, such as a protector who is all-knowing and insightful.

The frame of this story is versatile and has always worked using many themes, including handicapped toys which the other toys accepted and which some impoverished customer ended up buying for his otherwise toyless child for Christmas.

Other versions

Note. For more sophisticated groups, including third graders: By 3rd grade skills can extend into miming activities, telling any story, and acting it out. The drama as it's presented is neutral and many additions can be accommodated (see Extensions, p. 165, and Chapter 3, Analogy).

Would any of you be willing to be buyers who represent stores from all over the country? Would the toys walk out here, say what kind of toy they are, show their toy's movement, and anything else they want us to know about them? Will the toymakers have a talk with their toys, find out these things, and get ready for the buyers? Who are the buyers? You need to decide the kinds of toys that are important for stores to buy now and generally what kind of toy you're looking for to become stock for a store.

Generic exercises which are useful to include posing for the newspaper; the leader narrates an "in-place" journey as in Exercise 27, p. 130 while the toys become human as in the story of Pinocchio.

Animals

Introduction

Children's identification with animals is as natural and instinctive as their identification with toys. When set up so that each child is either a judge, a trainer or an animal, there is the condition of interdependence and hence mutual responsibility between these three roles which works well as a control factor. In this way the drama has a built-in degree of tension and, in this sense, works like the toy drama.

As the toymaker takes pride in his design, the toy is also proud. In the dramas in the Animal section, the animal, trainer, and judge are analogous to the toy, toymaker, and the customer in the Toy drama.

However, unlike all the children becoming toys, if all the children were to become animals, and no external awareness of their being a character grew, the children would become wild in their enthusiasm and no drama would be possible. In other words, "becoming an animal" would be literal. Warning!

The Fair, The Zoo, The Circus
(LA, Soc Stud, Sci) (K-3)

Objectives
1. To instill pride in children for their contributions.
2. To guide them toward cooperative interchanges with their peers and taking responsibility.

Materials
A tambourine, paper for writing

Concept
Children are given the opportunity to practice what is familiar to them, gaining self-respect, trust, and a discipline for form.

Strategy
The leader guides the group in movement exercises in an effort to help them internalize their roles. After they've begun working in small groups, she can become any of the "authoritative" roles suggested: mayor, sheriff, etc. The children become responsible to each other as trainer/performer.

Story
Animals will be on show either for a circus, a fair, or in a zoo. The children as one group may choose to be part of anyone of these situations. As a result, they are given the choice between becoming a trainer or performer. They may reverse roles if desired.

Motivational activities
Ask the group for the kinds of animals they think would be in a zoo, circus or fair, depending upon which drama is being carried out. Either write the list on the board or keep it in mind. The children's drawings can be put up as advertisements to announce the coming "show."

Depending upon how much movement is needed by the group, carry out a movement exercise to incorporate the suggested animals.

The game, "I am thy Master", can be used. (See glossary.) "I want you all to be big, grey, slow elephants---." (Use two beats for freezing.) And when I do this (two beats) you must freeze. Or a circle journey is taken, and the two drum beats are made to remind the children when they need to establish equidistance. Whatever

animal tricks or scenes the leader has in mind are introduced here as the leader guides them in a circle: **Show the lion is standing on his back legs--**
Show the horse rearing--
The rhino is moving his huge head from side to side.
A practice parade can be introduced here: **"Let's see all the animals following me in this big circle. We want to keep walking like our animal. How does the animal move its legs? Its head and neck? Carry its weight?"**
(Questions covering different parts of the body are asked.)
We want to impress the judges so that they'll choose correctly. We want them to see how well our animal walks and how proud we are of it.

Planning

Stop the action to ask: **We'll need some judges and animal trainers, as well as animals.** It may be necessary to remind them that only a few judges are needed; however, there can be two trainers for each animal, or two animals to one trainer and groups can vary.
First, since this is a zoo, fair, circus— (Ask which event they'd prefer) **what do you think the judges will think is important?** (Whatever the children say is considered and written on the board.) **Will the judges please go over these and write down the things they think are most important either from this list or ones you make up?**
Whatever criteria for judging they think is important for the animals and trainers can be decided here and introduced at the beginning of the "show." If the children can't write yet, have them draw their ideas. The judges will need to explain to the rest of the group what they think is important for the animals and trainers to do.
While the judges are working, will the trainers all come over here, and the animals over here? We've got a lot of work to do to please those judges so they'll choose us to go to the fair, circus, or zoo.

Drama possibilities

If the children are in 2nd or 3rd grade a meeting can be held to decide on the kinds of activities they want to work on, like: a two-legged walking horse, a dancing elephant, a lion jumping through a fiery hoop, a talking gorilla and the list goes on. The circus routines would be the most flamboyant, the fair next, while the zoo animals mainly concentrate on simple movements.

For 3rd grade, the animals can either speak for themselves or the trainer can introduce them. For less sophisticated and less verbal children the leader needs to group them by handing out small pieces of colored paper. Being sure of the ratio between animals and trainers, she hands out the same color to the animal(s) and trainer(s), so the groups are randomly determined.

For older children, the leader can have written the routines on cards which the children can improvise on in their smaller groups. They have some idea, having had the meeting as suggested above, as well as the journey in which routines were narrated by the leader. If the leader wishes for very little noise, she suggests that the animals cannot talk. The only way the trainers and animals can communicate is by showing each other what they mean by using action and a nod or shake of the head to signal yes or no. If she's not sure they can conform to this rule, then in role as the barker, or head show person, she demonstrates with the help of a child who volunteers as an animal. As well, she suggests there may be spies from other animal training facilities, whom they don't want to know how they do their secret routines.

At this point, she can divide her time between the various groups, giving advice, help, and encouragement. It may be necessary to bring chairs out so they can be used as part of the children's acts. At any moment she can leave this "shadowy" role and claim back her role as the "barker" who can take charge instantly either through vocal means, two taps on the drum, or both.

A number of elements can be introduced to increase the tension if needed. For example, any authority figure can enter at this point to introduce a complication: the sheriff can be looking for someone who is acting suspiciously and may be related to the most recent crimes against animals, introducing the ecological aspect of the need for animal conservation, care, and awareness.

The county health inspector can enter to ask for verification of medical records since an animal-related disease is a concern, and he can continue to congregate around the children to inquire about those signs or symptoms that are familiar.

A fire inspector can call attention to proper fire regulation procedures and institute a fire drill if wished.

A farmer and/or a scientist can call in to inspect the animal food because a bad chemical has been found in the food.

The mayor may want the group to move on because the last group of animals were not very good at entertaining and health problems were created.

Chairs may need to be placed in between the performing groups in order to help them concentrate on their own contributions. Also, twine can be placed as a quasi border and a reminder of space utilization.

Or, if the leader wants to introduce the mannequin, change hats, or simply change her voice and demeanor slightly, she can present any of the above problems, or areas that are part of the curriculum.

Next, a grand parade is announced; this time the circle is larger and the leader's narrative can include any of the activities she has seen. A kazoo can be used for this introduction as well as between acts.

The judges need to explain their criteria for judging during the performances. This provides control and need not become a pressure toward competitiveness.

Drama

The leader becomes like a barker, welcoming the contestants, taping numbers on their backs, and warning them about the decorum of presentation. She either introduces the act, or lets a child introduce it, and supports his introduction by repeating and/or re-emphasizing the child's words slightly differently.

The leader's attitude is one of anticipation and excitement as she walks around advising, introducing, keeping the children's focus, and complaining in role if children's attitudes are slipshod and careless. She can call on the judge's opinion and have the children repeat their scene, possibly slowing them down by her beats on the drum. The judges are continually brought in to make determinations, as well.

The leader can also introduce an antagonist by mail (see Chapter 4, Secondary Role), reading a letter which ridicules this event and provides a negative voice in order to unify the children and deepen their roles.

Roles can be interchanged and children can have a more varied experience so that new routines and concepts can be introduced.

Extensions

Posing for pictures, a reporter entering to interview and write up a story, the show needing to pack up and move on, some of the animals becoming ill.

Final questions
    How should we treat animals? What can animals understand?
What traits do animals have which are similar to those of humans?
Have you heard of the concept, "endangered species"? Do you know of
any animals now which are endangered like the dinosaur? Why is it
important to protect endangered species?

Let's put my turtle under the rain cloud.

Taking Care of Pets
(responsibility)(LA, Soc Stud, Sci)(K-3)

Objectives
1. To realize the importance of caring for pets (sometimes "pets" and "dogs" are used interchangeably).
2. To understand how one needs to be responsible to a group.
3. To make decisions based upon fact rather than emotion.

Materials
Pictures of pets: each child either brings a picture found in a magazine or draws a picture of his pet, a tape-recording of a whistle sound, different hats worn by the leader upon changing character, a white coats for the "vet" role, a prop to stand for a remote control radio (or miming it will work).

Concept
The children learn to become responsible (the second step in the affective domain) to the environment through their own natural empathic response.

Strategy
The leader takes on the "authoritative" role of a vet, dog catcher, and the "I don't know" role of reporter, unless she has the assistance of an aide who can take the role of dog catcher, or she may use the mannequin or a child.

Story
The teacher in role as a vet goes through home care procedures with the class; the dog-catcher arrives and asks the class to draw a picture of their pet; they are broken into family groups; a public meeting is held in which new information is announced. The children's pictures are pinned up; after new information is announced, pictures are torn down, signaling the dogs' demise.

Preparation
The children need to know about the following concepts: veterinarian; vitamins, penicillin, epidemic, hypodermic needle (optional).

Drama

(Leader in role as a vet) **I'm pleased to see that so many of you are here and ready to join our new campaign to keep our pets healthy. I work in the county health center as a veterinarian. Do all of you know what a veterinarian does? (response) You realize that no new dog license will be issued until your dog has been checked and cleared of any known disease. The reason for this is due to an epidemic that can spread and kill, if nothing is done.**

First of all, it is pet care that is basic to this problem. Today I'll take you through the complete care treatment so you can try it on your pet and work to prevent them from becoming ill. Of course we hope that this doesn't happen. First, I will demonstrate a simple method for keeping our pets clean. If you *imagine* **your pet in front of you, you can follow right along with me.** (All mimed) **You have before you a bowl of warm water and a sponge. First, place a clean towel in front of you. Dip the sponge into the water and wipe its eyes, around the mouth, and nose. Now add a little soap and gently rub its coat back and forth, all over. When you've finished pour the other pan of clear water slowly over the entire body and rub your clean dog's coat until it's almost dry. Now apply the medicated powder and rub it in all over, careful not to get any in the eyes or mouth, nor in an open wound of yours or your animal's. This powder is quite strong in order to kill any germs. Now wash your hands. That large pill is a vitamin. The way to get a pill down a dog is to hold it tight with one hand, open the dog's mouth with the other, and place the pill down into the throat as far as you can. Now, offer it the water bowl. If you have trouble giving your dog a pill this way, does anyone know of another solution to get the pill inside of it? Yes, put it into the food. As yet, we don't know how much this new disease has spread, so it is necessary to learn to use a hypodermic needle. This will enable the penicillin to reach the damaged or poisoned area as soon as possible. Please remember to keep the penicillin out of reach from children. This is a very special campaign we're venturing upon because the disease is spreading so rapidly. Now, I'll pass out the kits so that you can get started. We hope that these efforts will be taken up by people like yourselves so that the**

disease becomes no worse. (Leader mimes passing out kits.)
**Please inspect your dog's kit to be sure it's fully
equipped. The kit should contain the following items: the
special medicated dog soap; the sponge—any sponge
like this will do—but remember not to use this sponge for
anything except for washing your dog; the medicated
powder—just enough to last for four washings. At present
because of the epidemic, it is important not to waste the
powder; use it once a week. Directions and frequency are
written down and included in each box. It will be available
in the drug stores in about a week. The vitamins are next
—there are thirty—and the hypodermic needle with serum.**

**Please make a drawing of your pet and include any
distinguishing characteristics that would alert someone as
to its identity.** (Paper is passed out. After this, the papers are
pinned up and the children are divided into family groups.) **Be
sure your name is on your drawing, and your address.
These will be pinned up so that a record can be kept in
case your dog strays, is picked up by the dog catcher, is
killed, or runs away. The dog-catcher is here.**

Transition
     The leader either changes hats to become dog-catcher, someone
else becomes dog-catcher, or a mannequin is used.
     Dog catcher: **I see all of you are giving your dogs good
care. I've hired a lot of deputies to go around the
neighborhood to check on people who don't take proper
care of their dogs. I know it can't be any of you folks
because you came to this meeting. But you'll be seeing
either me or one of my deputies soon. And if any of you
want to keep up with what's going on, we've got a new
device that works right along with your TV and radio. After
you hear a whistle alert like this** (blows), **then you'll know to
turn on your radio and TV and hear the latest news about
the epidemic and any dogs that have been lost,
abandoned, or missing. Thank-you for attending this
meeting, and either I'll be by to collect your picture or
have one of my deputies come by. And if your dog checks
out, then you'll be issued a license. If not, then we'll put it
in the animal clinic and you'll have to pay for treatment---
even if the dog dies. Thank-you for your attention. I'll
check on any new reports.**

The organization of family groups may be developed by passing out to the class as many colored tags as are needed for children to be 5 or 6 in a group. So, if there are 30 children, then there will be 5 or 6 different colors. Establish where the groups are in the room by placing the same colors of 5 or 6 pieces of construction paper up in different parts of the room and have them take their pictures with them. In these groups children can finish drawing and then explain their picture to their peers to further expand and internalize the image of their pet.

Transition

Leader: (passes out colored paper) **Take this colored piece of paper and collect together with others from the same family by matching it with the same color on the wall. If you have a yellow piece of paper, then collect around the larger yellow paper that's pinned to the wall. Now explain to your family group how your dog looks according to your picture.** Allow this to continue for a few minutes and then play the tape recorder which has a whistle sound to alert the children. For younger children repetition may be needed.

Leader: **We need to remember what we've learned.** Leader guides children through bath process; vitamin taking; and inoculation of penicillin. Children will be using a form of dramatic play here. **Do you remember which part of the dog should be washed first?** (eyes, ears, mouth) **How should you continue to wash the dog? How to rinse? What's next? What should you apply next?** The same process is gone through again if needed, and the children respond collectively, recalling what they have just done.

Transition

The leader becomes dog catcher by changing hats. **There has just been a special alert. I'll turn on my radio here.**

She mimes listening.

Dog catcher: **I just found out that one of the officers in the police department has been bitten by an abandoned dog and is reported to have suddenly fainted and is now in a coma. We want to find out how the disease spreads. We must keep working.**

(At any time the leader can invent a reason for leaving and say that a reporter is coming to interview the children.) **I'm needed in an emergency–a reporter is going to be here any minute–.**

Transition

She changes a hat or any other item and presents herself as the reporter. **Good day, I'm from the local news.** The interviewing proceeds. She needs to go from group to group to keep the pace from lagging and to collect the pictures. After pictures have been collected they are placed at the top of the blackboard around the room. As the news items are heard, the pictures are torn down signaling the animal's fate. The children don't have to be warned about this action; however, it should be done dramatically so they receive the impact, non-verbally. Pictures are torn down non-selectively. **We've sent in the license numbers of these dogs on our computer with a health report. It has been decided that if any of these dogs are not found to be healthy, they will be destroyed.**

Transition

Leader: **Has everyone completed the care of their dog? Several parents have just phoned the department to say that a young baby and several small children have been attacked and the attacking dogs have been shot.**

As a result she mimes as though she's matching up the dog's license number from its picture with one that she possibly hears over her mimed radio device. The leader pulls down five more pictures. **We need to warn everyone to remain inside. Do not enter the area between Fourth Street and Eighth Street.**

The drama continues in this manner with the leader giving announcements and tearing down the pictures as she mimes checking the computer number.

Extension

As a reporter, the leader interviews them as a family group so all can hear. Asking questions about responsibility: **Who takes care of the animals in this household? Does the same person feed the animals every day? Who washes the animals?**

The leader has them get into their own space and carry out dramatic play as if they were coming home from school and found their pet. **Imagine your pet meets you at the door and is so happy to see you. What do you do?**

Even though you may want to do other things, what should you do for your pet right away?

For **older groups,** or a sophisticated 2nd and 3rd grades, the children need not be taken through the care procedure again. Calling them together in a meeting to interview the different group members about the problem can take longer with older children because they are more verbal. As a reporter she can summarize statements and keep adding new information as received from her incoming news-audio in order to continue to tear down the pictures. Those children who are left with their pictures still up are pressured to speak about solutions to the problem. As reporter, she continues to interview them while interspersing tapes like the following announcements. The following announcement is introduced with the tape of a whistle sound. **Please stand by. Following the news broadcast several minutes ago, it was reported that the officer who attempted to help an abandoned dog has died, and the dog has also died. This area is in the center of the city which is being carefully watched.** The leader pulls down the picture of the dog which died. This is continued from now on as news events are learned.

Another announcement. **Ladies and gentlemen, an entire section of four blocks has now been roped off surrounding the location in which a police officer and a dog have died because it is thought that uncovered garbage may have tempted other dogs to the same area.**

Final questions

Why is it important to care for your animals? What can happen if you don't? Do you need to be responsible for what you own? Are there other things you need to be responsible for? Why is this important?

Extensions

Use exercise, *Inanimate Objects* (in Chapter 9, Character) for carrying out the following, which may be done in small groups.

If your dog could speak, would it be able to give us some advice on how we could keep this disease from spreading?

A news article about a similar situation can be read to them at some point in the discussion or before the drama begins.

San Francisco Chronicle, August, '87: Future Looks Dim for 26 Dogs

Time is running out for 26 Oakland dogs confiscated from their owner---they could be sentenced to death tomorrow if new homes for them are not found.

Although the dogs are mostly a happy lot, they are generally considered too old for adoption. Most, if not all, will probably be put to death, humane officials said.

About a year ago, neighbors of 66 year old Alton Turner began complaining about his dogs' howlings and overpowering stench.

Community growling eventually reached Oakland Municipal Court, where Turner was ordered in May to get rid of the dogs after he was found guilty of maintaining a public nuisance and housing animals in inadequate shelters.

Turner, a retired engineer and contractor, also was ordered to keep no more dogs and to fumigate and remove all health hazards from his East 20th Street home.

Although his shelters perhaps were substandard, his dogs were not underfed or otherwise mistreated, officials said.

Turner, described as "stubborn but very principled," would not consent to an interview.

"He never physically abused the animals or was cruel," said his attorney, Deputy Public Defender Alex Green. "It was just a question of overcrowding. It was clear, (that many) dogs in close urban quarters just wouldn't work."

To comply with the court's order, the animals were taken to a friend's property, where they stayed in a makeshift kennel. But their new home was under the freeway near Fruitvale Avenue—a setting that reverberated the yelps and concentrated the stink.

Last week there was new residential unrest and the dogs were again removed, this time to the Oakland Animal Control shelter.

Animals usually are kept there for seven days to allow their owners to reclaim them said shelter supervisor Keith Lear. If they are not claimed—and if the animals are suitable and space permits—they are held for adoption. Otherwise, they are destroyed. This idea that animals are destroyed, ultimately, unless people take proper care of them needs to be emphasized.

The court will not allow Turner to reclaim the animals. Most of them are at least 6 years old, so adoption is unlikely. And because the seven-day period expired on Sunday, their shelter time has run out.

"Right now they are in a holding pattern until the investigating officer returns (tomorrow)," Lear said. "I can't say for sure what will happen. They are not in too good a shape. But it won't be easy (to find them homes) and we don't have too much space."

Gary Templin, executive director of the Society for the Prevention of Cruelty to Animals, said the SPCA will take seven of the dogs and hope for quick adoptions.

"We want to give them a reprieve, but having looked at the animals, it's going to be a task (finding them homes)," Templin said. "They are not in terrible shape, but people are not willing to accept animals that are older."

Templin said they would take more of the animals but his group also is short of space. "We will keep them until we need the kennel. If an animal comes in that's more adoptable, we'll have to play God and decide who we eliminate."

"The dogs are of mixed breeds. They range in size from medium to large and were primarily used as hunting hounds," Green said.

The whole article has been included so the teacher can choose any section which she thinks is appropriate to read to the class.

Other roles can be added to expand on the theme. For example, a person in role can be distraught because his dog is missing. One of the children has found it and given it a home; or it is reported that it has been run over because he has not kept it leashed.

The dinosaur has outgrown the building!

Save the Dinosaur
(Sci, LA)(2-5)

Objectives
1. To realize that the concept of endangered species is ultimately connected with the human race.
2. To gain practice using speaking skills which emphasize reasoning, decision making, and responsibility.

Materials
A book of dinosaur pictures; a "joke" leash; a letter; paper and crayons; the book, *The Enormous Egg* by Oliver Butterworth

Concept
The children identify with the dinosaur realizing its great strength was no match for the changes in nature. And if the human race is to survive, the "great mother" must be reckoned with.

Strategy
The leader will be in charge and in a "shadowy-authoritative" role throughout and can become the different characters as suggested, by changing hats, or using the mannequin. The leader can ask for a volunteer from the children to become any of several roles: a museum curator, anyone in Billy's family, including Billy, who could be played by a mature primary-aged student or most intermediate-aged students. Billy carries the "joke" leash to represent the dinosaur. The invisible role is given definition by the leash (see Chapter 4, invisible role).

Story
This drama is loosely based upon *The Enormous Egg* by Oliver Butterworth. A young boy raises a dinosaur from an egg. Word spreads and people become afraid that this dinosaur will become destructive. Scientists congregate from all over the U.S., and it is decided that the dinosaur must be killed, stuffed, and placed in a museum. The tension in the story is the answer to the question of whether or not it will be killed or freed; but if it is freed, it will become destructive (see book).

Motivational questions

While showing the pictures of dinosaurs, the leader asks the following: Do we know for certain that dinosaurs really existed? Was it a long time ago? Were people alive during that time? Does anyone know what the dinosaurs ate? Does anyone know why the dinosaurs became extinct? There's a theory that they may have received lead poisoning, another theory that they simply became so large they couldn't find enough food, or that the earth became so cold that there was no food for them.

Drama

I read in the newspaper that a 9 year old boy has been raising a dinosaur for six months. It started out as an egg and now word has gotten around that some scientists want it killed immediately so they can find out about its development. Also, the museum wants it for their collection, because finding the bones of baby dinosaurs is a rarity.

I wish to call this meeting to order. Today, ladies and gentlemen, we have to make a decision of whether or not we can allow a dinosaur to grow up in our town. There has been a great deal of discussion both for and against. A brief discussion is held; most of the children, if not all, will wish to keep the dinosaur alive. I want to read you this letter, for we may be able to convince the scientists.

Dear Billy:

We want you to know we will support your efforts to keep your pet alive for one year only. Beyond this time we feel it would endanger the community and lead to a tragic event that may cause not only your pet to be killed, but your family to be held responsible if any accident should occur.

We will be pleased to take your pet at any time, and take good care of it while we run experiments on its brain. These experiments will be used to help people gain better control over their bodies in the future. Dino's body would eventually be given to a museum where it would exist for the education of everyone.

Sincerely,

J.B. Patrovski

Representative of Scientists for a Better World

Our task is to reply to these scientists. But how are we to really know about the pet's threat unless we ask a member of Billy's family? This is Billy's mother. Mrs.----, we're having some trouble in coming to a decision over whether or not to recommend that Dino be given to the scientists, to a museum, or continue to be raised by your Billy. Has there been any problem so far?

A biographical sketch which includes some details of the relationship between Billy and Dino needs to be thought through by the adult or child playing this role. Billy's "joke" leash will work well if he refers to it with the belief that "Dino" is contained by it.

The drama continues as a city council meeting in which each child is given the role as some type of "expert" or town member, or chooses his own role. (See Chapter 2 on the sub-topic, "Children's reactions" and Chapter 4, "When children speak for themselves.") The leader continues to pose questions. The tension will remain constant as long as it is made clear that either way something tragic will happen.

Extensions

Other roles can include a scientist who tells about the need for studying the baby dinosaur in order to gain knowledge about the earth and possibly the human brain; a museum curator who talks about how they use scientific records in order to know what the dinosaur's surroundings were like. The curator can mention the need for accurate drawings resulting in either a collective mural, three dimensional forms, or individual drawings. The drawings can also become the basis for a manufactured dinosaur which can take the place of the live dinosaur. In this case, the teacher makes templates so the children can be part of an assembly-line to be responsible for creating different parts which are tied together as a copy of the original dinosaur. Each group can be responsible for developing one part and each child is responsible for doing his own bit in the process of creating the new dinosaur.

If the children have been able to draw their own renditions of dinosaurs during their study, then, the visual image will have become more concrete to the point of having been internalized. The pieces of tagboard are joined together and dedicated to the museum.

The art work may be done before or after the drama, or it may be part of it. If it is to be part of the drama, the leader needs to put forth the idea that this information they are contributing through their art work will help scientists in their studies of humans and nature in the future. Not only does this create more tension and meaning to the drama as a whole, but places an importance upon the children's roles, be they dishwasher or scientist (see Chapter 4, When Children Speak for Themselves).

Final questions:

How should we treat animals? What can animals understand?

Do you think it's important to treat animals the way we wish to be treated ourselves? Why? How can we insure that other endangered species are protected? Is the human race an endangered species?

The Old House

The house is used as a symbol of containment. We all have many associations that are connected to this symbol, and the questions asked represent many layers of familiarity. Upon showing a picture of an old house: **Do you think anyone lives here? Do you think it is haunted? What makes it haunted? If you were a real estate broker what would you say about it? What would be your favorite place inside the house? Why? What would you change about it? What stories does it tell? Is there a secret room? Why is it secret? Are there sounds you hear that want to communicate with you? What do they tell you? Can you create your house on this paper?**

A classic story, *The Selfish Giant* by Oscar Wilde, has been used many times as a stimulus for a drama highlighting a house which the children revisited in other dramas. The story and the character of the giant had become a familiar person who is destitute, separated from "reality", cantankerous, but vulnerable at the same time and whom the children grew to care for. The story is summarized here for the leader's background and as a reminder of the theme of caring.

It is such a beautiful garden because every spring all the trees flower and the children want to go in to play after they come home from school. One day they played in the garden as they had in the past. As they were climbing the trees and causing the apples to fall from the branches, they heard a loud voice yell at them: "This is my garden. Trespassers will be prosecuted." Upon seeing a large man advance toward them, they ran from the garden.

Winter came and the giant went to bed as always. He awoke to hear the hail and rain and wind thrash around the house. The giant woke up several times and wondered why spring was so late in coming. He looked out into his garden and noticed the trees were still bare, and he felt so lonely. Just as he realized his sadness he saw children creeping through a hole they had made in the wall by removing some bricks. Wherever they had placed themselves on the branches, the trees began to flower. "I've been very selfish," he thought. Without a moment's hesitation he walked out into the garden. Upon seeing him the children started to run.

"No," he called after them. "Don't go. This is your garden and you may come here and play whenever you wish to." The children came for many years to play in the giant's garden and they taught him to play with them.

One day he seemed more tired than usual and in the middle of one of their games, he slumped and fell. In his weakened voice he told them that he had left the house and garden to all of them. He hoped they would find it useful.

Since the giant's house can be easily imagined by the children it might be selected by the leader as a possible living quarters for many orphaned children. Working in drama with young children should be based on a project in which they are aware that their assistance is needed. When the importance and seriousness of the task is understood, their self-image gains stature.

They traveled through the forest to the old house.

Homeless Children

(LA, Soc Stud) (K-3)

Introduction

The most recent survey of homeless people suggests that the number may be as high as 3 1/2 to 4 million living in the streets in the U.S. It has been estimated that about a quarter of these are children. The following deals more with refugee children such as the boat people, although it is left ambiguous to provide more latitude for the leader to include parallel situations. . . such as the homeless or orphaned.

The first time this drama was carried, out an adult Chinese girl who was five feet tall entered to represent "refugee children." At the end of the drama she was taken by the kindergarteners/first graders to the playground. They helped her pick flowers and showed her how to use the playground equipment. If it had been possible, she could have become their permanent peer for they accepted her in this way.

Objectives

1. To help children understand the situation of being homeless and/or elderly.

2. To give children the opportunity of taking responsibility by the use of the "I don't know" role.

3. To help extend the children's imaginations by a journey (Js) to an old house, and to help them envision the surroundings.

Materials

A letter explaining a need for the house; a picture of an old house and a map which leads to it; music; pictures of homeless, either ethnic or anglo, refugee children; "best", but old, dress; green fabric to drape over desks, to represent the "outside"; props for old person, work apron, glasses, cane; hand-carried tape recorder with tape, see "story"

Concept

The children are introduced to the problems of children across the world. They become the caretakers for their own counterparts. In order for them to empathize as fully as possible, they take up not only the responsibility of house hunting but any concerns that will effect the children's futures. They also build relationships and develop empathy for the needs of the elderly.

Strategy

The leader changes roles from the beginning "authoritative" role of real estate broker, when she sends the children on their way with a map, to an old and/or a cantankerous person, also in an "authoritative" role, who meets them at the house. Here, she takes the children on a tour. She sends them back to the real estate office with the same map. By this time they have seen the leader in both roles, and they have become so absorbed by the drama that her transformation from the old lady back into the real estate person need not be as smooth as it first was.

In both roles, the leader tells the children to remember each thing so that the information can be conveyed, (1) from real estate person to old person, and (2) from old person to real estate person, making them responsible for accurate communication. A person in full-role may be brought in at the end of the drama, back into the real estate office, to represent one of the refugee children, but this is optional.

Story

The leader becomes a real estate broker, and the children are asked to inspect a house for her. As a neutral or "shadowy" character, she shows the children the directions to the house and while they are finding their way, she changes into the "old person" who lives there. Her cantankerous nature and poor vision or hearing contribute to the tension which draw the children toward the role. At the end of the tour, the old person has the children close their eyes to see if they can hear any disturbing sounds. During this moment, the old person turns on a battery-powered tape player with a tape which says, "I have come from faraway into your dreams, my people have been driven from their homes—we come from faraway to learn how to be children again—help us to learn how to play—." The recording can be made to represent the voice of the person taking on the orphan role.

Drama activities

1. Discuss topic.
2. Present problem of refugee children who need a place to live; the children must convince the owner of the house to move out.

3. Lead them through a "haunted" or scary environment while narrating.

4. Calm them down into a sleep state.

5. A person enters in role and the leader turns on a tape that contains the following, "I have come from faraway into your dreams, my people have been driven from their homes—we come from faraway to learn how to be children again—help us to learn how to play."

6. The children are led back to the real estate office.

7. The leader in "shadowy" role questions to find out about the children's experiences and in an "I don't know" role receives the play energy of the children.

8. The role of the "homeless child" may be played by a child or mannequin, or one may use a secondary role in the form of written material such as a diary.

Beginning questions

Have you ever had a favorite place to play? Have you ever known children who haven't a place to play?

I wonder why they haven't? Does anyone know?

That's what my problem is. (Pass out pictures of children and slowly read letter.) "To whom it may concern—These children are without a family and need a home. Their villages have been destroyed. They were found by the Red Cross wandering along the roadside about a month ago."

Do you think any of these children are American children? Why? Why not?

Have you ever heard the word "orphan" or "refugee" before? Do you know what these words mean?

Drama in real estate office

I've been waiting to find out if a bigger house has been put up for sale, but this is the biggest. I just don't know if it will be all right. Do you think you could look at it for me? (Show them a picture of the house) Do you think it's the kind of house that will be all right for children? I guess the lady still lives there. I wonder what kind of person would live alone in such a big house?

Do you think you could find your way to the house because I have to stay here and wait to see if any of the children will arrive?

If you think you can find your way, then I'll call the lady

to see if she'll be home to meet you.

(Using a phone that is mimed) **Hello, is this Ms. Gordon? I'm Ms. Adams at the real estate office. Do you remember that you put your house up for sale about two months ago? Well, we have a possible buyer.** (To the children: She's hard of hearing and so it's necessary to speak louder.) **All right. Yes, this afternoon.**

Would you be able to show your house this afternoon? I can't come, but there are many children here who can come to look at it. Yes, children. Is there some reason why you can't have children live in it? Oh, no, it won't be these children. They're just coming to look at it. All right. You'll be at the door looking for them? Yes, I'll point the way. Through the forest? Yes. All right. Goodbye.

Well, she said she didn't know if the house was a good one for children or not so good. I'm glad that you're all going because surely children like you would know what other children would like.

(Shows them a map. Js) **Start here and go down that street, right here, and then follow those trees around, then go straight, and that should lead you to the house.** At the same time the leader needs to walk around in the room and point out where the route really is in the room. Green cloth drapes can be thrown over the desks to resemble a pastoral setting. Or, the journey can be conducted by the leader as a visualization process while the children close their eyes, and she changes into the house owner.

Now, who will ask the questions? You have to speak very loudly because she's hard of hearing.

What do you think is important that the children would need? Can you remember that? You have to remember a lot, don't you? Don't forget anything because I can't go, and it's very important. Especially if the children are going to arrive today. Who will remember to show her these pictures of the children? It'll be a little dark through the forest. Specific children may be given specific responsibilities and referred to later. The leader can dim the lights, pull the curtain slightly shut, turn the lights off and use music if desired.

Transition

After the children have been sent off, the leader can change a few items of clothing out of view of the children—glasses for character, a work apron, a crutch or cane, and then take an obvious position to wait for the children at another place in the room.

Drama Activity at the house (This monolog requires pauses as well as reactions from the children.)
   Is there someone out there? My eyes aren't too good. Who are you? What did you come for? Are these American children? But is it right to take in all these foreign children? (The role needs to show some reluctance to sell the house, maintaining the tension.) **You'll have to convince me.**
   I'll take you on a tour. Some people believe the house is haunted. They say that's what caused the fire. Part of it was rebuilt. This is the spiral staircase that leads up to the old section where the children used to play. As the leader I have played the role by including in my biographical sketch the incident of my children dying in a fire. This event can be embellished creating a stronger connection between her role and the children.
   Follow me up these stairs. See if you think it's safe. You wouldn't want them to move into a scary place, would you? After it seems that the majority of children have traveled up these "spiral stairs", she invites them to sit down.
   I don't know if it's scary or not for children. It's not for me, of course. Why don't we close our eyes and see if we hear anything. (This recording should be made ahead of time to represent the appropriate group.) At this point a tape recorder can be turned on and the following is heard, "I come from miles away to a new land. My people are spread throughout the world. I have no family. No mother or father or sisters or brothers any more. Teach me how to be a child again. Teach me how to be happy. How to play." If the teacher is working by herself, these lines can be taped beforehand and played now. If a child is playing the role, s/he should make the tape and be the same person to appear at the real estate person's office to meet the children when they return. This step is optional. This statement can be written and phrased in any way to accommodate the person who may be in this role. If an older child or an adult is playing the role, the person should look childlike and not American, but ethnic.
   Well, what do you think? Is it scary? When do you think they'll arrive? That soon. Oh, I don't have any place to go. Do you think I could stay on for a little while? Don't you think the children would need someone like me around? Who will tell her that I want to stay on? You'd better get

started back. She points the way. Music can accompany the journey back. At this time the leader takes off the clothing additions and goes to meet the children.

Drama activity in the real estate office
What did she say? Do you think the house will be safe? Are there any problems?   When will the lady move out? She wants to stay? I wonder why? Is she lonely?   Do you think she'll be all right living there with the children? Do you think they'll be lonely?   What will they need to do to care for themselves? Do you think you would be able to care for yourselves alone like this? Do you think these children are different? Though this step is optional, at any time, one child can have arrived to substantiate the fact that this   is happening. It would be better if the child is a little older and from another class. If it occurs just before recess the children in the class can take the visitor out and show her/him how to play. This visiting child should not speak at all, seeming not to understand English.
   Thank you for going there for me. Let's sit down.

Final questions
   I wonder if there are many children like this? Do you know any people who have adopted these refugee children? Does anyone know why these children don't have places to live? I wonder if there are many? I've heard that there are many thousands.
   I wonder if everyone did what you just did if all the orphans in the world would have places to stay? It's very good to know that there are people like you who would look after these children.

Possible extensions
   1. Teaching the elderly lady to be more accepting and childlike by verbally communicating favorite aspects of childhood, e. g., games and or teaching them to her.
   2. Working in groups as individuals and in planning, each one can draw what is needed in the house if it is to be refurbished to house the children.
   3. Exploring the house, use of spacial memory and use of map skills.
   4. Learning global geography by locating where each child with a picture is from.
   5. Writing letters to these children.

The Island

Introduction

In this drama the children are concerned about their own survival. They extend themselves into an imaginary place which becomes more and more real for them as they create what seems like a sub-tropical paradise. The energetic optimism on which they thrive is evenly shared between groups. The amount of healthy invention, as well as their willingness to combine efforts with their neighbors, is an inspiration which the educational bureaucracy needs to recognize. I believe if adults could see this sharing as a way toward global survival, unlike the national prejudices between nations bound and bent by "the balances of power," they would encourage this kind of growth and training.

"We haven't found any water yet."

"We have. You can connect your pipe to our well. There's plenty."

"We found a cave and a lot of bones in it."

"Those must have been the person who left the footprint we found."

Wouldn't anthropologists in their "bone wars" feel some relief for these deductive skills being developed by seven, eight, and nine year olds?

Among children who have been participants in this drama, the motivation to continue on week after week, finding relics and multiple clues of long-lost civilizations, has been refreshing.

They have elected to continue the drama in order to build shelters, plant food, and build a boat.

Other tasks have included making axes, felling trees, reseeding trees, gathering food, shearing mountain goats, weaving a new sail, planting food, diving down beneath the ship, and catching fish.

A diary has been kept by the captain which can be selectively read in order to remind the children of the given circumstances up to this point.

The people in role have presented themselves as vestiges of the past.

A person in role as a pirate is found. She is aggressive, yet fearful for anyone else to find the treasure. The treasure map and code written on the map can be studied by the children and used to guide them toward the treasure. Since the pirate speaks English, she can provide as much information about the island and herself as is desired. She can be the one to alert them to the fire and smoke she has seen at the opposite end of the island, guiding them toward the other person in role as a native inhabitant.

A young woman around fifteen years old, the only remnant of her tribe who migrated to safer lands, is found. Her shyness and vulnerability attract the children. When they first come upon her, she's naturally frightened and makes a motion to run but waits, realizing that the children are peaceful. Both the group of children and the role sit with each other, waiting. Gradually, they begin to exchange a language of hand motions and signals corresponding with found objects, such as rocks, driftwood, shells.

Slowly each group begins to gain more trust. And just as slowly, the primitive learns to speak. She draws a map of the island in the dirt, represented by newsprint and felt markers. On this she shows the many shrines that she has created to contribute to her survival, as well as the sundial she has constructed.

"Sometimes there seems to be no time at all."
- Henry Behn

Gradually, she tells her story in this way and, like *Island of the Blue Dolphin* by Scott O'Dell, tells of her need to build a ship so she can escape and find her tribe again. Together, this task is carried out so that all can leave the island.

She teaches the children how to build a fire without matches and transforms this into a sacred rite which for her becomes a ceremony leading toward rites of passage. She also shows them more about obtaining water by building a well. Killing, drying, and preserving meat can be shown as well as knowledge about the properties of plants, either medicinal or poisonous.

If the reason for the mission has been to find out about plant life, then the primitive could be involved in picking up cues in English in order to communicate on these specifics.

Either a broken mirror or a flashlight can be used to communicate by sending light signals. Many planned out scenarios can be constructed with these two roles in mind. For example, the pirate could be found dying as well as bitter and afraid, while the primitive contributes knowledge about funerals and a link with the pirate's spiritual needs. This same difference can be acknowledged by recognizing the pirate's goal of wealth, and the primitive's need for a less temporal existence, but one respectful of the need to recognize connections with nature.

An obvious possibility is to have the island stand for an archeologist's dig. Objects such as fossils, stones, leaves, bones, shells, pieces of wood, including driftwood, pieces of metal, paper can all be included unless the leader has a particular agenda she wants included. She can then choose specific items which, then, tell their own story. Obviously, these would need to be carefully selected.

For an older class, ages ten and up, natural objects could be introduced which may look and be ordinary. However, if the teacher, as head archeologist, treats both the artifacts and the children as archeologists with respect, then their meanings will become significant. The leader guides the children through focusing questions and statements which also connect with the object so the ordinariness takes on a more uplifting meaning. The mood of seriousness needs to be developed and instilled, particularly if they are working in small groups, in order to play out their interpretations of how these objects were used. The leader simply needs to preface this step with an introduction stressing the concept of sacredness in order to remove the self-consciousness which some children may feel.

Such a statement by the leader could begin: "Let us not go unprepared into this new world we have discovered. Let us come to these relics with respect and wonder. May their history and the knowledge which they now share with us uncover a richer future for all to share." And with this experience at ritual creation the group can go on to create their own personal ritual as a class. By this means they will realize that they really have to know, in symbolic form, the elements that speak for the group in order to extol them through a ritual ceremony. From here knowledge is revealed that each town, state, nation combines in such symbols that are often not consciously recognized. A collection of symbolic elements to stand for a group of people can lead to a deeper consideration of how and why groups behave the way they do.

Of course, artifacts can be made and collected by the class. The homemade fossil is placed into a cut off milk carton with plaster which hardens around it. When the plaster dries the milk carton is peeled away so that it appears to be just like those found to be imprinted upon a rock. Such items as pieces of wood, fingerprints, footprints, small bugs, rocks, leaves, and old coins all work well.

This experience helps children adopt some appreciation for the past which can then speak to them through the present and into the future.

Island 1
(LA, Soc Stud, Geog, Hist, Sci)(2-5)

Research
Much of the information necessary is included, however, the leader may feel she needs to add essential aspects from her curriculum.

Objectives
1. To stimulate thinking about the ocean and how islands are formed so their importance can be appreciated.
2. To have an experience about being responsible in order to survive.
3. To stimulate their curiosity.
4. To nurture their feelings of cooperation.

Materials
Pictures of island formation and ocean life; sound of the surf; hats and clipboard for captain and first mate; items for lifesaving kit: pencil, sewing kit, flares, paper and pens, flashlight, compass, rope, map, matches, red flag, "radio" to represent walk-talky, orders to be carried out. Diagram of a submarine, showing interior and exterior, optional. Educational material about the ocean, e. g. Asimov's *Life in the Deep Sea*; pieces of newsprint about 2' by 4' go to each group along with enough pens for each person.

Concept
The idea of interdependence, conservation, survival, and primitive origins are all potentials for development.

Strategies
In *Island 2* the leader is in an authoritative role as the captain first. She lines the children up to introduce the tasks.   The children are in role as experts in different scientific fields. After the tasks have been introduced, they are played out until she introduces the problem of the accident, after which she takes them to the island using a visualization process. Next she introduces the crisis situation: they have hardly any needed survival equipment.   In *Island 1* the drama doesn't include working on tasks on the submarine. After the introductions and reasons for the expedition are communicated, she takes them through the visualization process that puts them on the

island. For both dramas: She gets angry at the second mate or the class as a whole for not bringing the proper life-saving equipment. Either an aide or a mature child can play the second mate. The children draw their maps or interpretations of the island's potential. They are encouraged to use any of the supplies they need to explore the island. This is really where the drama comes alive.

Story

As members of this exploring team, they are referred to as officers. In this capacity they board a ship and take up their jobs. The ship has an accident; (Island 1 begins here) all are taken through a visualization process, which shifts them instantly to the island. Tension becomes their need to survive without much survival equipment. In order to find out what is on the island the children draw their own images as a group in the form of a map, filling in the island's potential through their imaginations. From here, suggestions are given for extensions. Any of the children can be coached to become any of the roles found on the island, such as a primitive, fisherman, or whatever role is applicable to the curriculum.

Grouping

All are in one group except when escaping onto land and when working in small groups on exploration tasks.

Beginning questions

Have you ever heard of the Bermuda Triangle? Do you know what kinds of things have happened there? Do you think this was true? Have you ever heard of people surviving on an island? Do you think it's possible to survive on an island with few provisions or materials? How will it be possible? Question them on needs and necessities vs. luxuries. These can be listed on the board. Could we be explorers of some kind who may be trying to find a possible way to cure cancer? What could we call ourselves? What qualities would we have? Can you find these qualities in yourselves?

Beginning belief

Show pictures of island formation and sea life, as well as a specific island chart. Do you think it's cold down there? Do things grow? How does sunlight get down there? Read the following from Isaac Asimov's *Life in the Deep Sea*: "Without the currents that keep mixing the water of the oceans, from top to bottom and bottom to top, life couldn't exist anywhere on earth. Life began first in the sea, and only colonized the land billions of years later."

(Optional) Show a picture or drawing of a submarine which can be pinned up in front of the room.

You may begin with *Island 2* which is more formal as a result of the leader being in an "authoritative" role. Here in *Island 1* the leader begins in a 'shadowy' role.

Drama

We're going to begin the drama now and I'd like you to close your eyes. (The light changes, sound of waves is heard on tape, and the leader begins a transitional narration.) **We've been living on a submarine for weeks. We've seen and explored the ocean depths, and those who are divers amongst us, have taken samples of the plant life. As we were surfacing up through the blue green water of the ocean, we ascended too fast and the propeller hit a piece of loose coral, breaking the propeller shaft, and we were stranded and had to abandon ship. We swam ashore. Open your eyes.**

(Read orders.) **You are instructed to explore this island and gather the plantlife that is infected and diseased as well as that which has curative powers and has been helpful as seen from aerial photographs. Include your findings of newly explored areas on a separate map.**

(Oath) **Let us remember our oath. Please raise your right hand: I will be responsible for practicing life-saving and survival skills in my relationship to all crew members.**

The Captain goes through a packet of supplies and recognizes that provisions for emergency have not been taken from the submarine during the ship disaster. We have no powdered food, and only enough water to last 24 hours—some of the life-saving equipment isn't here—these people are scientists. They haven't been trained for life-saving—but now we must save ourselves. In this instance the captain gets angry at the first mate. The equipment mentioned above is inspected and found lacking.

Give instructions to groups about their responsibilities. Form in small groups: those responsible for shelter; food and water; rescue and signal senders; communication on the island; and locating and mapping special curative plants. **Meet back at sunset to report on your findings.**

The children are given large pieces of paper and felt pens to work with. **You will be mapping out the island as you explore it. Be sure to find or solve whatever your group is responsible for.** **Pay attention to all that you find on the island so that you can explain to the others what exists. After all we don't know how long we'll have to be here before we're rescued. Map the island and look for the curative plant life. Meet back here before sundown when you hear this whistle.**

Children can easily continue for 45 minutes to an hour wandering around the room, drawing on their paper, and borrowing articles from the packet that the Captain found wanting.

When they seem to be ready the Captain officially calls them back and has them present their findings to the class.

Final questions

Do you think this happens often? How was it possible for us to survive? Does the land have life-giving properties that help? Where did the land come from? Is it important that we take care of the land and oceans? Why?

Island 2
(LA, Soc Stud, Geog, Hist, Sci)(2-5)

Island 2 is more formal and can be used with children who are older and who also require more control in the drama process. All the other material up to and including the beginning belief is the same.

Strategy
The leader uses a much more authoritative role as captain, not a "shadowy" less defined role. An aide or child volunteer can serve in the other role. If it is a child, it is up to the judgment of the leader to determine whether he can take the "verbal abuse" which is leveled at him as a result of his irresponsibility in forgetting life-saving equipment, particularly since this affects the tension and needs to be strong.

Drama
When I turn around the drama will begin.

(Use an "authoritative" role.) **Attention. I'm Captain Pierce and this is Lieutenant Adams who is being trained to be in charge. All those who are coming on board, line up and sign on ONLY if you agree with this statement: All those aboard this craft will be responsible to the purpose of the mission and for practicing skills of lifesaving and survival such as have been learned in the course of the training. If there is anyone who does not feel that he or she can live up to these demands, please step out. Raise your right hand and repeat after me: I solemnly swear to uphold these regulations.**

Our orders have come in. We are to drop to a depth of 250 feet in order to find out why one part of this island is dying while the other part contains healthy plant life...from your own knowledge and what you have gained during the course of your investigations, can you make a guess as to the cause of this problem? Scientists are worried that this problem may spread and infect other plant life surrounding the island. But I'm not completely sure of this; there is some evidence that a plant root found both in these waters and upon the land we will be nearing may contain a rare liquid which in one form can cure certain kinds of cancer. Here are your individual

orders. The room is organized so that there will be 5 smaller groups, sitting and working at controls, pressing buttons, and involved in dramatic play. At each spot, a different yet simple simulated cardboard design of buttons and mechanical contrivances is offered so the children can follow their natural inclination to begin checking out their instruments. See the charts at the end for setting up this design. The leader sends each group to its section.

Those in charge of air-supply and temperature gauge be sure your channels are open and that all air-supply ducts are free so check your equipment. Five or six of you go to those chairs that are marked.

Telegraph and signal senders, be specific about what codes you are going to send, over there.

Periscope or snorkel induction trunk, over here with your group. Be sure that the mirrors are inserted properly to receive the images.

And your group is in charge of radio communications. Check your equipment using the control panels and be sure the electronic waves can be heard.

Radar and sonar equipment to be checked by this group. Be sure that your receivers are clean.

All clear as we begin descent, continue.   Begin descent—stand by Lieutenant—20—40—60—80—100 feet. (Continue to call out to each group what they need to be doing.) **HALT! dials are stuck. Lieutenant, please be sure the radar is working.   The craft is not moving and the engines are heating up.   Check the temperature gauge. Air supply—send air through vent into engine room.**

Lieutenant, check the life-saving equipment. A packet with life-saving gear is checked by the captain and found wanting. An attitude of anger and frustration is used to discipline the Lieutenant. This pressure and tension will help the children to believe even more in the situation. **Now   we must save ourselves.**

(Come out of role to say the following.) **I want all of you to come over here.   We're going to get to this island in another way, so I want all of you to close your eyes.** *The following is almost identical to Island 1* at the beginning of the Drama section which continues with a few changes. So all necessary steps are included.

The light changes, sound of waves is heard on tape, and the leader begins a transitional narration. **We've been living on a** submarine for weeks. We've seen and explored the ocean depths, and those who are divers amongst us have taken samples of plant life. As we were descending down through the blue green water of the ocean, we descended too fast and the propeller got caught in some kelp beds, breaking the propeller shaft and we were stranded and had to abandon ship. We have swum ashore.

(Read orders, stand, and turn off tape.) You may stand at attention now. You are instructed to explore this island and gather the plantlife that is infected and diseased as well as that which has been curative and helpful as seen from aerial photographs. Include your findings of newly explored areas on a separate map.

The group in charge of the air-supply and temperature gauge: you are now in charge of finding and constructing some kind of shelter that we can survive in.

The group in charge of telegraph and signal senders: use whatever you can from these few supplies to provide us with a means of rescue and sending out an SOS on this radio. (Hand them the laundry bag in which the life-saving equipment is kept.)

The group in charge of radar and sonar: you are now to explore the island, map it, and locate whatever plants you think are those which resemble the ones that have been studied or those which are new.

Those who were in charge of the periscope: locate food and water.

Those in charge of radio communication: be sure that our communication on this island is established.

All groups know what it is that needs to be done, and everyone is in charge of locating what is needed to survive, as well as carrying out the mission.

Meet back here by sundown and be ready to give a report. Good luck. Remember, if one person proves to be a hindrance to this mission or to the safety of the others, you will be demoted or discharged without pay.

Here is your paper and the pens to map your findings. (Hand each group a piece of newsprint about 2' x 4'.) Dismissed.

The group is attended to by the leader in a more "shadowy" type of role. It is necessary that the leader be helpful and encouraging while the children struggle with mapping the island and using whatever materials they find necessary in the life-saving packet.

The leader can call the group back together, end the drama, and ask questions, to conduct an evaluation by asking trial questions.

Final questions

Do you think this happens often? How was it possible for us to survive? Does the land have life giving properties that help? Where did the land come from? Is it important that we take care of the land and oceans? Why?

SAMPLE CHARTS for USE with ISLAND DRAMA no. 2

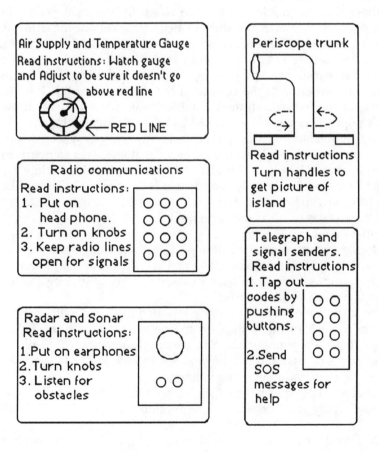

Nature and the Environment

Introduction

The concept of nature and the environment is so complex and vast that trying to simplify it seems to reduce its importance. Yet, children still retain a type of "conjunction mystic," a mystical connection with nature through animals and the objects they collect from the environment. Certainly their awareness is much more immediate than that of adults and just as immediate is the demise of us all if new conservation measures are not considered.

What are the things we enjoy about nature and the earth? What are things we don't enjoy?

These kinds of questions need to be asked. In how many years will the answers given under the minus category cancel out those in the plus category? How can each person work to reverse this?

Figures such as 1/4 of the world uses 80% of the resources while 3/4 of the world are left 20% of the resources in a year, seem devastating in terms of the education that is needed if this kind of usage is to be reversed. In the United States we have only 5% of the earth's population and yet we use 35% of the raw materials.

The understanding that the earth is an eco-system like a self-sustaining space ship has been used as an analogy. This comparison can go further. How is the human body like a space ship? How are we held together in the way the earth is held together? But unlike the earth, how are we not like a self-contained space ship? Do we need the earth as much as the earth needs us?

What do we need?

Does everyone need these things? Can these things be supplied forever? What can we do to maintain and sustain our use of the earth? These questions have been asked steadily, especially since Rachel Carson's book, *The Silent Spring.*

These questions are also silently repeated over and over without answers in each of our minds, to the point that apathy itself has become like a worse pollutant. Yes, we can do something, but what? Everything is so vast and it is beyond our minute ability to grasp all the intricacies of nature working in harmony.

What are those questions which we need to ask?

How many years does it take to develop the top soil? (1" = 10 years.)

Discuss the earth as a space ship by using a globe. From your questions establish that we're confined to the earth and why we couldn't live elsewhere.

How much land is there in comparison to water? Do other planets contain as much water? What is the difference between how the Native Americans thought of the earth in comparison to how the European ancestors did? What concept reflects the Native American philosophy?

In brief, the Native Americans believed everything was connected; the smallest thing was part of this interrelationship. As we can see most of nature is in a microscopic state, but each particle as small as an electron or nucleus is at work in this interdependent relationship.

Native American stories tell us that their respect for the earth was so great that they thought of the earth as a god or goddess, much in the same way Anglos think of it being Mother Nature. We can understand from their stories how animals can speak for these forces of nature, reminding people of their place in the universe. So grand was the earth for them that they offered prayers to their Great Father before taking anything from the earth when hunting or fishing. And they asked for blessings before planting. The prayer of Black Elk reminds us of this sacred connection: "Grandmother Earth, hear me! The two-leggeds, the four-leggeds, the wingeds, and all that move upon you are Your children. With all beings and all things we shall be as relatives; just as we are related to You, O Mother."

In contrast, what has been the relationship between nature and our European ancestors?

—Early settlers girdled the trees so that they died.

—Animals were shot for only choice parts or for the skin, whereas the Indians used the whole animal, even the bone marrow for lighting lamps and as a kind of ice-cream.

—Land was cropped every year until it wore out, which was one of the settlers' reasons for leaving Europe.

—Petroleum, oil, and coal have been removed in such great quantities that if we don't change our ways there will be none left for our grandchildren. The whole world needs oil, so we're all pushing our way into one small place in the world; it is only a matter of time before this runs out.

—Forests have been cut down so much that we're beginning to see the damage this has caused in helping to bring about the greenhouse effect.

—The ozone layer, which is the specially dense layer of oxygen between 20 and 40 miles above us, has two large gaps in it now. The reason this is frightening is because this layer protects us from the ultra-violet part of the sun's rays; these rays can produce a type of skin cancer. Scientific experts think that one of the reasons for this is due to the cutting down of trees in some of the largest forests in the world; the oxygen usually given off by these trees has become less available. On this point, less than 1/6 of the earth's original timber remains, about 16%.

—Wild life has been killed off so that many species that once existed are now extinct. About once every two years a group of poachers is convicted of killing off many animals belonging to the endangered species category, for which they receive lots of payment. Since it's illegal to hunt these animals, the poachers can charge and make millions unless caught.

The important concept to understand here is supply and demand. Which has the highest value, clean air, redwood, clay, top soil, rock, salt water? Which is the most expensive, solar power, wind power, oil? Why don't we use solar or wind power?

For the following exercise make a collection of objects such as glass, aluminum, paper, tin, wood, rock, a feather, shell, soil, a plant, leather, coal, cloth.

Divide the class into two groups and hold up each of the above. Ask one group at a time to say what main resource the article is taken from and whether or not it is renewable or non-renewable.

Recycling

The most direct way to change and have some affect upon our dwindling resources is through recycling. Each person throws away 6 pounds of garbage a day in the U.S. In one year 144 million tons of garbage is tossed, enough garbage to make a road 16 feet wide and 1" thick stretching from the earth to the moon.

Show pictures of a primitive tribe from a National Geographic magazine and contrast it with today's family by showing a modern kitchen. Ask the children what they think is the difference between the amount of trash thrown away today in comparison with a hundred years ago. Why is there more now?

The Sacrifice

(Soc Stud, Sci) (K-2)

Objectives

1. To re-emphasize the meaning of giving and receiving in relation to the concept of sacrifice.

2. To acknowledge this meaning in relation to Christmas and/or nature.

Materials

An old cloth or shawl covering; a wooden stick for a cane; a battery tape-recorder and tape of Mussorgsky's *Pictures at an Exhibition.*

Concept

A story/journey which requires an attitude of calm from the children follows. This story combines the quality of Indian life and its closeness to nature with that of a Western Christmas, and may be used to explore the idea of ecology.

They followed the bird up the mountain.

Strategy
    The leader will take on the main roles: a "shadowy" role and an "authoritative" (archetypal) role. Using the shadowy role, she guides the children on a journey to the place where they meet the archetypal earth figure. When the children briefly have their eyes closed, she throws on an old dark cloth and picks up an old stick which will be laid nearby. She will have difficulty seeing and will stare off into the distance which will help the children's belief because it will make this somewhat awesome character seem more remote.

Story
    The children are met as forest animals and led to an archetypal earth figure who explains that whatever they take from the earth must be replaced in some form. If they understand this then they will receive whatever they need to sustain them.

Motivational questions
    The instructor can begin by asking questions basic to developing a drama. **What kind of little animal character would you like to become?** Within large groups, many different but small animal characters can be included. The attention of young children frequently requires continual re-focusing upon an object or action, in order to guide their thinking and imagination. **Close your eyes and see if you can hear where I walk. Don't open your eyes until I ask you.** The leader should make several patterns around the children before asking them to point to where she walked. **How would you walk on snow in order not to leave tracks? Think of something you want for Christmas, and draw it in the snow.** Response.

Drama narration
    All of you are little animals in the forest, and it is winter. You have found your own place to be warm deep down in the earth. But you also smell a hunter who is stalking you for prey. The leader becomes the antagonist and is gruff and stomps angrily. **Where are all of those animals I've been hunting here? I'm hungry and I need food for my family. There aren't as many trees now that they can hide in, so I wonder where they are?** After a time, the hunter finally goes away without finding anything to shoot.

Narration
As soon as the hunter leaves, all of you wait until night, then come out of your hiding places very quietly and take all your belongings with you. Because it is night, you have to keep your eyes on a tiny bird that is leading you through the mist. You also have to watch for danger. During these actions, the leader plays music to accompany the children's journey and intensify their search. The journey may be as long as the leader thinks children's energy can be sustained with some narration. Mussorgsky's, *Pictures at an Exhibition* is one piece of music that may be used. It is cold and dark, but you must follow the little bird. Since she is in "shadowy" role, she designates herself as the bird by standing in from of them and waving her arms. Here's a creek. Wait and be sure that all the little animals get across. We're climbing slightly and can see the bird reflected by the moonlight. We must continue to follow it because we don't want to get lost. We need to go through this wooded section so stay together and follow the animal in front of you. After traveling through the night, the bird alights on the outside of a cave. There is a voice inside which calls all of you. Inside the cave, there is a warm fire. Everyone sit down and warm yourselves.

Transition
The leader guides them into a circle and has them sit down. The bird has asked us to close our eyes so that it can change into the spirit of the forest. Close your eyes and think about an object that means a lot to you. During this time she changes into the archetypal old wise person by donning an old ragged poncho and leaning on a stick, if desired. Then using a mysterious voice or monotone: Thank you for coming. I asked the bird to bring you here. Are you hungry? There is enough food buried below you to satisfy your hunger. Take and eat what you need, and take all the rest to last you through the winter. I will pass you these seeds to take with you also. After the children have acted out the digging, eating, and receiving of seeds, the leader should again narrate using the mysterious voice. Are you willing to sacrifice your most treasured possession, or Christmas present, for food that will last your life? If not, you may have to remain hungry. If you are willing, then it is time for you to throw your object into the fire as a sacrifice. The leader may stop only to receive

their decision or she may wish to carry out the ritual of having them verbalize what they are sacrificing and mime placing it into the fire. **Now that you have eaten and are warm, I will tell you why the bird led you here. I am old and will soon die. When this happens, you are to spread my ashes through the forest so that in the spring a new forest will grow to protect you. Now, you must be tired and need to sleep.** With this announcement, the voice fades away and the children close their eyes.

Transition
The leader takes off the poncho but continues to narrate. **In the morning when they awake, all the animals notice that the spirit of the forest is gone, but in its place the bird stands over a pile of ashes.** She mimes sprinkling ashes and passing them. **They all take the ashes, and place them carefully into their pockets, along with the food and seeds.** Accompany their mime and begin leading them by blending the narration with the movement, leading them back the same way. **Then the bird leads them through the forest back to their homes. Each has plenty to eat for the winter, and soon the sounds of spring can be heard. The animals remember the ashes and spread them throughout the forest.** As the leader narrates and mimes the action of replanting the children follow her. **In every place that they scatter the ashes and seeds, trees begin to take root. Soon, the forest is a thicket of trees and bushes, and the animals easily hide from the hunters. Whenever they are in danger they follow the little bird back to the cave for protection.**

Final questions
Did you help the animals? Will they be safe? Have you ever heard of the idea that you shouldn't take away things from the earth unless you can put them back? If you cut down a tree then how can you replace it? Have you ever heard of people cutting down trees and not replacing them? What could happen eventually? Do we need to protect the earth? Why?

Ecology and the Ocean
(Sci, LA, Soc Stud) (K-3)

Objectives
1. To enable children to understand the importance of the ocean to our lives.
2. To help them become more aware and concerned over how humans abuse the environment.

Concept
Emphasizing the interdependence between life on earth and the ocean.

They grew from the ocean floor.

Strategy

The leader works with the whole group at once guiding their "in place" journey and their sea journey. Before the drama begins stations in which "clean garbage" is placed are set up around the room, building up to the climatic meeting with the Corong. The Corong can be played by the animal mannequin or another adult wearing some draped fabric in order to represent an undersea creature. Otherwise, the children are in role as "experts," and the leader is in a "shadowy" role.

Story

The children are led on an expedition in the ocean to find medicinal plant life. Instead they find a "monster" who complains that he's being used as a scapegoat for all the pollution found in the ocean.

Preparation

The children can draw a mural of the ocean floor in small groups.

Materials

Paper for drawing the ocean floor.

A book showing pictures of the ocean floor; "clean garbage", containing no liquid, but plastic, tin, and paper containers; black plastic garbage bags to hold the garbage; two black plastic bags cut up and strewn across the floor, used to represent debris and oil (all this should be set out away from the children's view until after they meet the Corong; Debussy's *La Mer* playing during the journey; a simply drawn map; an educational booklet by Asimov, *Life in the Deep Sea*

Beginning questions

For younger children:

Discussion of an eco-system can be analogously related to what the children need as humans in order to live and grow: food, water, etc., particularly if they're in kindergarten and first grade. Scientific questions and information can then back this up.

What is it like underneath the ocean? Are there plants? Colors? Fish? Do things move fast or slow? Is the ocean important to our lives? Climate? (Use pictures.)

Continue, depending on the maturity of the children:

What are all the things you depend upon to live and grow? This is an eco-system. (Put the following on the board as a drawing in combination with words and symbols and discuss.) An eco-system is a community of living and non-living elements that are considered together as a unit. A person is part of this. 1. If you live near a body of water would that affect your eco-system? In what way? (winds, weather, amount of moisture) 2. Do you suppose there are plants in the ocean? 3. (From Asimov's *Life in the Deep Sea*, an educational booklet) "Without the currents that keep mixing the waters of the ocean, from top to bottom and bottom to top, life couldn't exist anywhere on earth. Life began first in the sea, and only colonized the land billions of years later." (Show a picture of plant growth in the ocean.) The same process takes place many hundreds of feet deep down in the ocean. 4. Does anyone know how the ocean may be used in the future? (food, fuel) 5 . (Hold up plastic containers.) What does this come from? (Oil) (Bring out a tin and a paper container.) 6. Which do you think lasts the longest? (plastic) We used to think that these plastic products were the best to have because they lasted so long. But, then, we find that they last forever. Is this good? Why? Why not? (They are not biodegradable and plastic sends pollutants into the air which destroys the ozone layer.) Let's find a place on the floor to become one of those plants (referring to picture) . (Dim lights and turn on ocean sounds.)

Preparation

(With younger children, K-l, use exercise *Small to Mature* in the Space section.)

The analogy of plant life is used with human growth.

As the leader speaks she also gets into a ball shape with chin between knees and chest up against thighs. **I want you to get into this shape and also to tuck your head in. Imagine you're a little seed moving deep down in the earth. It's very comfortable here. A tiny sprout begins to break out of the seed and like your finger it moves down into the earth forming roots. After the roots are formed the top part breaks out of a shell and like your finger, it moves gradually upward through the rich earth towards the warmth of the sun.** (Mime growing.) **It breaks through the earth being drawn by the sun's rays and slowly cells begin to add more and more fiber to the stem which is strengthened by its width. More buds form and leaves appear. The cells take on a bark-like appearance and the fullbodied plant continues to rise being constantly fed by** the moisture of condensation, the minerals from the soil and the sun's rays. The moisture that is being drawn up by the roots goes to the leaves and combines with sunlight and carbon dioxide to form sugar and oxygen. The oxygen is given off to us and the sugar stays to form more green leaves. It continues to grow until it becomes full and beautiful as it is gently blown by the breezes carrying new seeds to pollinate its little flowers. During this time the group slowly rises and spreads its arms, in imitation of the leader. Any scientific concepts that are being covered can be included. And now we expand and grow taking in the oxygen we need, just as the plant needs carbon dioxide and gives off oxygen. We work in harmony with it. Return room to regular condition. And now let's begin our drama.

Drama

Leader: **Good morning. Is this the right group? The ocean explorers?** (read letter):

Dear Mr. Z (name refers to teacher or leader):

We wish to inform you of the need for underwater exploration which has been increasing during the last two decades.

Our records show that you are training experts from various fields and will be prepared to explore the ocean floor and take samples of plant and sea life to be used for scientific research. Medical research is on-going since we have found no cures for many diseases. As well, research is also continuing to convert plant and sea life into nutritious food supplements for hungry people all over the world.

We know that in one of the deepest gorges of the ocean there are many forms of plant life which must be found; however, there is a section (as seen on the map) **of unexplored caves in which several deaths have occurred so we advise caution.**

We hope your people are in good health and above all are courageous to meet the unknown.

May luck be with you.

Sincerely,

Admiral John C. Wilson

9th Fleet, Pacific F624

Will all the explorers please stand at attention. Divide yourselves into two groups. The shorter people stand in front, and the taller, in back.

This will be an exploration of the ocean depths for future food and medicinal plants which can help in curing some diseases. We must find a cure for certain diseases and we are sure that some of the plant life in the area of this deep ocean chasm has produced the necessary antibodies that have been effective in treating certain infections in the past. You must be sure to pay attention to any possibility for this ocean gorge is one of our last hopes.

I will hand out these suits and demonstrate how we're going to use them. These suits are for warmth and protection when we're moving deep down on the ocean floor. Put it on over your uniform and be sure all the fasteners are used, on the sides and in front.

The leader comes out of role now to explain the transition.

Transition

Now close your eyes for a moment and concentrate on the sound. A tape-recorder of undersea sounds is heard again. The lights are turned off or dimmed. A wad of black plastic and other forms of pollution can be placed now.

According to this chart we will be descending 1100 ft. into one of the deepest gorges to view the plant life.

Narration: **As you see, garbage has been dumped here. It has taken this time for the heavier amounts to fall to the ocean floor. It is unfortunate that this whole area may have been affected.** In a corner of the room a single person (or 2 or 3) is wrapped in black plastic, representing a type of creature like the Gollum from the Hobbit, unless a mannequin is being used.

We are descending into the deep---slowly we begin to feel lighter even though there's much pressure from the water on top of us. We feel still lighter as we seem to float through warm currents, then cooler currents and see the changes of color from dark green to light green, and bright colors of pink, orange, yellow appears in the flowers. We put our feet down on the ocean floor as we drift through a tunnel made of rocks and look into the caves to search and explore the area. The leader can guide the children in a line if there is room. A whole undersea journey can be designed to include subject areas that are being covered in the regular curriculum.

Other props may include old bottles with slips of paper inside warning about the menace that is to come. Upon his first appearance the 'Corong' can seem like the epitome of evil but turn out to be kindly and almost offensively matter-of-fact. He or she can challenge the class to think of solutions. Pollution from nuclear waste can also be included as a problem area if appropriate. This monolog represents the basic attitude the character takes which can be improvised upon or changed to represent a different attitude. It can be expressed in any way the actor wishes.

The Corong's monologue: **I could see pollution coming down and settling here in the deepest area nearest the coast and no one would help because they didn't believe me. Because I have a black body even you can't see the oil on my skin from the pools of it around the spills from ships and leakage from the drilling. They all complain as though I've polluted everything. It's not me; it's the people up there. What can I do?** Questions can be asked of the children by the Corong, which is set up beforehand by the teacher. If she is using the mannequin it has been positioned at a strategic place so the class happens upon it. She sets up their questioning of the Corong. After their 'mission' has been completed, and they have communicated with the Corong, the leader guides them back and solidifies the information they are going to pass on in some form by asking the final questions.

Final questions

Many of the same questions asked at the beginning can be asked again.

How is the ocean important to our lives? How can we take care of it? What can we do now and in the future?

Some ways of following this up can be carried out, like writing to a political leader in either letter form or petition form and deciding to follow through on policies that will protect the environment in general.

Follow up/ variations

Following the journey exercise, make a transition into a slow motion journey in the ocean by adding: "Now we're moving much more slowly, as a plant in the bottom of the ocean; we want to remember some of the things we find here, but most of all we want to remember how beautiful it is. So close your eyes and let's see as many things as we can remember." The leader has used pictures, music, and images to introduce the children to the ocean. Now she wants to remind them about these images and help them to construct their own.

"I see a ---, what do you see?" etc. This can be passive or they can be encouraged to make suggestions. From here, the journey can continue by calling on their responses and including them as part of the narration. The leader also continues to use a combination of her own narration, oscillating rhythmic patterns (See Chapter 2, Narration/Journeys; Chapter 3, Slowness; Chapter 6, Rhythm), the children's contributions, and drumbeats when desired.

Variation

A variation which has been used: The Corong blames a mermaid (can be played by a child or the mannequin) for all the pollution which has come about due to an oil spill.

Corong: What's going on up there--? I see dead animals floating down through the ocean. There's no sunlight for the plankton to grow. (Explain the cycle on the board or use a chart: little fish eat plankton, big fish eat little fish, whales eat big fish, etc.) But ever since she came around this has been going on.

Mermaid: I've been trying to tell him, but I communicate with my tail and my arms and hands.

The Corong's monolog can be like the one already written.

The children become the communicators between the mermaid and the Corong.

Endangered Species (The Eagle)
(LA, Soc Stud, Sci) (K-4)

This drama can be altered for use with any bird, particularly since the eagle has been taken off the endangered species list, or other animal species.

Objectives
1. To reinforce the connection between nature and humans.
2. To realize that with each endangered species the human species is also endangered.

Materials
A bird costume may be a cap with feathers and bird wings made out of fabric (see illustrations on next page); a few feathers; lyrical music; taped sounds of birds (eagles); an airplane, and three gun shots

Concept
To enable the children to identify with the vanishing eagle population by briefly becoming eagles themselves and experiencing a sense of freedom that is eclipsed by the terror of pursuit and perhaps ultimate death.

Strategy
Helping the children to internalize the bird's vulnerability will build both their empathy and their understanding. The leader guides all the activities. She announces "off stage" action which works to increase tension. She may either use another person in role, the puppet/mannequin, or can change in front of the children to become the bird herself while their eyes are closed. At this point in the drama respect for the role has been assured.

Story
After the children are guided through some beginning preparatory exercises they are given facts about the diminishing eagle population and are initiated into the Audubon Society, becoming experts who can deal with the problem directly. They are taken up a mountain path to visit the remaining eagle(s). On the way, the leader uses a mimed pair of binoculars to deliver "off stage" action to the children, reporting a continuation of man's interference in the form of an airplane and gun toters. This makes the situation

much more tense for the mother eagle who is nesting.

They are encouraged to interact with the bird(s). If needed, a "devil's advocate" role can be introduced in the person of someone who still believes that Nature should be subject to human control.

Eagle costume, made out of flannel

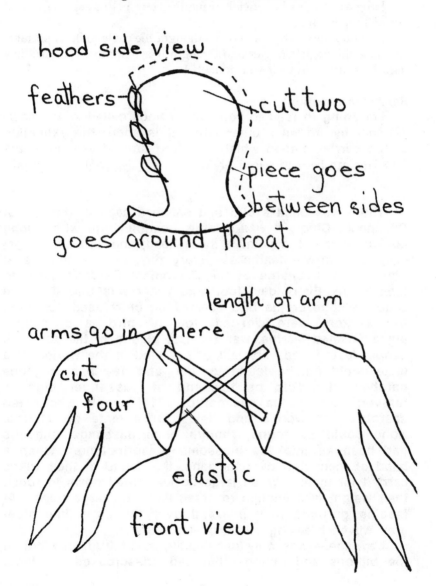

Beginning questions

Do you know why there are so few eagles left? (chemicals and human interference; people have believed that eagles are to blame for having destroyed much more livestock than is the case, and so have purposely killed them.)

How are eagles beneficial to man? (They help keep the rodent population down.)

Do you know why the Indians thought the eagle to be important? (Because the eagle's power and strength was a symbol for war; they used its feathers in their war bonnets.)

Related information

I'm going to read to you from a book called *A Vanishing Thunder* by Adrien Stoutenberg. It is about the extinction of the carrier pigeon which occurred around seventy years ago. This can be read selectively or told, but eye contact must take place.

There was once a bird that sat in a cage in the city of Cincinnati, Ohio. It was a large, beautiful bird with a long tail that came to a point, a sleek head, and soft blue, rose, gray, and brown feathers. Every day, and sometimes at night, men in charge of the Zoological Gardens came to look at it. Every day, food and water was placed in the cage. Whenever the bird seemed ill, or refused her food, the workers were worried, for the bird, a passenger pigeon named Martha, was the last pigeon at the zoo and, people feared, the very last of her kind in the world. If a mate could not be found for her, and new baby pigeons hatched, it would be the end of passenger pigeons forever. So, in the summer of 1914, people who cared searched the woods and fields for a mate for Martha. None could be found, though once passenger pigeons had been as thick as blossoms in springtime. When a band of them flew over the land, the sound of their wings carried for miles. When large flocks settled down to roost, their weight was enough to break limbs off large trees. At feeding grounds they billowed over the earth like blue-gray waves breaking on an ocean shore.

Now there was only one lonely, silent bird, one out of the billions and billions that had crisscrossed the land.

How could it have happened?   People asked each other. How could it be that seemingly endless flocks of passenger pigeons had so suddenly disappeared?   It only seemed sudden.   It had all begun many years before.   On September 1, Joseph and Sol Stephen went to Martha's cage.   She lay motionless, a small feathered heap, dead. There was no wind to ruffle or lift the long, quiet wings, and no way to relight the once burnished eyes that had gleamed orange-red through sunshine and shadow.   There was no way to restore to the sky the countless, throbbing bird bodies that had once passed across it like a blue snowstorm.   Today Martha stands mounted on the perch of a tree branch, the branch supported by an old-fashioned mahogany stand in a glass case at the Smithsonian Institute.   The stuffed feathers never move. The glass eyes look out and see nothing.

Drama

The leader begins by explaining that she has received word from a prominent Indian leader that the eagle population will face extinction unless a concerted effort is made to educate the public. The Audubon Society is reaching out for volunteers to help educate the public about the problem.   Here is a feather that the Indian medicine man gave me from one of the last eagles to be seen in this area.   It is his suggestion that the best way for us to find this eagle is to become eagle-like ourselves, as the Indians became like the animals they most admired.   In this way they developed a kinship with them. Close your eyes and listen to the sounds. A tape of sounds is played, and/or John Denver's song, "The Eagle and the Hawk." The last line has been changed.

I AM THE EAGLE I LIVE IN HIGH COUNTRY

ROCKY CATHEDRALS THAT REACH TO THE SKY

I AM THE HAWK AND THERE'S BLOOD ON MY FEATHERS

THE TIME IS STILL TURNING THEY SOON WILL BE DRY

AND ALL THOSE WHO SEE ME AND ALL WHO BELIEVE IN ME

SHARING THE FREEDOM I FEEL WHEN I FLY

COME DANCE WITH THE WEST WINDS AND TOUCH ON
THE MOUNTAIN TOPS

SAIL OVER CANYONS AND UP TO THE STARS

AND REACH FOR THE HEAVENS AND HOPE FOR THE
FUTURE

AND ALL THAT WE CAN BE THE BEST THAT WE ARE.

(The last line has been altered)

Motivational exercise: (similar to exercise in Space, from *Small to Mature* Jin)

Become as tiny as you think a baby bird is inside an egg. It's very dark and warm. You feel a sense of motion in your body that needs to be released, and you begin to break your shell. It takes a lot of work, and it's very hard. You stop to rest but still you know you must continue, and you do, hour after hour because it takes a long time. After several hours, you find yourself in a sticky mess. It takes you another spell to try to lift your wings, and oh, so many days, weeks, even months to learn to fly. You've watched your mother and father go and return and now you must perform this same task... It'll be fun----but— scary. What if—I fall? Is this what the others think? Oh, there she goes. And another. Whee-—just lift up and then glide, lift up—whew, that's the hard part. This type of journey may be modified depending upon the children's ages. For ages 5 to 7, use narration that allows the children to feel like the bird in the shell, so that they slowly become it. In like manner, the journey to the bird(s) needs to be gaged in accordance with the room space. For ages eight and older this can be used as a visualization process.

Transition

Lights should be dimmed, and the same music can be replayed for the background during the journey.

Journey narration

(Keep the journey physical. Js) **We're going to meet the eagles now. We must climb this treacherous path up the mountain to their dwelling. Their eyes and ears are so keen that soon we'll hear their call. They're the only eagle family in the area for hundreds of miles. I hope they're still around. They were spotted just last month, and it is thought that this is the year when they will breed their young. Perhaps they're afraid if we come now.** (Mimes using binoculars.) **I'll use these binoculars to see if I can locate them. —I think I see one of them. It must be the female because here comes the male bringing food to her. She's not leaving the nest. What do you suppose that means?** (She's nesting) **It takes many weeks for a family of baby eagles to hatch, and they take 3 to 4 years to become adults. All conditions need to remain the same or else she'll lose the birds.** (Suddenly, an airplane is heard coming closer with the use of the battery-tape recorder.) **This seems to have made the father eagle angry. He's flying toward the airplane. I can't see the mother. Oh, there she is, still sitting on the eggs.** (A gun shot is heard.) **Did you hear that? The mother just left her nest. Oh, no. She may have gone to find the father. But the babies may not hatch if she's gone for over a minute. We may not be able to see them if they've been scared away. Oh, she's back on the nest, and the father's flying above. I see him darting down.** (Another shot is heard.) **Oh, no. He's rising up and darting again. He's really angry now.** (Another shot is heard.) **He's falling. He's been killed. Do you still want to continue toward the nest? The mother has no help now to gather food. She has to remain on her nest. Do you think we could help her gather food? Let's approach quietly. Maybe we can gather food on the way and put it out for her when we arrive. We're just about there. She's sitting right up there. We can't startle her because she's been through a lot lately, and she may fly away and lose the babies if we seem to threaten her. I see her; she's right up there.** (The leader uses a whistle in the form of a bird call.) **She sees us, and she's not moving.**

Transition

The leader may become the eagle by having the children close their eyes.

Close your eyes and imagine yourself sitting high above the land, one of the last remaining eagles. During this time, the eagle role is taken by the leader who puts on the wings and cap; or by a mannequin; or another child.

Monolog

I am one of the oldest and most endangered soaring birds still left in North America. I existed in the days of mastodons and sabre toothed tigers which are now extinct. The Native Americans revered me as a symbol of power and freedom. I remember the green fields having been laden with trees which was part of our protection, for we lived high up in the mountains. Now we are hunted and hated. Those who come to help us only seem to harm us, for we know humans as our enemy. Thank you for coming. Your interest has given me new hope.

An interchange takes place between the children and the role who draws from her biographical sketch containing any factual information she will need to draw on. At the end of the interchange, the role can thank them for coming because now she has been given the will to raise her babies, in spite of all the interference. And the eagle population may continue to survive, at least a little longer.

Final questions

Are you more hopeful now about the eagle population having at least a chance to survive?

Do you think you helped in this effort?

What will it take to be sure?

How can we continue to be of help in the future?

Do you think if we protect the earth in small ways that people will become more interested in having a peaceful world?

Can you think of how we may do this?

The Forest
(LA, Soc Stud, Hist, Geog, Sci) (4-7)

Introduction

Forests, parks, and wilderness areas are gradually being diminished all over the world by commercial development, the need for more agricultural areas, and the basic human impact. Forests are like a great greenhouse and the greatest producer of organic matter and absorber of carbon dioxide. The forest floor contains an accumulation of humus—a combination of dead leaves and nutrients—that rebuilds soil. It takes about ten years to build one inch of topsoil. Topsoil is eroding faster than any other natural resource, and without it we can grow no food. Another grave problem, and one that is reversible only with great difficulty, is the depletion of the ozone layer. The ozone layer is losing the oxygen it needs in order to absorb the ultra-violet radiation of the sun. Forests give off oxygen, but because they are being cut all over the world, the ozone layer is shrinking.

This drama has as its theme an Indian child who is running away. There are many white children who have been raised by Indians, and many Indian children who have been raised by whites over the years. In almost all cases, the children want to remain with the parent or parents they know best and have learned to love, no matter who the blood relative is. However, the courts almost always rule with the natural parent who, in most cases, is usually the mother. Recently Indian groups have become more and more aggressive about trying to reclaim their Indian children so they can learn their heritage.

Objectives

1. To learn about the importance of careful observation and communication.

2. To value the reasons why the environment needs protection.

3. To become more in touch with and better able to appreciate the traditions of the Native Americans.

4. To understand and compare this historical tradition with that of the present day population and the destructive consequences of this latter trend.

Materials

A battery-powered tape-recorder; a tape of Indian lore which includes two poems on p. 230 ("By loving...") and p. 232 ("No longer...") from Dan George, *My Heart Soars*. Both are introduced by a drumbeat; a tape with several gun shot sounds; a back pack; three cards with scene suggestions; a copy of a statement about park and forest care; clip-on lights; green and brown cloths; clean garbage to be used as litter by the first group.

I am carrying the secrets of my tribe.

Concept

Two different groups show their use of the forest or park: each represents the attitude that nature is to be dominated, which often is synonymous with abuse. One of the children plays a runaway Indian child who represents the idea that nature must be respected.

Strategy

The leader is in an "authoritative" role as head forest ranger. One group of children are 'experts' as forest rangers. Three cards are given out with directions for each group before the drama begins.

Card 1. You are a family having a picnic in a forest. You enter the forest with your picnic basket. You take out a blanket and spread it on the ground. Each member takes out several items from the basket and mimes eating. During the course of your stay you violate most rules for keeping the forest clean and safe: throwing trash, leaving a fire going; feeding animals; picking wild flowers; chopping a tree for wood; leaving food. The dialogue begins as in Exercise 25, *Body Language*, and the following is only an approximation of what could be said.

—over here, let's lay it all out

—maybe there'll be some bears we could feed

—look at that flower—I'll add it to my collection

—ew, this place looks creepy

—hey, there's a cute animal—grab it

—there's no trash container—let's burn it—just get this wood going and it'll burn all this stuff

—what about the bottles?

—just toss them. There's no trash can here.

You have a conversation about how poorly the park looks and upon leaving, the head ranger gives you a warning concerning how you've left the camp ground as well as the violations your group has incurred. In payment you must now spend some time cleaning up the mess you've created.

Card 2. You are a family who has come to hunt. When you come upon some trash you complain, but also leave some of your own trash. At least one of you shoots indiscriminately at any moving thing. This happens two or three times and complaints are heard by the others in your group. One of you sees a doe and fawn running through the forest and runs to them calling out, "Oh, look a deer and its baby." At the same time you receive a minor wound from a stray bullet which comes from another source, and you complain to your group about this. A member of your group responds by shooting into the distance. Another thinks he sees the wounded deer, and runs to it. A gunshot is heard in the distance. The head ranger together with other rangers approach and asks why you are shooting into the trees. As the rangers find other dead animals, there is the realization that poaching is going on. The poaching group remains ambiguous. The head ranger points out to your group that what you are doing by shooting blindly is just as dangerous as what the poachers are doing.

Card 3. One child is given the role of an Indian child or white child that has been raised by Indians and is a runaway. He can be a runaway from an Indian home or an Anglo home, depending upon the theme desired. Whether or not the child is Indian or Anglo, and running in either direction, to or from the above homes, he is enacting some type of ceremonial ritual which can be taught to the whole group. Both his verbal and non-verbal attitude speak for his search to find his Indian heritage reflecting a closeness to Nature. His "running" symbolizes this search.

While the three above groups are planning, the leader organizes the remaining children who will be the forest rangers. She explains some of the difficulties that they will meet which are included in groups 1 and 2. The leader, as Head Ranger, guides the drama. At first she meets the majority of the children who are playing the rangers and announces the difficulties with campers during this holiday season, telling them to distribute themselves all over the park with their (mimed) walkie-talkies.

After all have tested their instruments from some paces away, the first camping group enters. The leader edges the rangers to the side while the campers appear oblivious to them. After reprimanding group 1 in role, she steps to the side lines, and the 2nd group enters while the rangers carry out their duties in an improvisation. As the head ranger, she plays the battery-powered tape recorder, treating it as part of her equipment. After directing the second group to the sides in role, she motions the Indian child on. She plays the tape of the Indian ancestor, which is introduced by a slow drumbeat.

> By loving the earth the joy of creation is known. My culture speaks through nature—through the trees— soon it will be too late to know my culture for our values have been forgotten. Many young people have been shamed and have forgotten the Indian ways. My

> culture is like a wounded deer that has crawled away
> into the forest to bleed and die alone.[1]

The Indian child has started to move as though carrying out a ritual, oblivious of all the others who are watching. The child and the leader have worked out this ritual beforehand, and it is one that can be taught to the whole class in an attempt to help others understand. The child is also carrying a large pack which he positions as the clue to the forest rangers that this person is a runaway. He may mime taking out a knife at first, as if to defend himself. The longer the role is silent, as has been mentioned before, the more tension will be created to deepen the drama. The child in role as the runaway needs to be shy, scared, stoic, and slow to speak. All of these qualities will add tension and work to capture the attention of the other children. The leader as head ranger needs to supply the most information so that the child's reaction can be less verbal and, as a result, will provide the needed tension. The forest rangers have been watching him and, as a result, have made some deductions about his identity; they are more accepting of the runaway than of the tourists. Some dialogue is given in order to provide an example of the type of communication that can follow. With the leader in charge, the Indian child reveals the motivation for his search. Anything he says is accepted by the leader while he remains within this attitude.

Head ranger: Excuse me, you know that this park isn't to be used for overnight visitors?

Runaway: I am staying there. (points)

Head ranger: Looks like you're moving in.

Runaway: I'm traveling.

Head ranger: You're passing through?

Runaway: Yes.

Head ranger: Looks like you know what you're doing.

Runaway: I'm following my destiny—

Head ranger: What?

Runaway: I'm—following my tribal ways—becoming initiated into my tribe—it's secret.

Head ranger: You do understand that none of the animals or plants can be used or killed, don't you?

Runaway: Yes.

Head ranger: I know what you're thinking. This land was once yours and now that it's been taken away from you and your people, you must uphold new laws.

Runaway: Yes—but it is better that all others have a right to it if it is to be protected. I am carrying with me the secrets of the past. I have been to the oldest one who is still living. He has taught me that I must walk out a pattern and chant.

Transition
Runaway: I will read this—the old one has written it in our old language. (He reads it. Both the leader and child lead the class as they repeat the two last lines together. Since there is a great deal of symbolism in these lines, the leader needs to question the class and include any references with the curriculum that seem appropriate. The Indian child asks all to help him walk out his ritual as they sit and repeat the last few lines. These lines are broken into phrases as marked and repeated as a chorus by small groups or a single speaker.)

(The following can be written on a grocery bag to resemble bark or on the board, and be enhanced by being taped and played. As the Indian child repeats this he needs to focus on some fixed point in space. The lines in parentheses can be deleted.)

> No longer can I give you a handful of berries as a gift,
> No longer are the roots I dig used as medicine,
> No longer can I sing a song to please the salmon,
> (No longer does the pipe I smoke make others sit
> with me in friendship,
> No longer does anyone want to walk with me to the
> blue mountain to pray,)
> No longer does the deer trust my footsteps.
> Please say this with me:
> The faces of the past/ are like leaves/ that settle to
> the ground/
> They make the earth rich/ and thick,/ so that new
> fruit/ will come forth/ every summer.[1]

The child in role with the assistance of the leader can continue by teaching the others.

Beginning questions
Does anyone know what the rules are when visiting a forest or park which is protected?
Do you have any ideas why forests, trees, and wooded areas are so valuable?

Does anyone know what the regulations are about adopting Indian children?

What can we learn from the Indian heritage?

Preparation

Drama preparation can take place the day before, particularly if the children are new to the experience. If this occurs, the room can be prepared so that the classroom space is transformed, (perhaps during recess on the day of the drama), into a forest setting, dimmed with some clip on lights at different points with green bulbs in them. Green and brown pieces of material are draped over desks and conspicuously placed.

Drama

After the leader has handed out the two cards and worked with the child who is to play the Indian runaway, learning his simple ritual and his biography (this has to be done separately before the drama begins), she begins in role as the head park ranger and addresses the whole class on the values, rules, and responsibilities of camping and visiting in these areas. She introduces the foresters to the campers and briefly addresses the foresters as to their responsibility. **Let us enter the forest-park area. This is the area where you can cook and eat—. These are the trash receptacles, over here—. Now we are going to ___.** At this point she takes the child foresters to the side-lines to begin instructing them, **Come over here. There are several dead trees that need to be carried away.** Next time she takes them off to the side-lines as if they're going off into the woods to carry out duties. The first group of campers carries on their improvisation, and the campers appear oblivious to the others who are watching from the sidelines, becoming an audience (see Chapter 2, Audience). After their scene, the head forester reprimands them. A 'warning' is given and recorded and the understanding about being on probation is explained. She then reads an official sounding statement: **The state of___ is hereby authorized to warn visitors if any violation of the national park and forest system seems imminent. Leaving refuse or lighted fires, disturbing any wild life such as the taking or killing of animals or plants, carrying any firearm without a permit, leaving open fires and generally not leaving the wilderness as you found it are all punishable by law.** They may argue, and all step to the sidelines while the second group enters. Using the tape player the leader plays the taped gunshot sounds. She questions the second group about the stray shots and checks their licenses. Since the origin of the shots is still a mystery she asks if they know of any other members of their party who are around and may have delivered the stray shots. She reprimands them in a similar way. As they are winding up their conversation, the Indian child enters stealthily.

The leader (in role) alerts the rest to watch. **People say that it's possible to hear an Indian chief's words when the breezes blow through the trees.** She turns on the prepared tape of the drumbeats followed by the voice of the Indian chief who chants the poem beginning, "By loving the Earth ..." (p. 230), on tape.

The child playing the role should remain mute and seem frightened even though he pretends to see no one. He carries out a ritual which the leader has helped him with. At first he is walking around to find the right 'place,' standing and lining himself up with a 'tree,' and holding his arms out in an angle out from his body as though to bring himself into a proper position in relation to the objects in the forest. He is concentrating heavily and carrying himself as though he is walking to an inner drumbeat. The Indian child completes his ritual by digging a grave and collecting the dead deer which he gathers up a few feet away, burying it. He states, "Your life was meaningless because the white man killed you for no reason, just for sport. Now I'll place you in the heart of the Mother Earth where your spirit will rise and protect the earth." (The second poem may be taped, and the Indian child repeats the last two lines; or, the whole poem can be taped while he moves as suggested; or, he can read the poem, and the leader can lead all in chanting the last two lines.)

Final questions
How did the Indians treat the earth in comparison to the white man?

What have been some of the problems with this?

Why do we need to understand their reasons for protecting the earth?

Follow up exercises
Have the children plan a **ritual** to emphasize an important value in relation to the land. The leader continues to narrate as the children carry through with action.

Human Nature

The kinds of dilemmas we find ourselves in are likely to have a universal trend because they are based upon dwindling natural resources. Better use of resources, for example implementing programs in solar energy, are constant needs throughout the world.

Many of the new jobs that have been created have been in the military preparedness area... which is also a reverberation of the same refrain, that of wasting natural resources, because these products aren't redistributed back into the society.

The skilled jobs which have been developed largely seek out and attract young trainees and require a specific talent and temperament, such as those in information systems. In short, a large spectrum of society is not being provided for now nor in the future and social problems abound.

Blue collar jobs have diminished, partly due to dwindling natural resources and mechanization; retraining programs have translated into service jobs which often hover around minimum wage. This change in job status means suddenly that people who have provided for a family can't do it alone anymore. And even if the wife begins working the income may still be near the poverty line because in most cases, neither wife nor husband hold skilled jobs.

Because of the increasing wedge between the haves and have nots, this social oppression can evolve into political oppression unless recognized and dealt with.

The surest way it can be realistically dealt with is if people are educated. This means not simply inheriting the problem and finding oneself up against a closed door, but looking at the problem now and anticipating changes which implies a transformation of values within the educational process.

William Glasser , in his book *Control Theory in the Classroom* (see p. 97, Cooperative Learning), looks at the institution of the public school. Unlike many current and oppressive findings which state that public schools aren't doing the job, he defends the task as having an inherent flaw. In the past the past, before Sputnik, children weren't required to remain in school as long as they are now. The reason for this was that these same students could drift into the public sector and find the kinds of unskilled jobs that are the same type of service jobs today. However, unlike the past, these jobs are a dead end. One can no longer make boxes in the factory and find any hope of working up because the skilled jobs don't exist; a McDonald's may be run by a corporation so that there's nothing in between waiting on customers and being a member of the board. The other reason is that the next step requires skill, either computer or management skills which require some post-secondary education.

Glasser maintains that the argument which has been used to keep teenagers in school so that they can get a better job is no longer valid. As well, the rewards are too remote for them. Glasser's main thesis is that since the need to insure physical survival is no longer a driving concern, other needs are now more pressing such as the need to belong, gain power, be free, and have fun. He basically contends that no teenager can sit in a competitive classroom and receive any of these satisfactions unless he is successful. Glasser bases the student's needs upon "the picture he carries in his head." If he has had experiences which support a view of himself as someone who succeeds in school work based upon these needs, then he will continue to apply himself. However, this picture must be nurtured if it is to continue. Glasser maintains that for 50% of the students, the pattern of individual competitiveness doesn't lend itself to "gaining power, belonging, having fun, or being free." As a result, illicit activities, particularly drugs and alcohol, do provide for these needs in the short run, yet are disastrous in the long run.

He debunks the past s/r (stimulus/response) theory which supports the idea that behavior is caused by the forces outside of us. Instead he states,"...it is an axiom of the control theory that no one does anything, simple or complex, because someone tells him to do it. All living creatures, and we are no exception, only do what they believe is most satisfying to them, and the main reason our schools are less effective than we would like them to be is that, where students are concerned, we have failed to appreciate this fact.."[2] In place of the traditional teaching practice of having the teacher up in front of the classroom lecturing, with the student working to achieve the best grade possible or not working because his own mental image is not nurtured, Glasser recommends placing students into teaching teams, a teaching strategy which he says helps the student to feel he belongs, can have fun, lessens the feeling of powerlessness, and if it does not let him feel free, at least mitigates the oppressiveness of the classroom.

We know that peer influence becomes stronger and compensates for lack of family support and encouragement as children move into their pre-adolescent years.

This form of cooperative learning is a hold-over from the late 19th century. It lends itself to the form of learning which is dynamic and stimulating because the student is creating his own learning with the teacher's guidance.

The dramas in this Human Nature section, *The Dead Bird*, *The Soldier*, *Nutrition*, and *Addiction*, deal with some human and social problems that may lead to alienation.

The drama called *The Dead Bird* deals with the problem of death. A teacher asked for this drama to be done because she had a child in her first grade class whose father had died. She told me that he had talked to his mother about the drama afterward. He had said, "I know why drama is important. It helps you to understand life better." Children are very wise. We need to reach them in time, however. It has been suggested that death is seen in the slow suicides amongst members of the drug culture. Death is the primary cause of our national debt: ". . .our enormously sophisticated super-weaponry of global destruction is the product of a high intellect---but one devoid of intelligence, since intelligence will not operate against the well-being of its species."[3]

Note: All of the dramas in this section are full role dramas. Except for the *Nutrition* drama they are all dealing with life and death issues. For this reason it is necessary for the role to be mature.

The Dead Bird

(LA, Soc Stud)(K-2)

Objectives

1. To more fully understand that the experience of death is universal.

2. To understand that the emotion of sadness is a legitimate experience and deserves expression.

3. To empathize with a person's loss by helping and observing them.

Materials

A book with bird picture on the cover, a drawing containing a wounded bird (see drawing), a map including a cross, a picture of a hunter aiming a gun at a wounded bird in flight, a feather, a shawl.

Concept

It is very difficult to present the concept of death to children. This drama uses a bird, and the children empathize with the feelings of the survivor.

Strategy

A person in "full" role is brought in who carries out everything non-verbally—a technique which allows the children to be more deeply affected than if speech were used. The leader guides the drama as a 'catalyst' slowly to sustain the intense involvement.

Story

A young girl's bird has died and she wants to bury it. She induces the children to help her, and through mimed signs, guides them on a journey. Upon finding the "mimed" bird, they bury it, and she places her shawl on the grave site. She guides the children back and leaves.

Beginning questions

In general, children are usually empathic with things which seem helpless, and in particular, with animals. However, knowing that the mood of bereavement is needed, the following introduction is used: Have you ever had a favorite pet or toy? What if something happened to it—it was stolen, became ill, was lost or died? How would you feel?

Drama
   I think that's the way the lady I'm going to introduce
you to feels.   When you feel like this, does it make you
feel worse if someone laughs at you?   So, we don't want
to laugh.   Here she comes.   I don't think she understands
English very well.   Here, the children need to be given time to
watch the role. She doesn't seem very happy does she?
Why don't we get up and play a game and maybe we can
get her to join us.   Let's make a big circle.   This game is
called Bird, Beast, Fish (or earth, air, fire, water).   I'll stand in
the center and point to one of you.   If I say, "Bird"—-how
does a bird move?   That's right.   You show it by moving.
Or, Beast, how does a four-footed creature move?   And
Fish—.   Good.   If I say fire and point to you, remain
perfectly still.   Play the game briefly, having about 6 or 7 take
their turns. The leader draws attention to the role who is not paying
any attention to the group.   Did any of you notice?   She looked
whenever you moved like a bird.   Let's go back.   The leader

quietly settles the group around the role and takes time to wait.The role or lady takes out a book and opens it up. Inside is a letter with a story drawn (show) on it and a feather. She takes these out and handles them gently. She has been focused on these symbols. The children are drawn toward her, thus creating aesthetic distance. After about 12 seconds of silence the leader begins asking questions. **I wonder why she's so interested in the letter? Can you see the cover of the book? I wonder what the book is about? Where do you suppose the feather came from? Would you like for me to ask her if we can see the letter?** The letter is passed around and the drawing is interpreted. **What's this mean?** Whatever the children say is accepted because we're not dealing with factual information. After the drawing has been seen and interpreted, the leader begins to draw the map of the journey on the board or if no board exists, begins to take over and explain where to go. **Maybe we can find this place.** At this point, the lady grabs the chalk and finishes the drawing, or interferes with the leader's "control". Then she beckons the children to follow her. She makes a wide pathway around the room to enable the children to follow her to a different spot. If the room is small for the number of children, a zigzag pathway may work better than a circle and will give the feeling of getting somewhere without taking too much time. It is also possible for the leader to play a tape on a battery operated tape recorder that will enhance and sustain the mood. As soon as we arrive at the appropriate spot, the lady puts up her hand as though to stop us. She, then, turns around, takes a few steps, and bends down as though to enter a cave. She cups her hands, makes a scooping gesture toward the "earth", stands up, turns around and advances toward us revealing the cupped hands. **What is she holding?** "The bird," they answer. (This lesson has been carried out with more than 300 children since 1974. There was only one child who did not respond by saying, "a bird." However, when he said, "I don't see a bird," his classmates communicated, partly non-verbally, the information that they did, and peer pressure won out.) She carefully takes off her shawl, lays the bird down on it, and begins to dig.) **What is she doing?** Burying the bird. **Shall we help her?** She stops, mimes collecting leaves and grass to place around the "mimed" bird. The children finish digging. By the wave of her hand she signals them to stop, pulls up a little more grass and carefully lines the hole with it. She takes the "bird", carefully lays it on the grass, and places more grass on top of it. She then begins to cover the hole. Some of the children may help. After this has been completed her anxiety and concern are gone, and she looks peaceful as she sits back on her heels. And for the first time, she looks at the children, smiles, as though to thank them. She places her shawl on the "grave", gets up, and leaves. We watch her go.

Final questions

Do you think she seemed happier? Do you think you helped her? At this point the leader pulls the shawl up to reveal the floor. There's no bird here. Is it all right that we imagined one? Is it all right to be sad? Have you ever had an animal which died? Have you ever known a person who died?

There have been several occasions when children have been deeply touched by this drama. I can especially remember two. The first time, the class was a second/third grade combination. After we had finished with the drama and were having a discussion, a little boy said, "My father died two months ago, and I really miss him, we used to go fishing together and play baseball—" The teacher knew nothing about this and was glad to find out about the child's problem. It was as though he wanted the other children to know about his hurt.

On another occasion, a teacher asked me to do a drama dealing with death because the father of one of her first grader's had died. She said that the boy was the least mature in her class and should be in kindergarten. After the drama the boy talked to his mother about it, and his mother told the teacher that he had said, "I know why drama is important. It helps you to understand life better."

Follow up

Create a ritual for someone or something for which you feel sympathy.

The Soldier

(LA, Soc Stud, Hist) (K-8)

Objectives

1. To empathize and identify with a person who's suffered in a war.

2. To realize that war is not an answer to problems.

Materials

Military papers, orders; a worn letter containing a dried flower and a picture of children; a small pad of paper and a pencil; an insignia; and military gear, especially binoculars; tape of war sounds; a biographical sketch for the person in role can follow those segments that are provided in the Drama

Concept

The whole idea of war is intolerable to most children, unless they think of it as "fun and games" due to the detachment that television brings. However, it is an extremely complex issue and cannot be easily dismissed in a single hour session. The "bottom line" message from this extremely exhausted infantryman is that he doesn't know who he's fighting or why he's fighting. He aligns himself with the uselessness of war and suggests that people talk first before fighting. Hopefully, a seed is planted.

Strategy

The leader prepares the children through questions and then brings them into the room to meet 'the soldier' who is played by a child or any young or middle-aged male. All the strategies of "full" role are used (see p. 69, Full Role) , and the leader becomes the "catalyst." A breakdown of questions is included. The children, ages six through eleven, have been able to sit for the hour because there have been a series of episodes and interactions that build on each other, thus capturing their attention. The soldier is speaking as if no one else is present (see **soliloquy**).

Beginning questions

Have you ever known anyone who's been in a war? (fathers, relatives, grandfather.) The person whom you are going to see may need your help. Have you ever felt worried or sad? When you're like this do you like people to laugh at you? We've got to be careful not to laugh because this person has gone through a lot.

Transition
Close your eyes. I want you to imagine that you're on a battlefield. At this time the tape of war sounds can be turned on and heard for about 30 seconds. **When we enter we'll find our soldier on this battlefield. Do you think you can believe in this? I want you to try to believe—can you do that? Because if you don't, nothing's going to happen to you?**

The leader takes the children into the room where they see a soldier. He's in a state of sleep or unconsciousness and over a period of about five minutes while the children watch him, he slowly comes to, but does not yet see the children. This must go slowly and can fill an hour. If it is rushed then the children won't experience the confusion and pain that would grip a soldier in wartime. Questions need to be asked in conjunction with the actions of the person in role. Each question can work as a cue for the person in role to begin the next action. These questions need to be asked about every 1 to 3 minutes, with follow up questions to keep the children connected to the role. For example: What's he reading, I wonder? Do you think what he's reading is pleasant? Do you think he's reminded of something he doesn't think is pleasant? How's he feeling now?

The following steps are a general breakdown of activities and possibilities which the children may pursue, but it must be remembered that this is not a script to be followed exactly for there is no way of knowing how the children may respond. (The questions of the children can work as cues for the role.)

Drama
I wonder what's the matter with him?
1. After the first 4 or 5 minutes, the soldier awakens slowly. He begins to wonder about his whereabouts; in an attempt to understand more fully, he may pick up his binoculars and observe. He may have a lurking suspicion that something bad has happened, but he cannot remember.

I wonder what a man in this situation thinks and feels?
2. This is a signal for him to get up. During this time he ignores his immediate surroundings because his memories and dreams are more real to him. He becomes aware of a limp. Something still haunts him. He may look at the emblem he is carrying.

Can you see what he's carrying?

3. Upon this signal he reaches into his pocket, sits down, and takes out a letter to read from his wife, while taking out the dried flower and pictures of his children. He looks at them as though he's not sure who they are. He holds up the flower, trying to remember.

I wonder what kind of a life this man has had? What do you think he's reading?

4. He's still trying to put together the letter with his more recent memories and he remains confused.

He doesn't seem to remember anything. Do you think if you ask him he will remember? You don't want to ask him to remember painful memories. What kinds of questions would you ask him?

5. This becomes his cue for being able to now recognize that the children are there. He takes out a pencil from his pocket and a little pad of paper and begins to write his wife a letter but can't because of his more recent memories. As though to get inspiration, he looks at the flower then at the insignia and his papers, trying to put it all together.

Why don't you ask him one of those questions you had in mind?

6. This is a signal for the person in role to begin to respond to the children's questions.

The soldier can still seem confused about all of the above aspects and go off in any direction to attempt to understand his present condition. After a child's question, for example, the memory is still too strong and his response can be: The Captain—I—I—tried—but I couldn't—save him—.

7. **What can we ask him that will remind him of pleasant memories?** This question goes back to his family. **How can we help him?**

8. I need to write a letter to my wife, but I can't tell her this--what shall I say. What should I tell her?

Final questions

What can he tell his wife? Do you think we'll always have wars? What causes wars? What will we have to do to not have wars? Do people always win? Why not? Who wins? What do they win?

(Wife's letter can be read by the leader to the class.)

My dearest husband,

No word from you since you left port. The war news seem to grow worse and worse. Molly Franklin has received news her youngest son, only 18, is missing in action and presumed dead.

I don't understand why the war gets worse and worse while the peace talks get longer and longer.

Since you've been away Carry has begun taking her first steps. Oh, how I wish you could have been here to see her. Thomas has begun to say a few words like Mommy, doggie, ball, and flower, I tried to get him to say Daddy, but he couldn't.

The roses you planted last spring are blooming, and so I've pressed one to send you.

Thomas looks a lot like you, I think. Lisa has also grown. Teddy and Toby say hello. And we----

I can't read the rest, the ink seems to have run.

This drama has been used with young children, ages six through eleven. It has also been used with older children, ages 10-13, in the drama called *War and Conflict* and in a drama on the Civil War. In both of these latter dramas, it was used presenting reasons against the concept of war, and the 'soldier' was present for only about 12 minutes during the hour.

Nutrition

(LA, Sci, Health) (K-8)

Objectives

1. To understand the importance of diet and its relationship to the four basic food groups.

2. To empathize with a particular person's need for better health.

3. To work co-operatively by making a machine to represent the body's reactions to food and other habits.

Materials

Pictures of the four food groups and a chart of the human body, detailing anatomical functions depending on age; pictures showing the effects of malnutrition, if appropriate. (see Follow-up)

Concept

The idea of processing the correct combinations of foods in order to obtain the most functional level of activity possible is considered. Other health factors, like diet, overall habits, exercise, and attitude can be included.

Strategy

The children are in role as "experts" who need to keep up with the newest ideas in attaining good health. Or, they could be Peace Corp or Vista volunteers who must find out about their assignments in other parts of the world. As part of their training, pictures of children who are malnourished from their field areas are shown as a stimulus to their need for training in the area of maintaining a balanced diet. In the midst of their meeting, a person in "full" role is introduced by the leader as "catalyst." The athlete needs help due to his lack of vitality and the added embarrassment of having been kicked off the team. Slowly his biography is revealed: he has broken the rules of training, poor diet, smoking, etc., and though he still has a keen desire to win or be on the team, he lacks will power. However, he is extremely interested in machinery. The desire to show him how the body works by using the machine may be used, as well as the pictures. A machine is built by the leader and made out of the children to show the effects of diet and habits. (However, the machine may be deleted and other aspects of the drama can be embellished.) The subject of this drama has many extensions which are applicable across a wide range of ages and purposes.

Story

The athlete in role is introduced to establish his need and to place pressure on the children as experts. The leader develops the concept of the four basic food groups and their effect on the body. Next, the machine is created to test the food groups and the design of an efficient exercise program is designed.

Beginning questions

As experts in health and nutrition what are some basic ideas we can recommend to people who need advice? The leader itemizes their answers on the board under appropriate headings such as: exercise; diet; daily activities and health habits.

Drama

A well-known athlete is introduced either in person or as an 'off-stage' problem which the children begin to work on. The athlete can then enter later. He's been kicked off the team because of his bad health habits which have slowed him down: bad food, smoking, not getting enough rest. His anger over having been kicked off the team is also contributing to his poor health.

Leader: (introduces the visitor) **He doesn't seem to be very energetic.** The person in role is interviewed by the class, and they discover his "biography" which can include as many problems as the teacher wishes to work on.

The leader becomes a dietician who plans menus from the four food groups. Posters and charts are introduced to the class to explain how these food groups can be combined into a weekly diet.

Daily diets of three meals a day can be planned on a weekly basis by the whole class or by smaller groups who must use the four food groups.

All children are in role as experts in some field related to health and are given special assignments in relation to the machine. They are, then, responsible to keep track of any information which the body machine emphasizes.

A machine is built from volunteers to represent the human body. If the group is young the machine needs to be built in one large group and be directed by the leader. Older ages can work in small groups planning their machines according to curriculum references. An added control factor can be introduced such as the production of a media event.

Here is a possible way for building the machine:

(1) The most important organ for sending blood? Have the heart stand, represented by one person.

(2) The most important organ for sending oxygen through the body and keeping the air circulating? The lungs stand on either side of the heart represented by two persons who face toward the heart and can join hands, showing expansion and contraction when breathing.

(3) The organ for making decisions? Place the brain on another side of the heart represented by one person.

(4) The systems that help us lift things, walk, move? Place the muscles and bones on the other side of the heart both represented by four persons who alternate, muscle, bone, etc. and are lined up in a semi-circle surrounding the side away from the brain.

(5) The organs for digesting food? Place the stomach and intestines represented by two people in between the muscle-bone section and heart section, stomach nearest the heart, then intestines.

(6) The system that holds everything together? The skin should be placed completely outside the other systems represented by as many children as needed, in a circle.

These questions are asked as children are chosen to take their places and become organized into a body machine to show the other members of the class how the body works.

The machine is now put to work and the leader narrates—the brain decides to take a bite of food which travels on its pathway; the brain has an idea to walk and move. The brain takes a big breath and the lungs expand and all the organs begin to work better. We give the body some orange juice and see how much stronger it becomes. The leader can narrate items eaten from the different food groups showing the difference in energy output in comparison to fat intake, sugar, vegetables, etc. Each "system" jiggles energetically or slumps, showing fatigue. Narration needs to be done straight forward and direct in order to make it significant.

These directions need to take place in one segment of the lesson plan and then the children should sit down. The children are in the role of experts and are either divided into groups in order to work out plans or can be handled by the leader in one group. If they are divided into groups, the following areas can be covered:

(1) drawing a "health machine" for the athlete to use in order to remind himself about taking care of his body;

(2) planning a diet or menu;

(3) developing physical exercises to teach body control, breath control, and relaxation. Each one can be tried out.

Groups can go one at a time to participate with the person in role, while the rest of the groups are working on their task. Or, the groups can finish, after which the drama is opened up to the whole class while individual children or groups volunteer to work with the person in role, and the others watch while filling out a form and responding prescriptively as an expert. Children in lower grades can draw. Their roles determine their concern. If they are doctors trying to find a cure for an epidemic or world leaders who want to find a way to control world hunger (and population), the teacher needs to motivate them by finding their personal link with the athlete. They must care for the athlete and have a reason for doing so. He may be a local boy who's headed for national recognition or a stable boy who loves horses, but must find a way of maintaining his frail health.

Take a big breath to get ready for this mission.
As astronauts we need to keep in shape.

Final questions

Why is it important to be in good health?

As advisors what can you tell people who ask you for ways to keep or improve their health?

Follow- up

Using the exercise *Inanimate Objects* (see Chapter 9, Character), children become the different kinds of foods, physiological systems, cells, and speak for them. Combine this with the exercise *Talking Hands* (see Chapter 9, Imagination).

Variations

For children who are fascinated by athletes and "winning," the biography could also include the athlete's use of other harmful substances such as drugs. Lack of will power, yet wanting to win, becomes the tension that serves to motivate the child experts in trying to change the athlete's habits. The athlete must want to achieve but be unable to.

When used with younger ages, K-2, someone becomes a germ hovering around the athlete on cue. As a result, the machine registers negative, having been fed too much junk food, and the athlete registers certain negative symptoms.

Addictions

(LA, Soc Stud) (4-adult)

Introduction

Although there are many problems involved in addiction, a symptom of addiction is to ignore everything except the object of the addiction. Children in upper elementary school grades from 9 years up will empathize with the person who has the addiction.

One of the problems in families of addicts is referred to by me as the "garbage" theory. This is a psychological theory that any aberration in an adult's life is unconscious to the adult, but subconsciously the frustrations are passed on to the bewildered child. Since the adult can only make things appear "right" on the surface and the energy to do more is used to repress the problem, the problem seems to disappear in the adult but actually reappears in the child.

It is the child who has no outlet to express the problem and hasn't developed his personality to the degree that repression works. It is a possible theory for why children are drawn to empathize with the 'addict' in this drama. In order to insure that this happens, the person in role needs to be in a state similar to a catatonic, cut off in his relations to other people. This will create distance, drawing the children into the 'addict's' world. The distance or remoteness will produce tension. However, the children must not think of the role as being a "mental case", or they may lose respect for him. Make whatever contact and preparation is necessary for the role to be believable.

Objectives

1. To realize that a person's early years are valuable to his development.

2. To be in a position of expertise in order to help a person make connections with areas that may be new.

3. To critically analyze a person's actions through observation and make decisions about problems.

4. To help this person develop a self-image and a positive relationship with others.

Materials

(These depend on the scenario chosen. See end of drama.)

Tape-recorder, junk food, ball, juggling balls, cheer-leader's pom-poms, white coat, clip board, any needed articles for TV characters, pads of paper and pencils, sports equipment. Props are used by leader, children, others in role to get the attention of the role.

Concept

The children project their feelings onto a young person whose problems may remain ambiguous but nevertheless serve as a reflection for their own concerns.

Strategy

The leader is in a professional, "authoritative" role as head of a hospital or a professional friend of the patient, and moves in and out of the drama introducing the episodes. A slow pace is important as she serves as catalyst keeping the focus on the patient. It is best that the person in "full" role be silent throughout the drama only reacting occasionally to outside stimuli. However, if he does speak, it is only to himself (see soliloquy). The leader will also become the "catalyst," The children are in role as "experts."

Story

A person is addicted to TV and it is the hope that "we" the hospital staff, the children in role as experts, and those who have known him are brought together to find a way of providing treatment for this person.

The children are asked if they want to make a choice among the following types of work or roles: child psychologist, experimental psychologist, toymakers, family psychologists, video game manufacturers, baby sitters, and other roles that are related.

All of these professions can be discussed in relationship to the kinds of activities each category of professionals pursue in their work.

The experimental psychologist may need more explanation than the others. They are the kinds of psychologists in John O'Brian's *The Rats of Nimh* who use mazes, control groups, and mathematical statistics to compare different groups and their performances. Finally, as a result of these comparisons they are able to make predictions and offer warnings. The children can choose to represent any of these working roles and they, then, question the person in role as though they were fulfilling the requirements of anyone of these roles.

Beginning questions (See final questions.)

Drama

Leader: **As you know this clinic specializes in different cases—cases which seem to have no known cure—hoping we can find a cure for the future.**

During the past few years we've had more and more cases of young people, particularly around the teen years, who've seemed to withdraw from society. It is a great problem, not only to them and their families, but for society as well, since these years should be spent actively preparing for their futures.

We've organized this convention of concerned citizens and professionals in the field to try to understand this type of illness—not physical, nor mental, but emotional.

I think if we could understand this case we'd be able to understand many more which aren't this extreme. We need to ask: what do they get from TV that they don't get from life, or are they simply withdrawing from life?

We know very little so I can't tell you much. We have a few doctors who have observed him, and you'll be free to observe him, although he seems to have lost his memory.

One thing we're doing more and more is to place articles around the patient that he may or may not remember. If he does use them and remember them, this can become an important link to regaining his identity.

More tension is created if the person in role is not brought in right away. During the time preparation takes place each member receives: (1) the Conceptualization Form (a legitimate counselling form is included at the end of this lesson plan) which is reviewed and followed as closely as needed, and (2) some background information.

An air of ambiguity is created in order to add tension and extend the moment, providing thinking time and hence depth.

The leader knows "everything" that is possible and answers any questions that the children ask. Props are useful to expand upon experimentation and any possible reactions. Separate objects are offered to the person in role and the reaction is noted. Any object can bring an association that helps the patient to remember.

Other characteristics can be stated here by the leader in role or during the observation period when the patient is viewed, such as: **It is our doctors' finding that his memory is weak because he has never achieved an identity.**

Two different scenarios are included from previous dramas. Many scenarios are possible.

Scenario for 15 year old boy

Sam has been found in the greyhound bus station where he was trying to catch the bus. He didn't have enough money and became belligerent when he wasn't allowed to board the bus. His mother had become ill and was taken to a hospital, leaving him alone. His intention was to look for his brother and sister since he was alone.

He had gone to the Greyhound Bus depot on other occasions because he liked watching TV, but because he had created a nuisance he was taken to an emergency mental clinic.

As a result of the sickness and ill health of his mother who had to work, no father, and siblings who were much older, Sam had developed very little ego strength. The television set became his friend as he sat passively, feeling protected by its existence.

Five children can create a simple video game through movement. They can be "carried" in by six others, 3 on one side, 3 on another, walking zombie-like until they are put down. The leader pushes the mimed button and the machine does its work. The patient can ignore it thereby making the attachment to the TV even stronger. Or, he can seem puzzled, or become somewhat interested, showing the possibility of becoming diverted from TV.

After this event he retreats inside himself and becomes detached again. At this point one of the objects can be introduced from among the props. It can be any item from the list. It is decided beforehand that he will ignore anything placed before him at this point. A new understanding of time is experienced by the audience in the role of experts who watch him. It is the kind of time that people in institutions live with. As long as he is in character, in short, alienated, he will provide a focus.

Since he's not paid much attention to the video game, (depending upon the decisions made by the leader), a mimed TV is brought in. Students will have developed exercises which they now carry out in groups as though they're the TV show. Either the audience, the leader, or the person in role changes the channel by miming the action and by saying the number: for example, "7" can be the cue for those involved to begin using their spontaneous dialogue in accordance with a particular style and type of program. The patient's concentration upon the set is intense as the program melds into a commercial on breakfast cereal.

At first he gets very excited and begins to grab the cereal that has been placed on the shelf nearby. He also reacts noticeably to violent sections by engaging in mimed fighting. The cereal is forgotten but a bear is grabbed and fought with until part of it is pulled apart. This worries him and he becomes fearful and unresponsive again.

At this point one of the class members can volunteer as a child psychologist and find another toy to try to get his attention. He turns away from the volunteers because this is the only toy given to him by his father. The mother mentioned that his father had wanted him to be better coordinated for playing sports so gave him the ball but only played with him once.

Another commercial comes on and as the virtues of the product are being elaborated upon, Sam grabs the aspirin and begins to wolf it down. This emphasizes his lack of ego strength as he is unable to resist the sales pitch of television and thus swallows a dangerous amount of medicine without supervision. In short, it can be deduced, he eats only when influenced by TV. The next commercial is for dog food. The commercial is mimed, and the boy mimics the commercial by miming the process of feeding an imagined dog, after which he pets it and pulls it toward him. But realizing his hands are empty and reacting to the audience with embarrassment, he grabs the toy bear which he has wrestled with. He sees the bear's vulnerability and tries to get its parts to stay together but realizes the damage cannot be rectified.

Scenario for girl

In comparison to the boy, she is more integrated psychologically due to the fact that she had the attention of both parents. However, she is very hostile toward her mother whom she blames for her father's having left. This hostility is expressed toward anything that may remind her of this situation.

The fact that she had been a cheerleader in her junior year of high school, and upon trying out in her senior year had not been chosen, collides with her already inferior self-image. The two disappointments, her father's leaving and her not being chosen cheerleader have been the factors contributing to her depression. Her mother had worked temporarily at a counselling center so she entered her into this experiment hoping to receive some financial assistance. Since her mother has been rejected, the TV set becomes even more important as an indirect parent. Commercials are prescriptive, and she turns to the props as the commercials suggest.

During the first time through, the leader may want to plant definite cues and to order them in a progression so that the chosen facts are revealed. It is better to allow information to accompany the actions and reactions of the patient rather than pressing too many facts on the observers before the patient is brought in. This way, fact is coordinated with feeling, and the impact is greater. For example, she relishes anything connected with her father, but turns away from her cheerleader's paraphernalia.

Schizophrenia, autism, alienation, depression, drug dependence, attempted suicides are all illnesses which are continually occurring in our society, and the symptoms can be identified and recognized by children as a factor in prevention. It is also possible that increased understanding and self-empowerment through drama will enable children to develop empathy rather than a caustic attitude leading to criticism and abuse toward people with mental illness, because knowledge is replacing fear.

Final questions
It's all right to ask these after the drama because the children have developed some empathy.

Do you know of people who are mentally ill?
Do you ever feel threatened by them?
What are signs that you recognize about mental illness?
What causes mental illness?
Can you think of ways that it can be cured?

If the leader thinks the children are socially healthy enough not to automatically categorize the role as a "mental case, weirdo", these same questions can be asked at the beginning of the drama leading into the concept. When the leader in role decides to bring the drama to a close she can ask several of these questions again, but rephrase them slightly.

Do you think you would still feel threatened by them? If not, how has your thinking been changed?
As a result of your position as an expert in the field, do you think you are able to recognize signs and causes of mental illness?
Do you have any ideas now that you think could work to cure mental illness? Are these ideas different from those you had at first?
If there is interest in filling out the form, the leader continues in role, guiding them and answering their questions.

Conceptualized Form

Name_____Case#___Date_____

Length of interview_____

Presenting problem: Indicate to what extent each of the following is a reason the client came for counseling.
career___educational___personal___ interpersonal ___ environmental___

Specifics:
Check each of the following that is now present
suicide considered ___ suicide attempt____
excessive drug/alcohol use____ sleep disturbance ____
eating disorder____ other_____

Check if each of the following is a major source of stress in the client's life
health___ school___ work ___ relationship ____ family ____ other_____

Relevant history:
medication____ specify
_____
previous counseling _____ specify
_____
mental status, describe
_____
_____
_____
_____

Recommendation:
type of service recommended
1. individual counseling 2. couples 3. group   4. walk- in

To what extent do you think the client benefitted from counseling?
 none 1 2 3 4 5 greatly

History and Oppression

Dramas about oppression can be difficult because the children must feel oppressed or there's no reason to do the drama. In order to have the license to oppress them, they have to allow themselves to be led into whatever type of oppression the drama is dealing with. If the leader gets their conscious consent then a single look from her during the drama will remind them of that delicate thread necessary for belief (see Chapter 2, Negotiation).

A very simple way to start and one which will give them a direct experience with history is to PLAY SCHOOL following the tradition practiced about 100 or so years ago whereby you, the teacher, have absolute authority.

Each individual has experienced oppression in some form by their acknowledgement of an authority figure which at times may not have been their choice. The leader can help the students draw many analogies to their own lives and the lives of those they study in history. In this way they can also get a perspective in relation to how modern the concept of human rights is. It is hoped that this concept will develop appreciation for the fragility of the human condition.

The classroom of 1899

At the Museum of the Colorado Historical Society in Denver children experience the type of classroom that existed at the turn of the century. First, they see slides of the city and the period, which of course includes information about the Colorado gold rush. They are also given instruction by a person in role as a cowboy who teaches them about branding, roping, lassoing, tying knots and baking a cherry pie. (The pie is baking during the lesson.) Of course, at the end of the session, they also get a piece of the pie and the recipe.

I was struck by the edifying arrangement of the museum, because they have made history so available to a wide range of onlookers by their application of a time-line, using the scale of an inch to represent a year. Within this display individual items are extended by a pole horizontally jutting out toward the viewer. In the classroom simulation, the schoolmarm is in "shadowy" role, going into role to represent the period and coming out to ask questions and explain background to the children. These particular children were in the 3rd grade, and it was summertime, so they were a little hyperactive and at times giggled, but in general internalized the experience, and I'm sure could have written an essay about it.

Here is a glimpse into the classroom of 1899.

The teacher: Good morning, children.

Out of role: My name is Miss____ and of course all the children would say hello to their teacher.

Children: Good morning, Miss_____.

In role: Shall we stand for the flag salute?

Out of role: Do you know who the president of the United States was in 1899? None did.

It was President William McKinley.

And of course, it would be much cooler weather than now. You would have had to walk to school because there were no school buses. When I was young growing up in Denver I had to walk four miles to school. You needed much heavier clothing. It would be left in the cloakroom in back of this room. That's also where you'd leave your lunch pail, which you'd have to bring with you because you couldn't go home, and there were no cafeterias. We ate our lunches in one large room, sitting on hard benches. Even if we finished our lunch in five minutes, we still had to sit for that half hour without talking.

Sometimes, the teacher would check to see if hands were washed after playing outside before school.

(Back in role) Hold out your hands, palms up. As soon as recess comes, you go and wash your hands. (Designating a particular child.)

Now let's all stand up. (Flag salute.) My, what about those shirts sticking out? Tuck your shirts in. Sit down, please.

On these cards I want you to write your name. Your full name. No nicknames. Please pass them forward. Now, I will call your name according to where you're seated. Please sit where you're sitting now. And stand when I call your name.

Each time I call on you, you are to stand. And whenever you speak to me you are to say, ma'am, no ma'am, or yes ma'am.

Now we're going to practice our penmanship circles. We can't use pens today because Gerald stuck Suzy's pigtails in the inkwell last week. Are there any left-handed people here? You know, you're supposed to write with your right hand. (Out of role.) And you know that those who were left-handed were usually forced to write with their right hand at this time.

(Back in role.) All right, let's practice these circles, in the air. On this paper I want you to put your name in the left-hand corner.

Now we want to use our exercise bar. Pass these back. Stand up, please. Hold the bar with both hands and move it around in a circle in front of you, to the sides, over your head.

Oh, I see _____ doesn't have his shirt tucked in. That means he needs to stand in the dummy's corner.

If you want to stand up here, you laugh again and you will.

Next, can I have 1 person from each row pass out the readers? Remember to stand when you read. All right_____will you begin on page 34, please.

(Out of role)

This was generally what took place within the hour.

Background

If one goes back through history reviewing this topic of oppression, it can be seen that the vanquished were expected to carry out the tasks for the victor's survival, as were the peasants for the lord of the castle.

Even though in Russia under Alexander II, the Emancipation of 1861 granted the serfs personal freedom together with allotments of land, serfdom did not end in Russia until the revolution in 1917; in Japan, until 1946; and in China not until the fall of the last dynasty in 1911. Even now, 80% of the population of China are still peasants using an ox and plow.

During the hunting and gathering period of history, slavery did not exist in the form we know it today. It's real beginning was during the change when going from a subsistence economy to a market economy. At this time large tracts of land were taken over by a few wealthy landowners. Slaves were mainly obtained through capture, or imprisonment resulting from crimes, birth, and sale. There are still vestiges of some of these conditions lasting into the 20th century, but in the main, the practice has not survived.

Until 1946 in French West Africa all able-bodied males had to work 15 days a year on the roads; even now in the People's Republic of China, the situation exists whereby each peasant must give 10 days each year to the government for road work and other public projects.

In Greece and Rome, just as in the South of the United States, domestic slaves were treated with more dignity than were miners or agricultural slaves. Slavery was not considered wrong and relations between a master and slave could remain congenial as long as the slave wasn't mistreated.

Even in India today the caste system, which Gandhi tried so hard to eliminate, still exists. although the designation of pariah or untouchable, the lowest on the ladder, has largely been eliminated.

In Muslim countries today the role of women seems to outsiders to be comparable to that of a slave.

In America, the Native American population was sometimes used as slaves, particularly when working in the mines. However, unlike the Black, they were more difficult to subjugate and contracted the white person's diseases more easily. Also, since the country was familiar to them, they could escape. Usually mission life was not as hard on them as it was on the blacks because the missionaries wanted to convert them from "paganism." The Catholic fathers considered the need for temperance in order to win "souls."

The characteristics that follow embody acts of oppression and become part of the action in the *California Missions* and *Immigration* dramas:

    standing and waiting
    authority figures in complete charge
    humiliation (generally meted out)
    no self-expression, including talking
    no regard for safety, health or comfort

These same situations can be initiated by the leader through her questions of the children. "What would be some of the conditions you think oppressed people would have to endure?" If they don't come up with as complete a list as you'd like, then ask questions such as the following: "How did they suffer embarrassment? How were they frustrated about their situations? How were they mistreated?" Even if the students had no background external to themselves, they could deduce answers from their own common fund of knowledge.

At the beginning the leader would know which pictures to show them and the kinds of questions appropriate to ask.

Pictures need to be selectively chosen and highlighted through the use of questions. The questions included here are general.

1. How are the Indians' and whites' life-styles different now?

2. How was the Indian life different from that of the pioneer?

3. How did these differences contribute to allowing the whites to conquer the Indian?

4. How are these differences contributing to our life now? those of the whites? those of the Indians?

The constantly moving circle-spiral of economic dependence moving toward political intolerance comes into conflict over raw materials. This condition will be seen as a universal trend running through the events of all of our histories and is the single most common theme running through these dramas.

History is all of our stories. To take an event out of history and translate it from a narrative occurrence into a dramatic happening is the goal of these dramas. It is not a story with a beginning, middle, end, but "a line in a history book" (Dorothy Heathcote), or story in the newspapers today from 12,000 B.C. For the child it is making literature and history live in the present. Just because we were born into this world without this knowledge doesn't mean it didn't happen and doesn't effect us, because it did happen. To paraphrase George Santayana, those who are ignorant of their history are doomed to repeat it.

Gold? Are you sure?

The Gold Rush
(LA, Soc Stud, Hist) 4-8

Objectives
1. To teach plot construction through the use of frozen tableaus, (see Chapter 9, Plots)
2. To examine a period of history using a chronological sequence of events.
3. To become aware of the concept of greed and how it permeated society then, as well as now (see Chapter 3, Analogy).

Materials
Glitter to represent gold or nuggets; Western costume pieces, mainly hats and neckerchiefs; some type of an authentic noise maker such as a bull-horn, whistle; background music to play between scenes; cue boards; maps on grocery bags, made to look old; pictures from Social Studies/History texts from the period.

Strategies
Present-day technology such as a television studio is used as a setting to tape a program in which school children will perform for other school children. The leader provides background material in the form of narration between scenes to acquaint the child audience with a historical perspective and to provide a bridge between then and now. Cards are used with short statements outlining task activities for the children to participate in. During the "takes" the leader as director, in an "authoritative" role coaches the children in their roles by asking for more facial expression, more emotion, etc. and suggesting retakes when necessary. The leader can also pace the scene, slowing or speeding it up. "Quiet on the set," can be used regularly as well. The children are in role as "experts," actors.

Beginning questions
How many routes and which were used to make the trip?
How was John Sutter affected by this find?
Did the miners become rich? Who did? How was the Gold Rush important to the movement West?

Drama
Exact dialogues are included to give the leader some idea of possibilities. However, the leader needs to ask the children to assume an <u>attitude</u> (see Chapter 4, When Children Speak for

Themselves).   She also needs to have them ask questions of themselves such as those which would be included in a biographical sketch. Specific questions also initiate their thinking. What do you think Sutter would have said? What do you think the Mexican landlords said?, etc. In this way they can use their own ideas and translate them into dialogue that becomes spontaneous.

Leader in role

Good morning ladies and gentlemen. As you may have heard we are going to make a videotape of those pivotal points in American history. Today the Gold Rush is our topic.   Do you have some ideas for scenes that may be part of this tape? Make a list on the board. After the list is made remind them that the events need to be listed in chronological order. They may be divided up into groups of about 4 or 5 children each to plan their dialogue and actions.   The leader can then watch each group in preparation in order to plan the transitional narrations in between scenes.

(Sutter is dressed up.   He requests land from Mexican ranch owners.)

Take one, Scene 1

(Two people representing Mexican ranchers are facing Sutter. He is initiating an offer to obtain their land.)

Sutter: I'll protect this land from being exploited by using it. I want to build a sawmill right here at this spot (refers to map), at the juncture of the American River with the Sacramento River. Since there are thousands of acres of forest land, trees will be brought to this point, and I'll charge a fee for cutting the timber. Other than what I need to make the place go, you'll receive the rest. Do you have any questions?

Those playing Mexicans can reveal their suspicions by asking questions which Sutter confidently answers.

Leader's narration

And we know that these Mexican leaders gave Sutter 50,000 acres east of San Francisco Bay where he built a huge farming, ranching, and trading empire.

Take one, Scene 2
(Another person plays Sutter, who builds a waterwheel to harness the energy to build the sawmill.)
Sutter: We have 50,000 acres to care for. Most of them are rich in timber and need to be logged. The rest of the land needs to be planted in crops. And then the saw mill needs to be built right here. (He goes into detail about its construction and uses a map.) Let's begin to clear this land right here; turn these acres over here; and now from this pile of wood that the Indians cut yesterday, begin constructing the sawmill. (One person becomes the water wheel; another rips the bark off the logs; another places the logs under the saw; another becomes the blade to cut logs; another sands the logs; and finally the process of stacking the logs begins according to the picture. (in their text) (The leader makes sure the cameras are on the whole group.)
Sutter's audience can include either businessmen from whom he needs support or workers whom he needs to inform about duties.

Leader's narration
Sutter sent John Marshall down to the south fork of the American River to test the sluice openings. The sawmill was working properly, but needed more power so (show) **he narrowed the openings, and left the sluice openings open all night to see if they were large enough.** The child playing the part of John Marshall bends down toward the river suspiciously. He continues to examine it. He takes a sample of the rock and another, and after some quiet reflection he suddenly gets up and calls to the workers.
Marshall: Finish clearing that ravine and then take the rest of the day off. I'm going to see Sutter at the ranch. I'm sure it's gold!

Leader's narration
It was gold, but he had to be positive, so he trucked for 40 miles to tell Sutter.

Take one, Scene 3
Marshall: Mr. Sutter, Mr. Sutter—, close the door—I made the test and then I ran—here, it's gold—what dya think?
Sutter: If you're right—then—do you realize what this means?
Marshall: Yea, we'll all be rich—
Sutter: (Shakes his head.) Don't let it out. (He holds his head in his hands.) Are you sure?
Marshall: Come yourself, and see.

Leader's narration
John Sutter had no illusions.   He knew his lumber
empire would change, but probably   never realized how
much.   Sam Brannan was the entrepreneur who spread the
word.   He came to Sutter's Fort to find out for himself and
decided that the miners would need supplies.   Within two
weeks, San Francisco had become a ghost town.   Brannan
was a Mormon who had preached—but soon realized
another future.

Take one, scene 4
Leader places groups of children: working on crops, cutting trees,
building a farmhouse, building fences for cattle.
Brannan: Did you hear?   Gold—right here in California—
that–a-way and you'll find a store that'll supply whatever you need.
(Groups interact with Brannan and question him about gold.)
Leader's narration: Word got out and it took from January
until May for the full impact to be felt.   Soon the hysteria
had spread as far as Hawaii, to the southern tip of South
America to the East Coast.   Thousands made the trip
across oceans, across the country, across Panama since
there was no canal as yet.

Take one, scene 5
A group of travelers are moving, pulling their load, carrying
babies and children. The leader calls, "Freeze." An interviewer goes
up to ask them questions about their journey, and they create a very
sorrowful story.

Leader's narration
By this time Sam Brannan had built as many stores as
he had time to.

Take one, scene 6
(Scene shows students: building, finishing and putting tools away,
carrying in supplies, and customers entering and looking for items. A
student becomes the proprietor of the general store as he's asked for
supplies.)
Proprietor: Here comes the dealer in claims. You have to pay a
little for it but that means no one else can mine on it.
Dealer: These here claims is for those mines that are still close
to the find, but they're going fast. This is worth $10 now, but may be

$20, $40 tomorrow. Here you are.
    Miner: How do we know these is real?
    Dealer: I'll take you out there.

Leader's narration
    The group traveled for several days. The claim dealer pointed the way. He said that it's right next to that rock there. "I'll be on my way back to town where you can find me."

Take one, scene 7
Everyone works together to get the camp site ready: gathering firewood, building a shelter, cooking, mining.

Leader's narration
    You've been mining for several days, but have found nothing. A stranger enters carrying a mimed rifle.
    Stranger: This here's my land and I want you off it before I count three.
    Miner: But, I purchased a claim here.
    Stranger: This is fake. Here's my claim—it's a deed to the property. There's all kinds of swindlers around.

Leader's narration
    Meanwhile John Sutter could not pay back all the money he had borrowed to buy supplies, pay and feed workers, and build up his ranch.
    After the '49ers had come many of them had settled down. California's population had risen from a few thousand to hundreds of thousands. Mexico had lost the war which was fought over this (use map) **southwestern corner. California soon became the 31st state in the Union.**

Take one, scene 8
(A sheriff enters where Sutter is seated, still holding his head in his hands.)
    Sheriff: In the name of the state of California, we're surveying this here property. It'll be divided up and auctioned off. I stopped by the sheriff's office to find your deed, but you don't have one. You're owing in land taxes beginning now, unless you remove yourself directly.

Leader's narration
Sutter went bankrupt. He filed his claim for the land in Congress, but it never was accepted.

Final questions
How was the Gold Rush important to the country as a whole?
Do you think Sutter was greedy?
What did he want to do?
(If he had been greedy, he would have reacted differently when Marshall made the discovery.)
Who did profit from the Gold Rush?
Do you think people are greedy today?
What makes people like that?
What happens when it goes too far?

Extensions
Use Exercise 26 and Exercise 29 in the Character section. More than two people can be involved. Suggestions are: a newspaper printing office upon hearing of the discovery; the meeting between a person with a false claim and the legal landowner; a believer in the Gold Rush making a business fortune like Brannan and a non-believer like Sutter who seemed to be in despair, knowing the consequences.

In the exercise section, Plots, show *Three Freezes* depicting specific scenes to which the class can give titles.

In the exercise section, Speech, use Exercise 34, *Reporting/ viewpoints*. Each person takes a different point of view about the Gold Rush: Brannan, Sutter, miner, swindler, Mexican government, U.S. government.

California Missions
(LA, Geo, Soc Stud, Hist) (4-8)

Research

An order was sent out in 1809 by the King of Spain to proselytize and bring the Indians into the white man's way of thinking since the former's gods were considered pagan. This step has been viewed as controversial and a contributor to genocide, since following it the Indian population dropped by 1/3. The last mission was founded in 1891. The Indians provided free labor and, like any vanquished people, were definitely bonded and in a state of slavery.

Preparation

For depth it is helpful if the children have time to design a symbol to place on their headband which stands for their Indian name. They may also plan hand movements to express their name.

Welcome my children. You have been chosen to do the work of the church.

Objectives

1. To look at a period of history dealing with oppression vs. freedom.

2. To emphasize the contradictory values of the Indians and their caretakers, the Catholic fathers.

Materials

A tape of Indian chanting; costume pieces will be required for optional roles, an eagle,1-2 padres, 1-2 soldiers, a drum for control and announcements, a sack with Indian artifacts, a bell, pictures of Indian life, Indian photos, headbands. (No feathers. Feathers encourage superficial stereotypical interpretations.)

Concept

Children are pressed into their roles so they can experience the type of oppression that many cultures and individuals have known at some time in their lives. As a result a shift in attitude is made from the negativity of resentment to a more true understanding of history through the leader's final questions.

Strategy

This drama has been carried out by the leader taking on all the roles which require the children to feel oppressed, while a few children were in role as her assistants. Except for these few who volunteer to assist, the rest become Indians. After the children are questioned as a group about the central topic, the type of negotiation which follows is essential for these dramas to work so that the children may really feel the impact of being subjugated. The fact that some may giggle in embarrassment is only in the transition of going from their pedestrian selves to their selves in the drama, that of becoming a subjugated Indian. They must feel their Indianness by repeating their Indian names. The leader continues in the role of the villainous padre/soldier who abuses and commands with one voice. She humiliates the messenger and the children in their roles as Indians. She needs to be centered in her "authoritative" role and go slowly in order to offer the children the opportunity of feeling their roles.

Story

The children are taken through what may have been a typical day of living and working in a California mission as enslaved Indians. The leader must be consistent in her use of pressure in role to keep the experience occurring. Toward the last half of the drama she has given the role of messenger to a child who will become her "devil's advocate."

Beginning questions

Pictures of Indian life are shown and circulated to help the children begin to experience their roles. As these pictures are passed, questions are asked to encourage a continuous thought process to occur.

How were the Indian beliefs different from the white man's?

How do most Indians live now?

What did we think the Indian should learn from us? (We didn't respect their way of life at all and decided they should speak our language, dress our way, and become Christians. Of course we learned how to plant beans and corn from them but beyond these two staples, they didn't use agriculture as a way of getting food.)

How did they find their food? (gathered)

How did this effect their use of the land? (Nomadic, no private ownership.) So, you can see that as a result of two conflicting beliefs, the two groups didn't get along.

Repeating the rules in the negotiation process

In order for this drama to work you need to believe in your role, and to allow yourself to be verbally abused. What happens is that many children begin giggling from embarrassment. But what will happen if everyone does that? Try to find a way into the drama that helps you to believe in yourself as an Indian person. Do you think we have something to learn from this past way of life? What?

Preparation

(Optional): Use the generic Exercise 16, *Talking Hands*, in the exercise section, Imagination; **think of your Indian name and find a way of showing it with the movement of your hands.**

I'll begin. (Speaking while using hands to illustrate): **My name is Laughing Water. I was born beside the waterfall. And you---** (Continue until all the children who wish to have expressed and/or said their Indian name.)

A visualization process is conducted: Put on the Indian chants and have the children close their eyes. Narrate over the tape. **We feel the dry wind from the desert and see the brown hills in the distance. For many moons we see people traveling through these hills. We see and hear that they make a**

stone temple to their gods and ring a bell before they
speak to them.   Our Indian brothers and sisters have
carried water from the river for them.   Now, the river is dry.
We must prepare to move to higher country.   Let us pack
our goods.   Open your eyes. Each "family group" rolls up the
skins which cover their dwelling.   At this point the leader changes
roles and becomes a soldier.

Leader as a soldier (or one of the soldiers):   I see you are
making your escape.   There's no need.   I will guide you to
a place where you will find all you need.   Food, shelter,
and water.   But most of all, people to care for you.   Follow
me.   Make a circuitous path so that ten steps, not more, are covered,
but it isn't repetitious. The music begins to fade out. Wait here.

Transition

The leader turns and exchanges her soldier's pieces for that of a
padre which include a black drape and a large cross.

Leader: (with a sterner tone) **Welcome, my children.   You
have been called to do the work of the church.   You have
been chosen because you are humble and seek to please
your maker.   Enter and form yourselves into two lines.** The
leader mimes opening a door, continues to guide them and marks with
her arms the area to be covered for one line and the other line.   This is
done so that room space is economically used.   Both lines are facing
each other.   She walks in between the two lines of children and
stands briefly at one end or the other. Whenever anyone whispers or
giggles the leader emphasizes quiet by calling out: **Silence. This is
the house of the creator. You will remain respectful. Take
this headband off.   Whatever your Indian name, you will
now think of yourself as part of this mission.   And you will
receive a new name.   I will collect the headbands.** An effective technique is for the leader to remove the headbands with a jerk
signalling their lower status. A small vessel holding water is mimed.
**You will step forward one at a time to receive your new
name and the blessing of a drop of water upon your
forehead.**   This ritual can be left out if time is a priority.   The
leader may travel to each separately, going up to dot their foreheads
with "water" and give them an Anglo name. It is a good idea to have
a lot of old fashioned names ready to be able to retrieve them
quickly. **You are Jane, Thomas, Lawrence, Harold, John,
Joseph, Peter, Louise, etc.** Another effective way of lowering
status is to rip off labels which contain their Indian names and to

complete this naming ceremony by giving them an Anglo name.

Leader: **Silence.** Say this only when necessary. **Bow your head. Please, our Creator, let these newly named be your servants, building a better future for us all.   Guide their newly christened lives and hands as we work the soil and haul water.** Instead of Ah-men, a phrase in gibberish can sound like a Latin religious phrase to finish the prayer. Lead them as though they were going outside. **Time to work. Clear the brush on this field.** <u>A repetitive chant which continues with the same rhythmic beat</u> is started either by playing the Indian chants on the tape recorder, and/or the leader begins to blend into the work while moving in harmony with the chant, demonstrating her demands by doing the work. **Follow me.** This way they can work in unison and their energy is directed. Allow for some work time as the leader participates in "shadowy" role chanting and moving for a few moments. As soon as their movement is coordinated, turn toward the bell and ring it.

Time for prayers.   Kneel this time. A similar gibberish phrase as last time is chanted by the leader. **Let our work be good; accept our humble hearts.** A gibberish, again.

Back to the fields.   Each of you must lift one of those jars of water like this, carrying it on your hip for they are quite heavy.   Slowly, let out the water over the soil this way. Again, the leader demonstrates and in order to keep the work synchronistically rhythmic, she bends down after a few beats to let some water out, and then stands straight and takes a step, bends down, etc., all to the same kind of beat as used before. After this has been going on for a minute or so, the announcement is made that prayers are in order again.

Bell is rung. **Time for prayers.   Kneel.   Bow your head. Bless this work. This land. May Your work be done by our humble spirits.** The same Latin sounding gibberish again. **Stand. Back to work.   Take these poles** (mimed) **and dig at the earth in order to loosen it.** The same example of rhythmic movement is shown and chanted by the leader. **Begin.** If there is another adult to step in at this time it would help to make the mood more one of assumed superiority toward the Indians. Or, after they're working the leader pressures them by demanding they work harder.

You're going too slowly.   Faster!   No dinner will be served this crew.   And you shall work one hour after the sun has set.   Silence! Keep them on task, and the leader reminds them of the rhythm again. **Remain together and work faster.**

At this point, beckon one of the children out of the group and give him a card with the following message on it:

You are to spread the word secretively to the others. You've heard from an Indian runner that many Indians at the next mission have been forced to work without food. They are dying of the white man's diseases and cannot use their own remedies. The child in role asks them these questions in order to stimulate their involvement toward anger. **How long are we going to stand for this? Isn't this our land that we're being forced to work?**

As devil's advocate becomes the oppressor's angel, the leader continues on in the role of the villainous padre/soldier who abuses and commands with one voice. She continues to humiliate the runner and also the children as Indians. She needs to go slowly pressing them into the feeling of their roles. The drama works from here to a climactic point as the leader continues to verbally abuse the Indians while the child in role as devil's advocate becomes the catalyst for her anger by standing up for the Indians. This need not last more than a few minutes, or until the time the children rebel on their own.

Final questions

Do you think you got some glimpse of how the Indians may have felt?

Was there anything or anytime in particular that helped you to identify with them?

What would someone have to take away from you that would make you lose your identity?

Can you think of other times in history when people were oppressed?

Extensions

The leader uses narration to bring the facts up-to-date. For example, the atrocities and injustices can be expressed right along with the concept of caring that was righteously acknowledged during that period. Together with this, the present-day concept of sainthood can be introduced in reference to Father Serra who is being considered for this honor.

The mannequin can be introduced as Father Serra. As a result of some research that has taken place, both among the children and the leader, questions can be put to the leader as though she, as Father Serra, has returned to the 20th century to be questioned about the inequities suffered by the Indians that the children wish to resolve. (Use Exercise 29 in Character section.)

Use Exercise 28, *Inanimate Objects,* in the exercise section, Character. Either accompanying the above lesson or separately, but in response to the feeling of humiliation, students can choose an object, such as their headband which they may have tucked away somewhere on their body, to speak for them while answering such questions as:

How did I feel about my owner being treated in this way?

What changes did I see in the way the land was treated? ----the animals were treated?

How did I feel about the kind of food that was eaten which was unlike the Indian diet?

How do I feel about the sickness and diseases which were being passed on to the Indians by the whites?

Why did the Catholic fathers think they were actually helping the Indians?

Can you think of this type of relationship happening elsewhere at any time?

Could it happen again?

How can people prevent this from happening? (Knowledge, having dignity, and goals.)

The First Thanksgiving
(LA, Soc Stud, Hist) (K-8)

Introduction
Before beginning this drama, the teacher may wish to engage the children in an art lesson: the Indians making headbands with symbols for an Indian name on the headbands; the Colonists making hats and collars. Before or during the drama, both groups can make maps of their lands and crops.

This drama can be the culmination of a unit and/or can be expanded in many directions. Basically the teacher guides each member of a group to identify with his character in relation to his group's life goals. At the end, she joins the groups while guiding them to explore their human quest.

Objectives
1. To understand the difficulties in settling a new land.
2. To experience two distinctly different cultures.
3. To understand how it is possible to share differences and cultivate friendships.
4. To develop an identity, thereby synthesizing ones own personality with historical concepts.

Concept
Though we know the occasion on which the Pilgrims invited the Indians for a feast, existed, we don't have any single factual account and so accept a generalized version. Perhaps the examples given to us from paintings exist as the common reference from which most people develop possible scenarios. The values of sharing, friendship, and trust are all implicit in this event.

Materials
Headbands: these can be strips of muslin around the forehead tied at the back   for the Indians. (No feathers. Feathers in headbands encourage superficial, stereotypical interpretations.) Shells, stones, feathers, and a mandala drawing (see drawing on next page) of Indian symbols; baskets of dried corn and squash for trading; collars and caps for Pilgrim women; hats and collars for Pilgrim men, (optional for both); a tape of waves, sea, and/or music depicting a storm at sea; newsprint and pens for making maps; any paintings

showing this historic occasion; a Mayflower Compact document which needs to be made.

Story/strategy

There is the romantic story about the first Thanksgiving when the Pilgrims invited the Indians for a feast. Since there are several different accounts, we'll include a generalized version as related by these different factual accounts. The teacher asks the children how they want to split up between Colonists and Indians. At least one-third need to be Colonists to make the drama successful. She goes back and forth between the two groups helping them to edge into the drama until she brings them together. The children are in the role of experts, as Indians and Colonists. The teacher provides narration and guidance by means of an intermittent and shadowy role. Each time she introduces a new segment in the drama, she speaks in such a way as to indicate the coming activity by emphasizing its significance and at the same time, her expectations for the class: For example, "Now let us validate this agreement."; "Now let us meet our new friends." Towards the end she brings the two groups together by asking for a volunteer from each group to become a spokesperson. At any time she can open up the activities of the Indian group to the eyes of the Colonists who become "watchers" as the teacher guides them in their rituals. If there is no child who can or will be in the role as the single leader who offers the blessings for the harvest at the end, then she will step into an authoritative role.

Beginning questions

How were the lives of Indians and whites different in the New World? (In particular, clothing, houses, food, religion, and relationship with the land.)

How did the religions differ?

Since there were many differences, did this account for the difficulty in getting along?

Do you think we can try to get closer to some of these differences in order to see that there were similarities also?

Planning

After the teacher asks how the class wishes to be split up, she gets those who are to become the Indians started. They choose from a collection of symbols any one which blends with their chosen Indian name, or they may make up their own symbol to fit the name they choose. These are then drawn on their headbands. After they are finished with their own individual headband, they work together to answer questions about their character and tribe. How old are you? What particular talents do you possess? What is your importance to the tribe now and upon growing up? What is your daily routine? Is it different in summer, fall, winter, spring? What are the important crops your tribe grows? What customs does your tribe practice? What kind of environment does your tribe live in? What is the history of your tribe? These questions can be rhetorical to stimulate thinking and need not be solely academic with fixed answers. Depending upon the maturity of the group, it may be necessary for the teacher to lead the class as a whole in answering these questions at the beginning. She may ask for volunteers to become the elders of the tribe and choose from the chart of symbols those that may represent it. These may be artistically placed into a disk, circle, or mandala, symbolically representing what the tribe stands for. After individuals or groups are finished with their own headbands and character questions, they write in their journals as their character, answering some of these questions. They can become apart of the group effort in choosing the tribe's symbols for the circle drawing. Another group task is to have them draw their crops of corn, squash, potatoes, wild berries and nuts. Some may draw a map that includes forests, rivers, birds, animals, burial lands, hills, mountains, ocean, ceremonial grounds, and living space.

While the group which has chosen to become Indians is working, the teacher leads the group of Colonists to answer the following questions: How old are you? Why are you coming to the New World? What are your dreams for the future? What are you leaving behind? Both groups can write in their journals as their characters. Collars and hats may be made before or after the children have considered their identities. A map of their living space and crops can be drawn at this time.

Since more children usually want to become Indians, the tasks above will allow for time to complete their identities and feelings of bondedness. She will then be free to begin the drama with the Colonists.

Drama (Colonists)

If possible, the room can be dimmed in one part and a tape of ocean sounds is played. **Breathe deeply and feel the rocking of the ship.** The teacher narrates the following visualization process; the children are encouraged to close their eyes. **I could still hear the creaking of the ship, the wind rumpling the sail, the splashing of water against the bow.** (The tape is faded out.) **We are the lucky ones. Many died on that journey, and the cold of the winter storms and influenza took many others.** (Excitement in her voice.) **Now we have planted corn and gathered berries. The earth smell is strong on our hands as we harvest out first crops** (Open your eyes.)

If we work hard as His servants, he'll see to it that we find our future to be bountiful in this new land. Let us now pray for a good harvest. Help us to fare well.

The Mayflower Compact: Although this agreement for governing was signed many days before landing, truth is being altered for artistic license.

Let us validate an agreement to allow our present leaders to continue to guide us in our new life. We will call

this historical moment, The Signing of the Mayflower Compact, a beginning of government in the New World. It asserts that each of you will continue to have responsibilities under the guidance of your present leaders and that each will be responsible to the group, etc. Will you be the first? If you cannot write your name, place an X in the space. (Each signs.)

Planning

After this beginning with the Colonists, the children plan their crops by drawing them. Some may wish to write in their journals.

Drama (Indians)

At any time the teacher may go to the group which has chosen to become Indians, having them sit in a circle to 1) share their Indian names using hand signs, and 2) have those who volunteer explain the tribe's symbols. (See Exercise 16, in Imagination section, Chapter 9 for the following.) **Let us share our Indian names, given us at our birth to represent our connection with nature and our value to the tribe.** Each one who wishes to can be involved. **My name is Splashing River, for I was born beside the river just after my father rode downstream to place the gill nets across it.** Each one says his name as he moves his hands miming the images implicit in the name. There may be time for those who don't share their names now to do so later when the whole class is together at the end.

Planning

Since it is difficult to know how long these activities will take, the teacher is free to go back and forth, keeping each group involved and focused. When it is time, each group chooses a spokesperson to represent it, then the two groups are joined together. During the planning sessions and before the groups join, there is no need for them to be seen by each other; however, after the teacher decides to bring the two spokespersons together, both groups are open to each other, and the teacher must see that the sightlines are maintained.

Drama

Upon returning to the Colonists, she engages them in dramatic play by having them harvest their crops, hang them for drying, and build a storehouse in which to preserve them. During this time she models the activities as they begin to pattern her. **It's time for** harvesting. **You two get that row; the others take on the next few. Remember these have to be dried. We need to pull these up and dry them before they rot. As soon as you get a bag full, take them out and lay them down in the sun to dry. You have to pick all of these rows. These are potatoes; there are beets and cabbages. Let's get that storehouse built over there before the rains come. According to the plan for the storehouse, this flat stretch of land would be best. Let's start digging this space... about a foot deep for the foundation. The others can help by placing these logs around the perimeter for a foundation.** After the Colonists have done their chores, a spokesperson is chosen to visit the Indians. (Before suggesting the Colonists become open to the Indian group, the teacher needs to be sure the latter are ready to be watched.) **Which of you will volunteer to visit our native brothers and sisters?** Suggest that all become the eyes of the spokesperson while watching the Indians in their life. Now the Colonist group is open to the Indian group.

Approaching the Indian group, the leader speaks to them: **This is a member of the Colonists. We wish to speak with you. I'll translate if necessary.** He can speak haltingly, using a simpler vocabulary and using his hands more than usual.

May we have a spokesperson from this Indian group? When a volunteer steps forward the leader's narration continues helping to fill the moment of unification.

Now, let us join together. It is a great occasion when those representing two completely different cultures are united. Let us realize the benefits of nurturing peaceful relations with our native brothers and sisters. Will they introduce themselves to us and tell us about their tribe? They share their names and accompany them with hand signs, and the concept of their tribe's heritage can be narrated as a story while using the symbols of the circle drawing. If the children seem involved, then the teacher asks, as though outside the drama: "What do you think they would want to know about each other?" She gets a shopping list from the children that she can write on the board: farming crops, helping each other out, illness, other settlers, the future, the climate, each other's customs. If they seem tentative, then she can bring them together to bless the food and the occasion. **Let us be seated; we are coming together in peace to bless this food and to thank these friends who have shared their knowledge of the soil and planting so that**

our lives can continue. (As she says this she can lift up any of the dried food.)

If the preparations and background have been adequate, both in relation to academic facts and internal identity, then the leader's guidance will serve as catalyst and encouragement. (See extensions.)

Final questions

Why couldn't this kind of peaceful state continue? How important is the concept of trust? Explain. Why didn't this concept continue? What was one of the overriding differences between both groups in reference to land? Does anyone know the status of Indians today? Though there were many "broken promises and treaties," today Indian groups are being listened to. However, many of the lands which they call sacred have been claimed for development. The philosophies of private ownership versus the public domain are still in conflict. The Indians' concept of no property being privately owned, however, has not been abandoned by many.

Extensions

Both sides can offer prayers to their deities, blessing the food. Each dish is passed and contents are mentioned as a means of informing the other group.

Any of the following could be set up by the teacher, and/or planned with the children. A problem can be created: a child from the Colonists' side has developed small pox. As a result, one of the Colonists can turn into a doctor and together with the Indian shaman, each can practice some healing.

Since we know that this was a peaceful occasion, a messenger can be introduced to bring news of encroaching danger, either from other whites or Indians. This could bring the two groups even closer together in creating ways to stave off the aggression. A person from either group could have become an outcast as a result of having been shamed or rejected by his group because he had taken advantage of the others, stealing food, etc. and hence, be the cause of the above danger. Or, the source of the information can remain ambiguous.

A ritual could be held bringing both groups together.

Any of these situations the leader could initiate or ask the children to initiate, or the children may come up with the ideas themselves.

At any time, the leader can step out when she feels the drama is going well. Or, if the drama seems to need more focus and direction, she can introduce any of these situations or those the children suggest by maintaining her "shadowy" role which is somewhere between teacher and taking a role in the drama.

This drama has been carried out in grades K through sixth. It is very open-ended and can include different episodes, depending upon the classes' needs.

Westward Journey
(LA, Soc Stud, Hist, Geog) (2-8)

Objectives
1. To acquaint children with knowledge of the West through an autobiographical approach, and with the literary genre of Tall Tales.
2. To have children experience this situation first hand (grades 2-5).
3. To enable children to turn these experiences into their own by making up a series of scenes to represent the period. (grades 6-8)

Materials
A map, crudely drawn; any pictures of pioneers such as those in the book *Women's Diaries of the the Westward Journey* by Lillian Schlissel; music of Aaron Copland's *Rodeo, Appalachian Spring,* or *Billy the Kid*

We're goin' to git farmland...to start our life over...

Segments of the drama
　　Beginning questions
　　　Lower grades
　　　　Introductory notes
　　　　Preparation for the drama
　　　　Beginning of the drama: the campfire; stories; bed-down;
　　　　　work;
　　　　Introduction of the mannequin: an Indian visit
　　　　Final discussion
　　　Upper grades
　　　　Teacher's narration
　　　　Scenes described
　　　　Final discussion and questions
　　　　Follow up

Strategy
　　The leader takes on an "authoritative role" as wagon train leader. The children as pioneers are in the role as "experts." Whenever the leader thinks it is appropriate, each player may speak his inner thoughts (see soliloquy).

Beginning questions
　　Why did people go West? What were their dreams and hopes? What were the dangers? How did they find water and wood for fires on the way? How and what did they eat? What was their relationship with the Indians?

Lower grades, introductory notes
　　The children will spend a "day" traveling to and settling in the West.
　　Each group of five will become members of a family or a group of individuals who have decided to make this trip together. The music mentioned should be played softly in the background. Various trails that the pioneers took are shown and traced on a map, showing the states and any natural barriers.
　　Leader: (This will be read by the teacher as though it is from a book. It is paraphrased from *Little House on the Prairie* by Laura Ingalls Wilder.)
　　A long time ago, when all the grandfathers and grandmothers of today were little boys, little girls or were very small babies, or perhaps not even born, families were traveling West. They'd leave their homes lonely and empty, never to see them again.

There were too many people around now. You could hear the echoing thud of an ax that was some one else's ax or a shot that came from someone else's gun. Wagons were slowly creaking past them in the road. On the day they drove away, the town looked smaller and smaller, but they knew no harm could come to them in their wagon. Days of slow-moving sameness continued until the day that they came to the creek. The wagon's canvas was tightened and secured. The horses began bravely to cross the waters in which they sank deeper and deeper. At one point you could feel the horses lurch; in a moment all seemed to sink. One of the settlers jumped off swimming toward them, grabbing the reins and leading them across.

We continued to follow the creek bed until it fell past us as we headed almost due West by our compass. We traveled through the rolling hills of prairie land seeing smoke of an occasional fire rise in the distance. Not as often, a cross looked as though it had been planted as a reminder of our human frailty. What could it have been, to cause this one's death? Illness, an insect bite---so many strange diseases we'd heard of for which there were no cures. After several days more we finally settled alongside a creekbed that meandered on a ways. On the first night, after we'd collected the firewood and water from the creek, we washed off the day's heat and dirt. We got some good hot food and black coffee or cider into us, and we sat to hear all the strange stories about our adventures.

Preparation for the drama

It's time to think about <u>who you are</u> on this trip, your <u>age</u>, and <u>relationship</u> to the others in your group. Will you talk quietly about that with the members of your group? While you're waiting, will you be thinking about yourself as this pioneering person by answering these questions: What will happen on this journey? What could make us turn back? Will we make it? Why are we going? For instance, someone has just commented on turning back because there's a lot of smoke rising behind the hills. One child has died, possibly from some insect bite, and you know there is much danger that lies ahead. So you wonder about turning back. It is at this point that every-one must decide if this is to be his future. If so, what are your hopes and even dreams for the future in this new and dangerous land? Please use this time with your group to discuss these questions and decide on your character. You'll have 2 minutes.

Beginning of the drama
  <u>The Campfire:</u>
The teacher comes into role as the wagon train leader and instructs them about any rules or procedures she needs observed. The families introduce themselves. Polite chatter can ensue as participants intermingle and learn of each others' plans, etc.

The teacher asks the group to join her on the floor. Stories are selectively told by the leader.

Why do you suppose people told Tall Tales? They used the exaggeration as a form of humor and as a way to draw attention to how they felt about the bigness of everything. Everywhere there was land going in all directions, and by comparison, they felt very small. This was their way of having fun and at the same time, expressing the smallness and perhaps inadequacy they felt during these pioneering days.

(Paraphrased) When Paul Bunyan decided to go West, and needed to cut down any trees, he'd generally go ahead of Babe, his Ox. Babe was 40 ax handles high, but Paul was 60 ax handles tall, and used his ax like a scythe, swinging it back and forth to make a path that he could walk right through. I remember one time he was on one of those trips, when Babe was a calf, and Paul brought him along to butcher. A young fellow there who was homesteadin' said he'd put the calf in the barn for the night, to keep him out of the elements and keep his meat tender. Well, the next morning when we got up we looked out and didn't see no barn. The homesteader said that some mighty powerful winds do blow on the prairie at night or anytime. But he didn't think that any had been blowing in the night.

Someone thought that they had some binoculars, and they handed them up to Paul, and he stood up and looked around everywhere until he could see his ox. He could see him in the distance. He stood up and had the barn all hanging around him. Now that's how much he had growed in the night.

There are lots of stories about how Paul dug the Mississippi River. That's right. And of course I was there to see. After he pulled up as many trees as he needed, he made a raft and began plowing out the river. He put the raft on the plowed up part with the Ox, Babe, pullin' the raft to be sure the opening was big enough for big steamboats. He kept going out ahead just pulling his plow behind him. As soon as there was an opening, the water just washed in, and it saved the plains from being flooded. It acts like a sink drain, I reckon.

The other story I remember is about that Johnny Appleseed. He was a big guy, too. When Johnny Appleseed traveled West he sprinkled appleseeds everywheres. Well, he must have run out at the Mississippi River.

It was the Fall season and Paul came along and could see that the apples from the trees were going to rot. So he gathered enough apples with seeds in them for Johnny Appleseed to plant all the way to the Columbia River and that's what they did.

Bed down

After the storytelling, all are instructed to bed down. A "watch" is called. During this time the teacher may softly narrate in the background to provide a transition into sleep followed by wakefulness, morning chores, and either preparation for the journey or settlement. After the night has passed she calls them together for chores.

Work

We want to spend our time as if it were a day on the prairie 150 years ago. If this is where you plan to settle then here's the area squared off. You got them trees along the creek bed there, the hills in the distance over there, and what we just came through in back of us. Best to get started building some kind a shelter before the wolves find us. (A crudely drawn map is used.)

Best place to dig a well is probably at that low spot right over there. Find you some wood along the river there for your common shelter. Let's find out who's going to do what. All the men and boys over here. A third of you need to collect the biggest trees you can find along the river bed. The other third will clean off the bark and prepare the tree for building, and a third will dig the well. All the women and children will gather the biggest rocks you can find to be used for cooking, storing water, and building the fireplaces eventually.

A list of jobs is written on the board to be referred to when needed: map the area, dig a well, take water from the river and store it in the ground, build a large common building, gather rocks for the fireplace fires and for the well.

As soon as the sun is high overhead we'll stop for some cornpone made by these ladies on this metal grill they brought, and water brung up from the creek bed by

these girls.   The older women are taking care of the young children. The teacher continues to supervise as all are engaged in work. After a few minutes she may signal for them to stop for the mid-day break unless she wants to keep them going in the drama for the sake of intensifying their belief. When she stops them, they talk over the work done and that which still needs to be completed. She sends them back to work reminding them of the wolves, and their need to complete this today. This last step of doing the chores can be skipped if there is only time to speak about the following in the larger group.

Introduction of the mannequin: an Indian Visit

Various monologs are possible. The one given here is a fictionalized version of a lone Indian woman represented in the myth called *The Inland Whale* by Theodora Kroeber, *The Buffalo Woman*, and/or *The Girl Who Loved Wild Horses* by Paul Goble. After the leader warns the group that an Indian person is approaching who is not carrying a gun, she moves the mannequin toward them:

I come for help. My child needs food. I am part white. My mother was white, my father Indian. He died in the hunt. Afterward the tribe would not accept us. My mother sent me to boarding school. Afterwards I live with her and marry Indian hunter, have boy child. My husband disappears, no one knows where. Afterward, the tribe will not accept me. I take the horses to the high country. Horses obey me and become my family. Still my boy and I are not accepted. Mother die. Now, I must feed boy. The children can be guided to develop a relationship with the Indian. She can offer to guide them (in the manner of Sacajewea); as payment, they invite her and her son to become part of their train.

Final discussion

Just before the end of this session, she stops them and calls them together to speak with the members of their group about those thoughts having to do with dreams and hopes for the future. (See final questions at the end of the lesson plan.)

Upper grades, 5 and above

The same introduction can take place with older children in upper elementary school. In their smaller groups, then, they can plan and act out a series of scenes.

Scenes described

(To bridge this introduction with the feeling quality needed to enact these scenes, the children should listen to the music with their eyes closed against the following visualization carried out by the teacher.)

The long days of traveling seemed endless. Flat lands extending to the horizon begged for interruption. When the interruptions came, the scenery seemed to swallow them up: a windstorm and rainstorm raged and any motion at all required all the effort they could possibly muster. Suddenly, without warning, insects would come down, tornadoes would descend, and Indians would raid. The endless days were broken up now with warning signs, smoke in the distance, a streak of lightening, the earth rumbling. All the members of the group became a single hand pulling against the odds.

Each scene will include an observable activity in which the family group is involved in an enactment of an emotional issue.

1) You are part of a close knit family. A dreaded flu is going around. Drinking lots of water is the best way to keep it from getting worse. The only way you know of getting water is to dig a well. The child you are trying to save is running a high fever and may die unless s/he is able to get water.

2) The strongest man in your family has just died of scarlet fever and needs to be buried. Two children have just died also. The rest of you are looking forward to the future and have thought about all the changes that will take place in your lives in spite of the sadness.

3) You see some Indian warriors approaching your camp. You're holding your gun as though you are ready to defend yourself. You could take them one by one right now, but you realize you've no ammunition in your gun. So you wait. You tell the others, and all are deciding what to do as you wait.

4) You see wolves all around your camp. You see the older man of the family and you want to warn him. The warning will be for his protection, but also for yours and your family's. You and your family are trying to find a way to keep the wolves from attacking.

5) A fire is working its way across the prairie, directed by the wind. You know the only way to keep the fire from your camp is to make a little fire ring around it, which then needs to be put out. If everyone helps, it can be done.

Final discussion and questions

In what way are the dangers we face now similar to those faced in the past? How different? What are the dreams and hopes that we have now? How are they different, or the same?

Follow up

The children are requested to write their impressions in diary entries, or are assigned to write a Tall Tale.

Old Medicine Person
(Soc Stud, Hist) (4-6)

Objectives
To help children understand what it's like "to live in another person's shoes."

Materials
Pictures of Indian life, Indian chants on tape, drum, headbands for all. (Again, no feathers; they encourage stereotypical and superficial responses.) An environment is set up containing six-inch rocks (or for a less mature class, small stones, one for each child); baskets; a rug or rugs; three letters, one carried by the government official, one by the Indian person, and one a note on a "bundle" representing a baby. The monologue in this drama is based on the journey described in the book *The Way to Rainy Mountain* by N. Scott Momaday.

Concept
Though the idea of genocide is not brought up, it is introduced indirectly through the beginning questions. The children begin to realize in role as Indians that "promises are broken."

Strategy
The leader begins in "shadowy" role and slowly evolves into the medicine man or woman, in an "authoritative" role guiding the drama. Towards the end, she becomes a "devil's advocate" to get the children to turn against the U.S. army officer. In this way the children will follow this example and be able to express their aggression without inhibition. A child or an adult may play this role. In either case the person must be aggressive.

Story
The old medicine person tells of the difficult journey traveling from a place which is now known as Glacier National Park in the northern part of Montana, to the plains in Oklahoma. This is a true pilgrimage, which is written about in N. Scott Momady's book, *The Way to Rainy Mountain*, about the Kiowa tribe's migration. The children in role as Indians hear of this journey, which is immediately connected to forced migrations made at the request of the U.S. military. When the old person informs them that they are now

ordered to move from their land, she also introduces the idea that a white baby has been left "at their doorstep" to be cared for. At the end of this monolog by the old person addressing the children, the U.S. Army person enters to remove the Indians from their land. After this order, the Indian role intentionally baits the children, and they defend their land.

Beginning questions

How were the Indian people and white people different? (land, religion)

Do you think these were reasons why they didn't get along?

Do you think if the white man had never come to America the Indian tribes may have been constantly at war? Why, why not?

Do you think we have something to learn from the Indians' way of life? What?

Drama

Begins with the leader in a "shadowy" role. The leader stands in front of the class and starts to narrate. **The drama will begin now.** The leader changes in attitude slightly to suggest a change in demeanor, taking on a "shadowy" role that leads into an "authoritative" role.

Leader in role

Today and hereafter you will begin to know more about your tribe. You must carry on the traditions—even though you are young—the old are dying and knowledge is gone—those in their middle years have gone off to work, to make money so we can survive—only we are left, the very young and myself, the last old one— so take notice of each thing we do, for each thing has meaning for our tribe, and the white man would have us learn his ways. Join with your tribal members now and let us renew our traditions of trust. (See Exercise 4 in Senses.) **Listen and sense your Indian brothers' and sisters' presence as they move their hands over one part of your clothing. Your eyes are closed. You must become alert and receptive to that which is outside of you in case of harm. Open your eyes and see if you can decide where they were moving their hands. Now that there is more trust, it is time that each one will tell his or her secret Indian name to those on each side.**

The children are instructed to choose an Indian name for themselves in order to begin a process of identifying themselves as Indian children.

For example, Singing Grasses—place one arm horizontally across the front part of the body, while the other moves up perpendicular, intercepting the horizontal arm line and continuing its motion, upward, as the hand moves back and forth to describe the grass's movement as singing. **As you share your name, you become a member of the tribe by moving your hands together to show your name.**

(A crude drawing marking out the journey is given so the children can identify with the feeling of traveling.)

Leader: **You'll follow this pathway as you travel toward the old Medicine person.   Begin the chant Ah-Na-Hoo, Ah-Na-Hoo. This will signal the Old Medicine person that you approach.   Close your eyes to imagine this route. Open your eyes. Now begin your walk to the back country toward the Old Medicine person.** (One of the class members or an aide can lead the group in a zig-zag trail or circle to give the feeling of movement as they are taken in a pathway pattern that conforms to the space available. (Ten to 15 steps are enough.) At this time the leader changes by putting an old tattered poncho over her head and standing slightly bent holding a wooden stick to express age, becoming the Medicine Person.)

Medicine person
Welcome to this land.   You may be seated.   We meet here at this site on which our Indian history is written in these stones.   These stones tell of many years of traveling from the rainy forests to this dry country and land of the great buffalo herds.

For mature classes. **I want you to know this story of our tribe as you** (pick up stones) **pass these stones, feel the story of our long journey over desert and plain, through rivers and mountains.   As you feel the stones know the road of our ancestors.** She handles the stones, passing them as she speaks, and begins to tell the story of the tribes' migration.

For less mature classes, a variation: instead of passing the stones a ritual may be practiced here, before starting. **Each one take a small stone. Hold it to your chest where your heart beats. In this way you belong to the land as your ancestors did. Follow me in this circle. As we walk, listen to the history of** the stone. Feel your union with it. I have come from the ocean and have been pressed by the land over time, first by wind, then rivers, until I fell broken from my mother earth. I will live again as you place me in the soil. (kneel) Now that you have carried me at your heart, I carry your will with me to become part of the land again. Let us bury this pebble and repeat together, Ah-Na-Hoo, Ah-Na-Hoo, our chant meaning: I am you. Together. Ah-Na-Hoo, Ah-Na-Hoo.

(The following should be used for mature classes only.) The leader looks off into space as if seeing a vision. We ascended from the deep valley of rain and then up to the top of the world upon the mountains where we looked down upon the continent to see the grass lands and rivers. The old chief was my grandfather. He had a vision of a large bird rising over the land to help us on our way. From that day on the journey became one of fortune as though we were being led by this bird. One day there were suddenly meadow larks and quail in the open land. The dark red earth seemed to glow with the setting sun. At that time of day there was a deep silence. It is as though everything had stopped to let the sun leave the land. And then we heard a sudden piercing call of a bobwhite, and we knew that this was where we must settle. Here on this land.

Now that you have felt a union with Mother Earth and know the story of the tribe's journey, let us sit and reveal our Indian names that only our tribe will know. (Use Exercise 16 in Imagination.) The Indian names they have chosen contain movement which they can show with their hands. For example, Singing Grasses: place one arm horizontally across the front part of the body while the other arm moves up perpendicularly, behind the horizontal arm and continuing its motion upward, moving back and forth to represent the grass's movement as singing. Once you say this name you become members of the tribe by having your Indian brother or sister place the headband that's around your neck, around your head. My name is Valley of Tall Grass. Said this way. (Accompanies this with hand gestures.) Now let us share our names with each other and if you wish, say why you were given this name. For me, it is because it was the place where I was born.

(Have some start and then continue until all who wish are finished.) **Now, you are welcomed into the tribe. And remember, never say your Indian name to a white man. It is for this reason that I have called you together today. The white man has come to claim this land. We need to have a council meeting to decide what we're going to do.** (becoming angry) **This is our land.** The white man gave to us after we were moved far across the plain, and now they want to move us again, to where? The white man visits us today. We have been told that since the last treaty all the land north to the next mountain and west to the river is ours. Can we suffer any more "broken treaties?" (At this point there is a cry heard and a bundle is brought in by a child to represent a baby with a note saying: I leave my baby in your hands. Please keep it from harm, and raise it as an Indian. Sincerely, Mary Fisher. P.S. I am not an Indian.) **Why do you think she wants us to raise her child? Shall we make this baby Indian? All right. I will teach you the dance our tribe made that night when we first saw this land. Let us stand. Repeat, and say to the baby, Ah-Na-Hoo, walk to the left, now to the right, forward, back. Now the baby has been blessed, and the baby is one of us.** (U.S. Military personnel come to remove Indians from their land.)

Soldier: This here the Injin reserve—? Ya got 24 hours to move yourselves outa here by order of the U.S. government. (reads) By order of the U.S. government, this land is hereby claimed to be used for its mineral deposits of iron and copper. All Indians are ordered to leave within 24 hours. Signed by the Secretary of the Interior, Calvin C. Judd.

The Indian Medicine Person takes out a note for one of the children to read: Know all men by these present that this instrument conveys ownership in the green grass valley of all land on either side of the river of the Kiowa Indian tribe to have and to hold as long as the rivers run and the sun rises. (Argument begins as encouraged by the Medicine Person.)

Medicine Person (The leader): **You're not getting us to move again when this land was promised to us—you're a traitor to your own government.**

Soldier: No Indian has a right to remain on land which the government of the U.S. deems is valuable to the interests of the country. (At this point the soldier sees the baby and wonders why it's here.) Where'd this white baby come from? I've got a second statement here which says that all you white children are to be taken back to Washington D.C. and be reclaimed by your white forefathers.

This outburst is built upon by the Medicine Person who uses the role of devil's advocate to entice the children toward verbal abuse and challenges the soldier. The children's own argument with the soldier can go on for as long as the leader thinks it is building the children's resolve. After about 5 minutes, the leader can decide whether to come out of role and call for the drama to end or to continue in the argument. When the leader does decide to end the drama, she says: **The drama is over now. Let's sit down and see what we've done.**

Final questions

How would we feel if someone claimed our land?

What can we learn from the Indian way of life?

Do you think the Indian tribes may have destroyed themselves and eventually the Indian population would have gradually died out—even if the white man had never come?

Does the study of Indian culture have value to us now?

How can we apply these teachings to our own lives?

When is war justified?

War and Conflict

Objectives

To address the world issues that affect us all and will continue for a long time to come. These issues can be general at first: disease, the energy problem, dwindling natural resources, environmental pollution, terrorism (among poor countries) versus technology (among richer countries), and the whole concept of supply versus demand. Any other problems that are preferred can be introduced.

Materials

Maps can be made to depict the information which represents each country; if *The Soldier* is used, his role may be presented using another adult or child or it may simply be in the form of a sound tape played to "represent the waste" of war. A U.N. type charter to be drawn up and read is mentioned in the drama. Pictures of bombings are shown as evidence. The leader needs a gavel.

Concept

The children are made aware of the finiteness of the planet and how nations are dependent on each other, which fosters interdependence and cooperation on larger issues, such as the environment. The countries A,B,C, and D are analogous to a pattern in today's world, which can be raised depending on students' maturity.

Strategy

The leader provides the needed information either on the board or on dittos. The leader may feel that this same information needs to be reviewed in the beginning on the board as part of the drama. The leader is in role as someone who is comparable to the Secretary General of the U.N. She takes charge of the meeting using an "authoritative" role.

Background

The leader enters in role explaining that the following meeting will be held to determine who is behind the terrorism which is being practiced against countries (A) and (B) in which innocent victims have been killed, including children.

The leader passes out four different pieces of paper with A, B, C, or D written in the upper left-hand corner on them. This will divide the class into four different groups.

Leader: **At this meeting any questions can be asked of you so be sure you can answer any questions that may be put to you about your country.** On these same papers the following information is passed out to each group.

A represents the Ariels, a developing country with dwindling resources which manufactures high 'tech' equipment that other countries want; B, the Boness, also a country with dwindling resources, is otherwise a developed country and raises many crops which other countries need and can't raise. It is thought that its water contains curative properties. Both A and B are suspicious of each other's completely different economies. Yet both have to get along because they each produce things the other country needs. Also, they are slightly more advanced than the countries around them and want to keep their place in the world scheme.

Both are worried about countries C and D because of their growing alliances and growing poverty. C represents Collady which is an underdeveloped country but possesses a large quantity of material resources. D is called Daphire, also an underdeveloped country which does not possess a large quantity of material resources yet has a rich cultural heritage, books, ideas, inventions, art, etc. Both of these countries trade and farm.

The most important topic of concern for A and B is how to get C's resources before D does; and how to acquire D's rich cultural heritage before C does. The impending problem is that terrorists have struck the countries of A and B and without warning are killing innocent victims. Terrorism is the tool of poor countries; technological warfare is the power behind wealthier countries.

The wife, son, and daughter of the leader of A have been killed in one of the terrorist attacks, forcing a blockade of C and D's harbors, which is illegal. This has brought all to the UN to participate in a World Telecom to which all nations can come and take part. Candid shots of disasters are being passed around in order to inform the group of the intensity of the problems.

A and B say the terrorism must stop; those representing C and D say they know nothing about it.

In line with the "givens" for countries A, B, C, and D answer the following questions in your group. What are your major resources? What is your main energy resource? Where do you get it? What is your prediction for the future of your country? What farm products are grown? What products are manufactured for export? for import? What symbol is important to your country's history and future? (For example, in the U.S. the eagle means freedom, and the stars and stripes in the flag also contain meaning.)

The children can use as much of this information as they want as a guideline and continue to invent from here as ideas are bounced around in the class discussion.

After the groups have worked separately for about twelve to fifteen minutes developing their countries' backgrounds, the meeting is called to order and the latest news is announced about the death of country A's ruling family in a terrorist attack.

Since this is a Telecom, a wide screen, telephones, video-tapes must be imagined as vehicles for bringing in information. As it is not possible to bring in a video-tape machine, pictures of war zones and/or terrorist scenes can be passed around to represent some of the damage that has been alluded to. Also, at this time, as an example of a video or audio release, it is announced that a tape of a soldier who doesn't remember which side he's fighting on will be shown or heard. (See *The Soldier*.) His monologue is represented by the following example, which can be improvised upon: I've been captured and am now a prisoner. I fight for whomever pays me—like my father used to—can't remember anything—I am a professional soldier—got my training in Ariel—guerrilla warfare—that's all I can remember—in the 7 days that I've been captured—can't remember being wounded—but have had part of my chin blown off—and one arm just hangs with no feeling to it—can't move it—it's my artillery arm—can't remember my name—or the country I'm fighting for—or even if I'm married or have any kids—I'm a non-person and getting weaker and weaker---losing blood--- (breaks down and sobs—this monolog needs to be delivered as though the soldier is in a state of semi-consciousness, in order to be effective.)

Drama
We wish to call the meeting to order.   This is the second World Tele-communication meeting.   We're sorry to have to announce that the wife and the two children of President Hadley have been killed by the latest terrorist attack made on that country.   Many other innocent victims have been killed and wounded as well.   We don't know the exact figure, but it has reached over a hundred at the last count.

(The following needs to be written up and presented like an international charter.)

I'll read the charter of the World Union.
WE NEED to consider that we are one world with

limited resources, but nevertheless one world with problems that everyone needs to solve such as disease, depletion of the ozone layer, and terrorism, etc.

WE NEED to be aware not only of the advancements, but the impoverishments that individual countries suffer in order to prevent a downward spiral in terms of the quality of life which could affect the world at large such as Brazil's cutting of the rain forest in order to pay debts.

WE NEED to consider that each country has its own unique and rich heritage that represents the underpinnings for its actions.

(Perhaps it is revealed here that underdeveloped countries are more likely to engage in terrorist activities.)

We need to protect the world at large from attacks by independent and radical minorities.

Do we need to amend this? How can we stop the terrorism?

At present the countries C and D are blockaded. What are we to do?

At this time I would like to ask country A if there has been any evidence of guerrilla training being carried out in your country? If so, how can we uphold a charter which speaks against terrorism?

Are we going to withhold any imported products from countries C and D until the culprits are found?

Is terrorism illegal, just as the blockade is?

Perhaps we can speak about the new cures which have been found in the waters of B? Will other countries be allowed to use this water and cure those diseases for which there are no other cures?

Do we need to organize an international secret police to solve these problems?

The leader may use any of these questions or others to start the discussion. The leader may offer her own agenda and write it on the board. "Today we must solve the following..."

The discussion needs to be controlled by the use of the leader's gavel along with time limits for each speaker. Participants need to stand, say what country they're representing, give their name, title, in what capacity they're representing their country, as military personnel, scientists, doctors, teachers, artists, government employees, etc., and their question or comment.

   This sort of discussion is always slow at first; it simply means that the leader has to present more information and ask more questions to stimulate the children to ask questions and to present their ideas. The leader's questions can be in reference to the pictures or tape (video or audio) for these are the only facts that have been presented to the group as a whole. The knowledge that each child has of his own country will be used as background as well. She is free to elaborate, to make up facts, to conjecture, to probe, to present evidence from a "world C.I.A." team, if there is one in the drama.

   Once the discussion gets going it is difficult to stop so the use of the gavel and maintaining a formal atmosphere is essential.

Final questions
   Do you think we'll always have wars?
   What causes wars?
   What will we have to do to not have wars?
   Do people always win?
   Why not?
   Who does win?
   What do they win?

Immigration
(LA, Lit, Soc Stud, Hist) (5-8)

Objectives
1. To help children become more aware of the physical as well as emotional hardships endured when immigrating to the New World.
2. To incorporate an affective method of learning topography and names of states.
3. To make children aware of their heritage.

Materials
Pictures of migrants and immigrants; a whistle; a white coat; a stamp pad and stamp; a map of Europe and of the U.S.; cards for each child with the "Newly Arrived Immigrant Card" pasted on them, and a copy of the IQ test and Health Record for each; signs labeling the stations, I--IV; a class list; an eye chart (see p. 317).

Is it hard to travel in a crowded boat for two weeks?

Concept

To realize that Americans are a nation of mixed identities and values; that our pioneering ancestors' chief motivation was survival on a daily basis.

Strategy/story

Before the drama begins the children should find out about their heritage. For the drama to be successful each child needs to know that his overriding objective is to enter the country; all difficulties are suffered with this one hope in mind. The children will be pitted against the prejudices, hostility, and boredom that awaits most poor and newly arrived immigrants. The leader is in role throughout using a combination of "authoritative" roles such as chief immigration official, customs officer, doctor, etc. Other adults or child volunteers can help if desired. The group will stand in line, be faced by authoritarianism, feel rejection and some humiliation in order to appreciate their legacy of freedom. It is the children's responsibility to remain in role, or "nothing's going to happen for you." If possible, one child can be used as a customs officer. (see p. 265)

The drama is divided into five parts: 1. working in the factory; 2. a conspirator whispers to the workers about America; 3. workers rebel and refuse to work or sneak away; 4. transition by ship; 5. at immigration center. In part three, the leader can go from an "authoritative" role into a "shadowy" role collecting the children together before going on. At this point she goes into a transitional narrative when they are on the boat. **I want you to close your eyes again and listen.** She turns on the tape of ocean waves lapping upon the shore. The room needs to have been set up so the transition can be smooth. This can be a recess period. At the immigration center the children are divided into four groups with seven or eight in a group. The station number at which each group begins is written on each card. Each group is in line at one of the stations, rotating after the immigration officer gives a signal. The first 10 items on the immigration card are filled in by the child. These are rechecked and questioned by the leader in role as the immigration officer when they get to item 11, the last station. Each card also contains a number that matches with the final list that the leader has and checks off, making a note of whether or not the person is to be admitted.

On 5"x8" reinforced cards (two glued together):
station 1 includes questions 1-3
station 2 includes use of maps, 4-8

station 3 includes use of two tests 9-10
station 4 is in front of the immigration officer, 11-13

Beginning preparation

The leader shows pictures of the immigrants that are available from the late 19th century, the turn of the century, and the most recent groups, while questioning students about the differences between the various groups concerning treatment and hardships. Questions are asked regarding geographical background concerning the maps: Where are you from? Where are you going?

Remind the children before the drama begins that each of them should find out about his own heritage.

Beginning questions

Has your family descended from immigrants? Where are they from?

Do you know why they immigrated? For what reasons have people been immigrating?

Why were the immigrants willing to undergo such difficulties?

Were the immigrants sure of a new life? Or, were they taking a risk?

How did they help each other out?

Do you see people who you think are immigrants?

How do you feel towards them?

How do you think people felt about immigrants during this time?

How do you think the Native Americans felt?

What type of work do you think most of these people were involved in?

Were they self-employed? Or working for someone? Can we agree that their work was not very rewarding?

Remind them that if they want to know how their ancestors felt they must allow themselves to be taken "there" in the drama.

Remind them of their overriding objective: to be an American and to understand the meaning of being an American (see Chapter 2, Negotiation).

Among the kinds of routine work which are most oppressive are field or factory work.

Drama

Leader: I want you to stand and slowly let the images I speak begin to work on you.   Just close your eyes and let the images form.

(For European immigrants.)You're employed in a factory and you're canning vegetables that the people on the other side are picking.   Both groups are part of the same factory.

(For other immigrants.)   You're all working on the land. You've been planting/harvesting (For Asians it would be rice; for Hispanics, fruit and vegetables.)   Your back aches.

(For all.)   Your work day is twelve hours long with 20 minutes for lunch.   You have a daily quota.   Your pay is cut in half if you do not meet that quota.   You can be laid off for any reason whatsoever.

Jobs are very hard to find.   People take care of their own families.   There are no labor unions; there's no welfare, or job security.   It's 7:00 in the morning and your job begins.   You've walked quite a few miles to get here. (During this time the leader's tone has become more harsh.)   Open your eyes. Half of you are on one side picking vegetables and half are on the other side canning vegetables. (Blow a whistle.)   Whenever you hear this, you stop working; if you aren't working, you then begin. The leader blows on the whistle and speaks in a stern voice. LINE UP.   Whenever there is giggling or talking: SILENCE, the next person who talks will have his pay cut or be replaced. There're plenty more out there to replace you. (Indicate the working space.)   The rows are here and here.   There will be the usual search for weapons and/or for papers about communism. This will be done one at a time. Blows whistle. TO WORK!   The leader goes up to individuals, takes them aside to search them or says, "Show me your pockets—" at which point they attempt to prove their innocence by emptying their pockets.   Work continues along with harassment. Faster—stand back so you can be watched—we don't like communist traitors—as soon as you've filled your bag, empty it into this box—no talking—the next time I hear anyone talk— everyone in that direction will receive no pay for today's work. Either one of the children who has been kept out purposely or another adult enters secretively   whenever the leader's back is turned. This remains secret and is set up before the drama begins.   As soon as the leader leaves the room, the "spy" announces, "Wouldn't you like to immigrate to America?" This will be like 'cat and mouse' but the leader needs to return and leave at unannounced intervals, not more than three times to set this in motion.

Transition

If the leader wants continuous involvement then the children should be taken away from the playing area so the room can be rearranged for the next part. A recess break would be convenient. Whenever they are taken, even if it's outside, a transitional narrative is used to keep them in the drama and in their roles.

The leader has them close their eyes while she narrates the following:

For Europeans:You have been on a ship for 2 weeks. The winter cold has chilled your bones; you are weak from hunger, for you have been ill and your skin is dry from lack of water. The days are so long. And then one day, like a dream, a statue rises up out of the water, a lady holding a torch and a book, and you know this is your country. Then you see a sign: U.S. Immigration Processing Center.

For Hispanics: You have been crossing the border. The winter cold has chilled your bones; you are weak from hunger, for you have been ill and your skin is dry from lack of water. The days are so long. And then one day, like a dream, you see the lights of a city in the golden land, and you run, hiding and running, until you are sure you're safe.

For Asians: You have been traveling in a boat for a month. The winter cold has chilled your bones; you are weak from hunger, for you have been ill and your skin is dry from lack of water. The days are so long. And then one day, like a dream, you see land and lights in the distant fog. You keep your almost lifeless body going.

Inside the classroom, processing stations are set up so the center of the room is cleared, and the leader can use a long table at one end together with either a student or an adult assistant to help with authority if needed.

All the immigrants are conducted back in and as they pass through the door they are handed the following card, together with the IQ test and the Heath record. They will automatically be divided into four groups. (They will start at the station of which every numeral is underlined in red.)

(Sample) **Newly Arrived Immigrant Card**

1. Name: old_____

           new_____

2. Trade:_____

3. Reason for coming_____

4. *Destination in U.S. address_____

         city_____state_____

5. *Relations in U.S.:   address_____

      city_____state_____

6. *Country of origin_____

7. *Tests_____

8. Money in possession_____

9. Language(s) spoken_____

      English (how well)_____

10. Tests, IQ and Health (see separate sheets)_____

11. **Eye test_____

12. **Baggage inspection_____

13. **Please sign: (fingerprint)_____

_____

(signature of new name and, if name has been changed, old name)

* Maps and IQ tests need to be made available

**Handled at end by teacher in role

Drama

The leader will be at the front desk or table. After passing out cards, along with the I. Q. test and the Health Record, she will announce the following.

Attention! There's to be no talking. You have reached the U.S. Immigration Processing Center. "Silence" can be ordered at intervals. She gives cards and the two tests, IQ and Health, to children as she calls them by name.

Each of you has a card to be filled out. There are Roman numerals at each station where you will stand to write the information needed. At each station you have something specific to do. At the first station you will only write. At station 2 you must find your country on the map and your final destination in this country. At 3 you will take a test and fill out a health questionnaire; at 4 I will check your baggage, give you an eye test and decide if you will be allowed in. (tension) **You will remain at each station until I call for you to change stations. You see a red line on your card marking the station at which you must start. All will be addressed in English. If you do not understand, TRY. Who would like to be our first volunteer to show the others?** This should inform the others so that there is no confusion, since the processing must be done smoothly and with no talking. The leader will be processing a few at a time and cannot be giving instructions during this time. The leader will be checking results quickly. In order to make this possible, the first six items are not an issue. One-fourth of the children will be at each station at a time. As soon as all the children in each group have finished filling in the items, they will move to the next station when the leader calls out the command to change stations. One through 10 are filled in independently. Four through six require maps, which should be tacked up. Item ten can be available on 2 separate sheets at station 3. The leader will conduct both the eye chart and the baggage inspection. In this way the leader can "run" all the groups through without help. However, if she wishes to elicit volunteers, they can become a visual authority by being firm while at the same time assisting in routing by saying "next; no talking; move on." The eye chart can also be used to deepen whatever feelings of paranoia may exist, for they will be asked to describe the symbol that they see. The leader can check over all the previous items, including the IQ test and Health Record. Finally, if the person is not permitted to stay, his card will indicate this and he can be conducted to one space, analogous to becoming an "outcast." The leader must be sure that those who are excluded contain the fortitude to deal with rejection. Depending upon this she may deliberately not exclude those who have problems with these tests.

Each card contains a number that matches with the final list that the leader has and checks off, making a note of whether or not the person is to be admitted.

Name	1	2	3	4	5	6	7	8	9	10	11	12	13

Final questions

Did you feel the immigrants were treated fairly? or harshly?

Were there any sections at which you felt more humiliated than at others?

Were any of you coasting and not involved?

Why were these things asked of the immigrants?

Do you think there may have been a natural suspicion connected to the immigrants? Why?

Do you see immigrants now? Can you tell if they are? How can you tell?

How do you feel about them? Do you think it's part of human nature to feel some suspicion upon encountering people who are different? Can this feeling develop into prejudice?

What do we need to do to prevent this from happening?

Is the U.S. the first country in modern times that has moved toward assimilation?

Follow up exercises

Small groups of two or three to role play using any personal facts together with historical accounts.

After brainstorming with the class, topics such as the following with the accompaniment of an attitude are used: the end of the day's journey and camping for the night; work in the factory ends and the family meets in their rooms; stuck in New York City; for Hispanics, traveling in a clandestine manner; for Asians, living in a boat for a month.

(Note to teacher: This is a large topic, but it is important to discuss. Although the U.S. does not have anything like a perfect record, what we have attempted hasn't existed in any other country. So, it is crucial that these children discuss this and also ways for making it work better.)

(Sample) I.Q. TEST

1. How many states are there in the United States? a) 24, b) 48, c) 55, d) 50

2. Your mother's sisters are your a) cousins, b) nephews, c) aunts, d) nieces.

3. The Declaration of Independence was signed on July 4 a) 1784, b) 1790, c) 1776, d) 1765

4. If you have $5.00 and you spend $3.88, how much will you have left? a) $.22, b) $.48, c) $ 1.20, d) $ 1.12

5. The capitol of the United States is a) Washington, D.C., b) Philadelphia, c) New York, d) Boston

6. The Constitution of the United States contains one of the following: a) All men are created equal, b) All American citizens are entitled to free medical care based on the provision, "Providing for the general welfare—", c) All male citizens who are able bodied must provide for the common defense, d) Americans are free to practice whatever religion they choose.

(Sample) <u>HEALTH RECORD</u>

Mark the known diseases which members of your family have died from:

typhoid fever _____, small pox _____,
measles: black___ red___, mumps_____, chicken pox _____,
scarlet fever_____
(the following, if checked, mean automatic rejection)
tuberculosis____ , lung disorders _____, undulant fever _____,
heart problems_____, kidney troubles _____ , ulcers _____,
intestinal troubles _____ , head injury or headaches _____,
paralysis of any kind _____, difficulty breathing___

(Sample) <u>EYE CHART</u>

¡   ¢   ∞   ᵃ   ±

"   –   🍎   Ò   ◊

Í   Ï   Ô   +   =

NOTES for CHAPTER 10

1 George, Dan
2 Glasser, p. 8
3 Pearce, p. 73

Appendix

According to the *California Visual and Performing Arts Framework, '89*, correlation means relating the arts with subject matter areas; integration means relating the arts of dance, drama, music, and visual arts together. In this text drama is viewed as a catalyst for learning in subject matter areas rather than as an art in its own right.

Subject matter areas are indicated and keyed to the dramas in Chapter 10. They are abbreviated as: LA (Language Arts), Lit (Literature), Geog (Geography); Hist (History), Sci (Science), PE (Physical Education).

The exercises in Chapters 8 and 9 have also been correlated with subject matter areas. In this appendix the following list of these exercises (1-46) further correlates them to match the areas of the *California Visual and Performing Arts Framework*. (When appropriate the *California Language Arts Framework* is referred to.)

The terms used in this framework are: Components, Goals, and Objectives, followed by levels, I, II, III.

Components:

I. Aesthetic Perception - speaks for a multisensory awareness of stimuli through the learners' own experiences.

II. Creative Expression - includes the development of drama skills through "doing."

Goals and objectives for each of these sections are a further breakdown of these headings. Levels indicate I, II, III as beginning to advanced.

Because this text concentrates on process (and a correlation of drama with subject matter in the elementary school) and not on product, which is usually addressed in the upper grades, almost all of the last two components from the *Framework*—III Drama/Theatre Heritage and IV Aesthetic Valuing—have been omitted. Aesthetic Valuing addresses the development of criteria for evaluation. Also the area of formal acting, directing, stage managing, and technical design have not been included. There are and have been thousands of books written on these last two components and are considered to be the material for older ages. Though these categories are somewhat ambiguous, the Arts Framework offers guidelines for setting up a comprehensive school program.

The following is from the *Arts Framework*, pp. 39-40.

Component One: Aesthetic Perception—Multisensory
Integration
Goal I: To experience dramatic elements, actions, and
characterizations
Objectives: The student will be able to:
1. Become perceptive and selective in observing and
responsding to the environment.
2. Use movement as the external expression of an
internal idea, intention, or feeling.
3. Use the voice as an instrument for the expression of
meaning and feeling, whether in speech or
nonverbal sound.
4. Respond spontaneously and collaboratively to
rapidly changing, unanticipated stimuli.

Component Two: Creative Expression
Goal I: To develop skills in storytelling, playmaking, and
playwriting
Objectives: The student will be able to:
1. Retell and perform a story.
2. Perform an improvisation which is structured,
played, evaluated, and replayed.
3. Write original scenes or plays from improvisations.
4. Create appropriate design and technical elements
for such scenes or plays.
Goal II: To develop an awareness of the collaborative
nature of playmaking
Objectives: The student will be able to:
1.Participate actively in the planning of a
dramatization.
2. Perform group dramatizations.
3. Evaluate group effort in exploring and expressing
ideas.

One component in the dance area of the *Framework* correlates with a few exercises in the text. The following outline is from p. 12 of the dance portion of the *Framework*.

> Component One: Aesthetic Perception---Multisensory
> Integration
> Goal I: To develop the student's awareness of the body, a
> sensing of the communicative potential of body
> movement, and a capacity for spontaneous
> movement response.
> Objective: The student will be able to develop an
> awareness, identification, and image of the body
> as an instrument of expression in space and in
> time." This is the only part of the dance section
> which has been used.

The following paragraph is quoted from the *Language Arts Framework*, p. 25. Exercises 1-10 of the text consider the correlation between writing and drama.

> In studying a work of literature, (for example,) teachers must plan classroom activities to help students first to get into the work by reading a portion of the work aloud or playing a recording to evoke a desire to read. Second, the students will explore the work, understanding it by looking carefully at quotations or dealing with critical questions about central issues. and, finally, the students will go beyond the work to dramatize or illustrate it or in some other way connect it to their everyday lives. (Underlined is mine.) As they explore a work, students must also encounter strategies for thinking; that is, how to understand and how to compose, when to ask questions and how to answer them. The challendge of teachers, then, is planning classroom activities so that all students discover the way to learning for themselves.

The following exercises are included in Chapter 9, and are here correlated with the *Arts Framework*.

Exercise 1.   Drama: Component 1; Goal 1; Objectives 2,3,4;
                       "Rhythm and movement," "move
                       abstractly"
              Dance: Component 1; Goal 1; Objective 1;
                       levels I, II, III
Exercise 2.   Drama: Component 1; Goal 1; Objectives 2,3,4;
                       "Rhythm and movement;" level I,
                       "move as an object or animal or as different
                       types of people;" level II,
                       "represent moods in movement"
              Dance: Component 1; Goal 1; Objective 1;
                       levels I, II, III
Exercise 3.   Drama: Component 1; Goal 1; Objectives 1,2,3,4;
                       level III;
                       Component 2; Objective 3; level III,
                       "improvisation of images in a poem"
              Dance: Component 1; Goal 1; Objective 1;
                       levels I, II, III
Exercise 4.   Drama: Component 2; Goal 2; Objective 1; level I
Exercise 5.   Drama: Component 2; Goal 2; Objective 1;
                       levels I, II
Exercise 6.   Drama: Component 2; Goal 1; Objective 3;
                       levels I, II;
                       Goal 2; Objective 1; level I
Exercise 7.   Drama: Component 2; Goal 1; Objective 3;
                       levels I, II;
                       Goal 2; Objective 1; level I
Exercise 8.   Drama: Component 2; Goal 1; Objective 3;
                       levels I, II;
                       Goal 2; Objective 1; level I
Exercise 9.   Drama: Component 2; Goal 1; Objective 3; level III,
                       "Playmaking"
Exercise 10. Drama: Component 2; Goal 1; level III,
                       "Playmaking"
Exercise 11. Drama: Component 1; Goal 1; Objective 1; level I
Exercise 12. Drama: Component 1; Goal 1; Objective 2; level I
              Dance: Component 1; Goal 1; Objective 1; level I
Exercise 13. Drama: Component 1; Goal 1; Objectives 1,2,4;
                       level I
Exercise 14. Drama: Component 1; Goal 1; Objective 1; level I

Exercise 15. Drama: Component 1; Goal 1; level I
Exercise 16. Drama: Component 1; Goal 1; Objectives 1,2,4;
                      evel I
            Dance: Component 1; Goal 1; Objective 1; level II
Exercise 17. Drama: Component 1; Goal 1; Objective 1; level I
Exercise 18. Dance: Component 1; Goal 1; Objective 1; "Space,"
                      levels I, II
Exercise 19. Dance: Component 1; Goal 1; Objective 1; "Space,"
                      levels I, II, III
Exercise 20. Dance: Component 1; Goal 1; Objective 1; "Body
                      awareness," level II, "Focus attention on
                      kinesthetic sensations with inner felt
                      experiences of movement"
Exercise 21. Dance: Component 1; Goal 1; Objective 1; "Body
                      awareness," level I, "Respond
                      spontaneously in movement to varied
                      stimuli---"
Exercise 22. Dance: Component 1; Goal 1; Objective 1; "Body
                      awareness," level II, "Observe and follow
                      movement of another person as in follow-
                      the-leader" and "respond to the feeling of
                      observed movement"
Exercise 23. Drama: Component 1; Goal 1; Objectives 2,4;
                      level I1
            Dance: Component 1; Goal 1; Objective 1, "Body
                      awareness," level I1
Exercise 24. Drama: Component 2; Goal 1; "Pantomime," level I
Exercise 25. Drama: Component 2; Goal 1; Objective 2;
                      "Improvisation," level I1
Exercise 26. Drama: Component 2; Goal l; Objectives 1,2,3;
                      levels I, II, III
Exercise 27. Drama: Component 2; Goal 1; "Pantomime," level I
            Dance: Component 1; Goal 1; "Body awareness,
                      levels I, II
Exercise 28. Drama: Component 2; Goal 1; Objectives 2,3;
                      levels I, II
            Dance: Component 1; Goal 1; Objective 1; level I,
                      "respond spontaneously in movement to
                      varied stimuli--"
Exercise 29. Drama;   Component 2; Goal 1; "Pantomime in story
                      lines-"

The following exercises are correlated with Language Arts.

Exercise 30. Drama: Component 2; Goal 1; Objectives 1,2,3;
                        "Improvisation," levels I, II, III
Exercise 31. Drama: Component 2; Goals 2, 3; Objectives 1,2,3;
                        "Improvisation and playwriting,"
                        levels I, II, III

The following exercise is correlated with Language Arts,
Literature, Social Studies, and History.

Exercise 32. Drama: Component 2; Goal 1; Objectives 1,2,3;
                        "Improvisation and playmaking,"
                        levels I, II, III

The following exercises are correlated with Language Arts and
Social Studies.

Exercise 33. Drama: Component 2; Goals 1,2,3; Objective 3;
                        "Improvisation," levels I, II, III
Exercise 34. Drama: Component 2; Goal 2; level I
             Visual Art: Component 2; Goal 2; "use artistic skills,"
                        level I
Exercise 35. Drama: Component 2; Goal 2; level I
Exercise 36. Drama: Component 2; Goal 2; Objectives 1,2;
                        levels, 1, 11
Exercise 37. Drama: Component 2; Goal 2; Objectives 1,2;
                        levels I, II
Exercise 38. Drama: Component 2; Goal 2; Objectives 1,2,3;
                        levels I, II
Exercise 39. Drama: Component 2; Goal 2; Objectives 1, 2;
                        "presentation of characters," level I
Exercise 40. Drama: Component 2; Goal 2; Objectives 1, 2;
                        "presentation of characters," level I

The following exercises correlate with the Language Arts
Framework, p. 28, "Because good speaking also takes practice,
students must experience in the early grades a variety of activities to
expand their speaking repertoire, such as puppet theatres, "show and
tell" times, and opportunities for telling stories about experiences or
pictures."
Exercise 41 through 46. Drama: Component 2; Goal 1; Objective 2,
                        levels I, II

Music

BACKGROUND

Bartok, *Concerto for Orchestra,* for adventure in which chases, searches, discoveries, exploration and dramatic and intense moments are interchanged with whimsical and mysterious, romantic, optimistic feats of triumph.

Copeland, *Music for Movies, New England Countryside* from *The City,* quiet, majestic, romantic, pastoral; *Barley Wagons* from *Of Mice and Men,* rural, folk life, warm, happy, sunny; *Sunday Traffic* from *The City,* jazzy, whimsical, jaunty; *Story of Grover's Corners* from *Our Town,* enduring, tender, moody, slow—a scene painting; *Threshing Machines* from *Of Mice and Men,* the onomatopoeic sounds of machines and rye, it is rhythmically musical.

Grieg, *Peer Gynt Suite,* morning and the day's beginning, strong yet gentle and soulful, good for growing, or stretching and release.

Mussorgsky, *Pictures at an Exhibition,* gradual build, and decrecendo.

Vivaldi, *The Seasons,* descriptive and broken into four parts: Spring, Summer, Fall, Winter. No strong contrast or gradual crescendos

CLIMACTIC

Beethoven, *Pastorale,* quiet, gently rising to a climax, useful for rising and stretching.

Berlioz, *Symphony Fantastic,* a continuation of individual segments which round to a climax, each stretching slightly further than the one before and building from slow and low to fast and loud; useful for a dreamlike fantasy and journey.

Holst, *The Planets,* strong, intense, dramatic.

Stravinsky, *Firebird Suite*. *Inferno* for a conflict situation and growing and reawakening.
Petrouchka, a puppet comes to life to dance and grow tired.

Villa-Lobos, *Little Train of the Caipiria*, steady locomotive sound effects played against a lyric string background building toward crescendo.

EERIE

Luening, *A poem in cycles and bells*, Composers Recordings, CRI 112, also includes *The Fortunate Islands* on the back, more serene. Useful for creating unusual atmosphere.

Mussorgsky, *Night On Bald Mountain*, also climatic and builds to a storm subsiding to calm.

Saint-Saens, *Danse Macabre*, increases in intensity, and frantic in quality, subsiding into longer moments building toward a climax.

Subotnick, *Silver Apples for the Moon*, electronic music synthesizer. Nonesuch H 71174, could accompany journey or story about space or any unusual atmosphere; there are intervals between mystical, slow and frenetic throughout.

HISTORICAL

Copeland, *Appalachian Spring*, each movement is different, contributing to the landscape of a gracious and strong land caught between moments of festivity and calm.
Billy the Kid, gently, intense, bouncy, and light moments in the life of the western cowboy.

Gould, *Spirituals for Orchestra*, many moods represented, depending upon movement used: bouncy, soft, bitter, rhythmic, sad.

MAGICAL

Dukas, *Sorcerer's Apprentice*, interludes mixed with sections of intensity; very slow building gradually toward a climax.

Mussorgsky, *Dawn of the Moskva River*, from *Khovantchina Prelude to Act I*, a transformational quality, building in strength.

Rimsky-Korsakov, *Scheherazade*, transformational quality building in strength. Transformations occur in a journey through a weather-worn environment that becomes more difficult and challenging.

LYRIC

Copeland, *Dance Symphony*, sustained and light at first, builds into an exchange between lyricalness and intensity.

Debussy, *La Mer*, flowing, builds slowly to a strong climax, useful for underwater environment.
L'Apres-midi d'un Faun, gentle, rising and growing.

Dvorak, *From the New World Symphony*, segments of slow flowing movements building toward a crescendo, intermixed with bouncy, active movements. A symphony about America.
Ravel, *Mother Goose Suite*, light imaginative fairy tales are being narrated, could be used to accompany journeys for young children in which a slight change in intensity is used to overcome an obstacle.

Sibelius, *Finlandia*, segments of light and heavy movements build gradually toward a climax; could accompany a secret journey which is tranquil, promising wishes.

Tchaikovsky, *Romeo and Juliet*, rhythmic tone picture which builds in poignancy and intensity until struggle begins, ending in confusion and rage. The final ending is lyric and accepting.

PROCESSIONAL

Bizet, *Carmen*, introduction to Act I

Borodin, *Prince Igor*, specific actions as part of ceremony are built up with festive climatic sweeps, good for circus, fair, celebration.

Kettelby, *In a Chinese Temple Garden. With Honor Crowned*, drums and brass instruments introduce a dignified personality---a march step, a procession of pageantry. *Persian Garden*, oriental marketplace setting with an important entrance.

Rosini, *La Gazze Ladra*, first few minutes.

RHYTHMIC

Beatles, *Magical Mystery Tour*, slower than most Beattles' music and appropriate for exercise and general physical movement.

Breuer, *The Moog Synthesizer*, stereo, faster than other rhythmic records on this list, useful for inspiring imaginative activities, that are kinesthetical and visual

Kettelby, *Jungle Drums*, percussive and festive.

MacDermot, *Hair*, electronic, stereo, 2013, useful for exercising with well adjusted upper grade students.

Nickelodian Music: Music of the Gay Nineties, audio fidelity, AFLP 1960, useful for exercise, marches, all kinds of movement.

Shankar, *The Genius of Ravi Shankar*, electronically recorded for stereo CS 9560, continaully involving and hypnotic, useful for movement exercises and concentration, best used with older groups.

The Wonderful Belgian Band Organ, AFSD 5975 useful for exercise, locomotor movement, circus music.

For specific tape recorded sounds, you may find the sound you want on sound effects records in the library.

Bibliography

Suggested reading for teachers:
Burgess and Gaudry. *Time for Drama: A Handbook for Secondary Teachers*. Philadelphia: Open University Press, 1986.
Cullum, Albert. *Push Back the Desks*. New York: Citation Press, 1967.
Henig, Ruth. *Creative Dramatics for the Classroom Teacher*. Englewood Cliffs, NJ: Prentice Hall, 1988.
Kase-Polisini, Judith. *The Creative Drama Book: Three Approaches*. New Orleans: Anchorage Press, 1989.
Moffett, James. *A Student-Centered Language Arts Curriculum*, K-13. New York: Houghton Mifflin, 1968.
O'Neill, Lambert. *Drama Structures*. London: Hutchinson, 1982.
Rico, Gabriele. *Writing the Natural Way*. Boston: Tarcher, Houghton Mifflin Co., 1983.
Morgan, N. and Saxton, J. *Teaching Drama*. London: Hutchinson, 1987.
Shuman, R. Baird. *Educational Drama for Today's Schools*. New Jersey: Metuchen, Scarecrow, Press, 1979.
Spolin, Viola. *Improvisation for the Theatre*. Evanston, IL: Northwestern University Press, 1963.
...*Theatre Games for the Classroom*. Evanston, IL: Northwestern U. Press, 1986.
Tyas, Billi. *Child Drama in Action*. New York: Drama Book Specialists, 1971.
Wagner, Betty Jane. *Dorothy Heathcote, Drama as a Learning Medium*. Washington D.C.: National Education Association, 1976.
Ward, Winifred. *Playmaking with Children*. New York: A.C. Crofts, 1947.
Way, Brian. *Development Through Drama*. Canada: Longmans, 1970.

Other references

Barlin, Ann. *Teaching Your Wings to Fly*. Santa Monica, CA: Goodyear Publ. Co., 1979.

Benson, Herbert. *The Relaxation Response*. New York: Avon, 1975.

Bettelheim, Bruno. *The Uses of Enchantment: the Meaning and Importance of Fairy Tales*. New York: Alfred A. Knopf, 1976.

Bloom, Benjamin. *Taxonomy of Educational Objectives*, Handbook I: Cognitive Domain; Handbook II: Affective Domain. New York: Davis Mc Kay Co., Inc. 1971.

Blough, Schwartz, Huggett. *Elementary School Science*. New York: Holt, Rinehart, and Winston, Inc., 1958.

Bolton, Gavin. *Toward a Theory of Drama in Education*. London: Longman Group Ltd., 1979.

Boorman, Joyce. *Creative Dance in the First Three Grades*. New York: David Mc Kay, 1969.

Bradley, Virginia. *Holidays on Stage*, New York: Dodd, Mead and Co., 1981.

Brown, George Isaac. *Human Teaching for Human Learning*. New York: The Viking Press, 1971.

...*The Live Classroom*. New York: The Viking Press, 1975.

Bruner, Jerome. *The Process of Education*. New York: Vintage Books, 1966.

Bry, Adelaide. *Directing the Movies of Your Mind, Visualization for Health and Insight*. New York: Harper and Row , 1978.

Butterworth, Oliver. *The Enormous Egg*. New York: Little, 1956.

Campbell, Joseph. *The Power of Myth*. New York: Doubleday, 1988.

Carr, Rachel. *Be a Frog, a Bird, or a Tree*. New York: Harper Colophon Books, 1977.

Carson, Rachel. *The Silent Spring*. Boston: Houghton Mifflin, 1962.

Casteel, J. Doyle. *Value Clarification in the Classroom, A Primer*. Pacific Palisades, CA: Goodyear Publ. Co., 1975.

Castillo, Gloria. *Left-Handed Teaching*. New York: Praeger Publ., 1974.

Chekhov, Michael. *To the Actor*. New York: Harper and Row, 1953.

Chilver, Peter. *Stories for Improvisation*. London: Batesford, 1969.

Cranston, Jerneral. *Dramatic Imagination*, Trinidad, CA: Jenfred, 1975.

Cornell, Joseph Bharat. *Sharing Nature with Children*. Ananda Pub, 1979.

Courtney, Richard. *Teaching Drama*. London: Cassill and Co., 1965.

Cullum, Albert. *Shake Hands with Shakespeare*. New York: Citation Press, 1968.

DeMille, Richard. *Put Your Mother on the Ceiling*. New York: Viking, 1973.

Dhority, Lynn, ed. *Suggestive-Accelerative Learning and Teaching*, A Summer Institute for CSUC Faculty. Long Beach, CA.

Erickson, Erik. *Childhood and Society*. New York: Horton and Co, 1963.

Ferguson, Marilyn. *The Aquarian Conspiracy*. Boston: J. P. Tarcher & Co., 1980.

Fitzgerald, Burdette, ed. *World Tales for Creative Dramatics and Storytelling*. Englewood Cliffs, NJ: Prentice Hall, Inc., 1962.

Furness, Pauline. *Role Play in the Elementary School*. New York: Hart, 1976.

Gallwey, Timothy. *The Inner Game of Tennis*. New York: Random House, 1974.

Gardner, Howard. *Frames of Mind, the Theory of Multiple Intelligences*. New York: Basic Books, Inc. 1985.

George, Dan. *My Heart Soars*. Surrey, British Columbia: Hancock House, 1974.

Glasser, William. *Control Theory in the Classroom*. New York: Perennial Library, 1986.

Goble, Paul. *Buffalo Woman*. New York: Aladdin Books, MacMillan, 1984.

...*The Girl Who Loved Wild Horses*. Scarsdale, NY: Bradbury Press, 1978.

Goldberg, Moses. *Children19s Theatre, A Philosophy and a Method*. Englewood Cliffs, NJ: Prentice Hall, 1974.

Gordon, Thomas T. *Teacher Effectiveness Training*. New York: Peter H. Wyden, 1974.

Haggerty, Joan. *Please May I Play God?* New York: Bobbs Merrill Co., Ltd, 1966.

Harmin and Sax. *A Peaceable Classroom*. Minneapolis: Winston Press, 1977.

Hendricks and Wills. *The Centering Book*. Englewood Cliffs, NJ: Prentice Hall, 1975.

Hendricks, Gay. *The Centered Teacher* . Englewood Cliffs, NJ: Prentice Hall, 1981.

...*Transpersonal Education: A Curriculum for Feeling and Being*. Englewood Cliffs, NJ: Prentice Hall, 1976.

Hodgson, John and Richards, Ernest. *Improvisation*. London: Metuchen and Co., Ldt, 1974.

Hunt, Albert. *Hopes for Great Happenings*. New York: Taplinger Publishing Co., 1977.

Jennings, Sue. *Remedial Drama*. New York: Theatre Arts Books, 1979.

Johnson, Sickels, Sayers. *Anthology of Children's Literature*. Boston: Houghton Mifflin, 1970.

Johnson, Roger, and DavidJohnson. *Learning Together and Alone, cooperation, competition, and individualization*. Englewood Cliffs, NJ: Prentice-Hall, 1975.

Johnstone, Keith. *Impro*. London and Boston: Faber and Faber, 1979.

Jung, Carl. *Man and His Symbols*. New York: Doubleday, 1965.

Klein, Melanie. *The Psychoanalysis of Children*. London: Hogarth Press, 1949.

Koste, Virginia Glasgow. *Dramatic Play in Childhood, Rehearsal for Life*. New Orleans: Anchorage Press, 1977.

Koch, Kenneth. *Wishes, Lies, and Dreams*. New York: The Vintage Press, 1970.

Koch, Kenneth. *Rose, Where Did You Get That Red?* New York: Random House, 1973.

Kroeber, Theodora. *Ishi, Last of His Tribe*. New York: Bantam Books, 1981.

...*The Inland Whale, Nine Stories Retold from California Indian Legends*. Berkeley: University of California Press, 1959.

Lazanov, Georgi. *Suggestology and the Outlines of Suggestopedia*. New York: Gordon and Breach, 1979.

Leonard, George. *Education and Ecstacy*. New York: Delta, 1968.

Mc Kim, Robert, H. *Experiences in Visual Thinking*. Monterey, CA: Brooks, Cole, 1972.

Momaday, N. Scott. *The Way to Rainy Mountain*. Albuquerque: University of New Mexico Press, 1969.

Moore, Sonia. *The Stanislavsky System*. New York: Viking Press, 1965.

Motter, Kay, C. *Theatre in High School: Planning, Teaching, Directing*. Englewood Cliffs, NJ: Prentice Hall, 1970.

Neill, A.S. *Summerhill*. New York: Hart, 1960.

O'Brien, Robert C. *Mrs. Frisbee and the Rats of Nimh*. Atheneum, 1972.

O'Dell, Scott. *Island of the Blue Dolphin*. New York: Houghton, 1960.

O'Neill, Lambert. *Drama Guidelines*. London: Hutchinson, 1983.

Ostrovsky, Everett. *Self-Discovery and Social Awareness*, New York: John Wiley and Sons, 1974.

Pearce, Joseph Chilton. *Magical Child*. New York: Bantam Books, 1977.

...*Magical Child Matures*. New York: Bantam Books, 1986.

Pearson, Craig. *Make Your Own Games Workshop*. Pitman Learning, 1982.

Perls, Frederick, S. *Gastalt Therapy Verbatum*. Lafayette, CA: Real People Press, 1969.

Restak, Richard. *The Brain, The Last Frontier*. New York: Warner Books, 1979.

Robinson, Ken, ed. *Exploring Theatre and Education*. London: Heinemann Educational Books, Ltd., 1980.

Rozman, Deborah. *Meditation for Children*. Millbrae, CA: Celestial Arts, 1976.

Schattner, Regina. *Creative Dramatics for Handicapped Children*. New York: John Day, 1967.

Schlissel, Lillian, ed. *Women's Diaries of the Westward Journey*. New York: Schocken Books, 1982.

Shaftel and Shaftel. *Role Playing in the Social Studies*. Palo Alto, CA: Stanford University Press, 1969.

Shaw, Perks, Stevens. *A Handbook in Drama and Theatre by, with, and for Handicapped Individuals*. Washington, D.C.: American Theatre Assoc., 1981.

Shepard, Richmond. *Mime: The Teaching of Silence*. New York: Drama Book Specialists, 1971.

Siks, G.B. *Children's Literature for Dramatization*. New York: Harper and Row, 1965.

Silko, Leslie. *The Ceremony*. New York: Viking Press, 1977.

Silverman, Charles, E., ed. *The Open Classroom Reader*. New York: Vintage, Random House, 1973.

Simon, Howe, Kirschenbaum. *Values Clarification*. New York: Hart, 1972.

Slade, Peter. *Children's Drama*. London: University of London, 1954.

...*Introduction to Child Drama*. London: Universtiy of London, 1971.

...*Experiences in Spontaneity*. London: Longmans, 1968.

Snitzer, Herb. *Living at Summerhill*. New York: MacMillan, 1968.

Springer and Deutsch. *Left Brain, Right Brain*. New York: W.H. Freeman and Co., 1981.

Stabler, Tom. *Drama in Primary School*. London: MacMillan Education, 1978.

Stoutenberg, Adrien. *A Vanishing Thunder, extinct and threatened American birds*. Natural History Press, 1967.

Taylor, Paula. *The Kids' Whole Future Catalog*, New York: Random House, 1982.

Thomas, Marla. *Free To Be You and Me*. San Francisco: Mc Graw-Hill, 1974.

Toffler, Alvin, ed. *Learning for Tomorrow*. New York: Vintage, 1974
...*The Third Wave*. New York, Vintage, 1980.

Turk, Jonathan. *Ecosystems, Energy and Populations*. Philadelphia: Saunders, 1975.

Vitale, Barbara Meister. *Unicorns Are Real: A Right-Brain Approach to Learning*. Rolling Hills Estate, CA: Jaimar Press, 1982.

Wagner, J. and Baker, Kitty. *A Place for You, Our Theatre*. San Antonio: Principia Press of Trinity University, 1965.

Ward, Winifred. *Creative Dramatics, for the Upper Grades and Junior High School*. New York: D. Appleton-Century, 1930.

Wilde, Oscar. *Complete Shorter Fiction*. New York: Oxford University Press, 1979.

Wilder, Laura Ingalls. *Little House on the Prairie*. New York: Harper, 1953.

Wilder, Thornton. *Our Town*. New York: Coward Mc Cann, Inc., 1939.

Williams, Linda Verlee. *Teaching for the Two-sided Mind*. New York: Simon and Schuster, Inc. 1983.

Witkin, Robert,W. *The Intelligence of Feeling*. London: Heinemann Educational Books, 1977.

Wittrock, M.C. *The Human Brain*. Englewood Cliffs, NJ: Prentice Hall, 1977.

Drama/Theatre Framework for California Schools. California State Department of Education, 1989.

Glossary

aesthetic
> beauty and form; a pleasantness contributing to; when a drama or scene works because of; at work in science and technology as well as the arts

aesthetic distance
> for adults this separation is not measurable in physical terms, but is a separation which resonates emotionally, leading to an identification with the actor and/or situation. When working with children this separation needs to be adequate to instill belief and identification; if too close, belief may not occur because of the need for more distance; if too far away, remoteness contributes to lack of belief; a comfortable distance to insure belief

affective
> the domain of learning which engages the feeling area of the individual child

analogy
> a comparison between two different things; a way of high-lighting relationships to bring out more information and meaning, enabling the thing compared to acquire a broader impact

archetype
> an original pattern, model, identity, from which something is formed or made; tends to be hallowed, god-like, heroic

beat
> a moment or several moments in the action of a situation which are connected to a single theme

biographical sketch data sheet
> specific questions which the player answers in order to gain knowledge and develop himself as this character

cartoon
> a style of acting and a genre which is bombastic, slapstick, and often chosen, not consciously, by children who are self-conscious

catalyst
causing an interaction; a person who causes an interaction to take place between participants and the drama

catharsis
an experience of releasing emotion, purging, after having made a connection with the main character or "hero" through identification

cinquain
a five lined poem which contains the following syllables, 2-4-6-8-2 and can be iambic

classical
a form which is balanced, large, specifically chosen; used with historical characters and topics to give them meaning and weight

classical speech
a type of speech which is especially chosen to stand for a particular type of person, unlike domestic speech which is everyday speech

conglomerate movements
a group of intertwined players, making up the whole, none of whom can speak as an individual; representing machines, objects; all members are part of the group; unlike tribal

cognitive
the factual, conceptual domain of learning which influences the participants' thinking

cooperative learning
children work together in groups and compensate for the lack of motivation, and so interest, among lower achievers

devil's advocate
one who purposely causes antagonism in order to provoke a reaction

dramatic play
when children are playing using a role

Earth, Air, Fire, Water (or Beast, Bird, Fish)
    a children's game in which the leader stands in the middle of a
    circle quickly pointing to one child then another. If she says
    "earth" (beast), the child responds as an animal on earth; "air",a
    bird; "fire", freezes; "water", an aquatic creature

educational drama
    drama which is practiced for the purpose of understanding,
    reflection and gaining depth in a particular concept; connected
    with the curriculum

eidetic imagery
    an association which forms a visual representation; a picture in
    the mind can be seen when one closes his eyes

emotion-memory
    recalling a past experience associated with a given emotion

equidistance
    a level of development whereby children move so that each is
    wary of his own space; guards against aggression and collisions

experience story
    a lived through adventure from which children dictate to the
    teacher as she writes down their thoughts

expert
    a role in which children rise to a level whereby they are
    considered particularly knowledgeable

frame
    to enclose within a theme which acknowledges a particular
    style, mood; identifies the drama; eg. a technological frame for a
    drama might use a television studio (Gold Rush)

generic exercises
    typifying, not specific or individually exceptional; common to or
    characteristic of a whole group or class; related to the dramas in
    this text and exercises which are a natural outgrowth of
    children's own play

genre
    a category or way of defining styles of writing, art, eg. a Gothic
    novel

give and take
> when groups share space so that only one group is speaking at a time; at first the leader calls the groups' numbers 1,2,3,4, etc.; next the groups TAKE (from another group) or GIVE (to another group) the space on their own without the leader's help

given circumstances
> the facts that answer the questions what, who, where, why and sometimes how, which have to be known by the "actor" before becoming the character

haiku
> a three lined poem which contains specific syllables for each line, 5-7-5

haptic
> a sense of touch; a learner needing, having a material presence and reality of an event by living through it; being involved experientially

hourglass questioning
> a process of using questions which proceeds from general to specific, constantly engaging the children so they understand both levels of a topic from its details and specifics to its broader implications; the alternation from general to specific has focusing value that keeps their attention

I am thy Master
> a movement game in which the leader vocally repeats "I am thy Master, and I want all of you to become ---", any animal is mentioned; after this all participants mime the animal which advances toward her until she points to another participant who becomes leader by taking up the same action, but uses another animal, and so on

Ideas game
> about four to six ideas are spontaneously verbalized and are then combined into a situation/scenario which is acted out

imaginative play
> children are guided in their play by a leader to take on roles

machine
> a movement exercise in which participants coordinate with each other to show the inner-workings of an object or idea

melodramatic
    a style of acting and a genre of plays which is overly emotional and exaggerated, often chosen by children who are self-conscious

metaphor
    a figure of speech in which one thing is compared to, or is used in place of, another to suggest a likeness

mirror
    a movement exercise in which one or more persons move in imitation of a leader

monologue
    the actor does not depend on verbal interaction with another player but holds the stage by his own continuous speaking, yet is speaking to other(s) on stage (see **soliloquy)**

negotiation
    the most important step of the drama, in which a verbal contract with the children is made, establishing their belief, cooperation, and willingness to engage in the drama

oscillating rhythm pattern
    an up and down pace which is purposely kept by the leader to guide children in a journey so their movements coordinate with their natural physical energy

pacing
    a rate of process, how fast a scene is going in accordance with meaning and levels of emotional tension

presence
    a public projection of the leader's personality which conveys inner calm and outer strength, based upon a projection of confidence

psychomotor
    the mind and body connection which relates to movement, includes kinesthetic responses

reflection
    a pause in which a participant's focus is intent and thoughtful, extracting meaning from the experience

ritual
a practice which is regularly repeated; a ceremony or rite helping the group participate on a transpersonal level

role play
dramatic play; during play a role is taken so that the player's identity has shifted to become the persona of someone else; playing out a problem by taking on another identity in order to understand the problem from a different vantage point

sidecoaching
the leader stands outside the drama verbalizing directions as a (transitional) narration so the participants can sustain the mood and feeling quality without interruption

Simon Says
a movement game in which the children move in imitation of the leader as long as she says Simon Says; if she doesn't say S.S and moves, any one who imitates her is out

soliloquy
the actor is speaking his thoughts and is overheard by the audience

subtext
information which is not in the script (text), but which the audience member infers from the action and emotion of the actors

subtextual
related to subtext

symbol
anything which stands for something else, usually implying an abstract connection; e. g., a key stands for encountering truth

tableau
a frozen picture involving one or more persons

tension
a time of stretching the child's mind when a new pressure or idea is brought to bear; closure is purposely not dealt with; the leader constantly introduces the unknown; distancing is used

transition
> a movement or change from one "beat" to another or one scene to another, which the leader tries to meld together with a transitional narrative

transitional narrative
> a narration that coordinates movement and mood which the leader uses to make a smooth connection from one part of the drama to the next to sustain the mood/feeling

tribal
> a group in which all are part of a tribe, yet each is a separate voice; unlike conglomerate movement

twilight
> a gradual way of going into role

Who Stole the Bacon
> a game in which two lines face each other and are numbered off as partners by starting with those farthest away; when called, the pairs run toward the middle of the lines where "the bacon" (any object) is placed; the objective is for a player to get the bacon back to his place before he is tagged by his partner

Biography of the Author

Jerneral (Jenny) Cranston is Professor of Theatre Arts at Humboldt State University, Arcata, California. She received her B. A. from Stanford University and her M. A. from San Francisco State University. She is the mother of one son. She has had extensive experience teaching in elementary schools in California and London, England. She currently instructs university courses in Creative Dramatics and T'ai Chi. She has also taught Acting, Mime and Movement, Women in Theatre, Children's Theatrical Literature, Improvisation, Storytelling, Children's Theatrical Production, and Asian Theatre. In 1986 she received the Outstanding Professor Award at Humboldt State University. She leads workshops in Creative Dramatics for teachers and children of all grade levels.